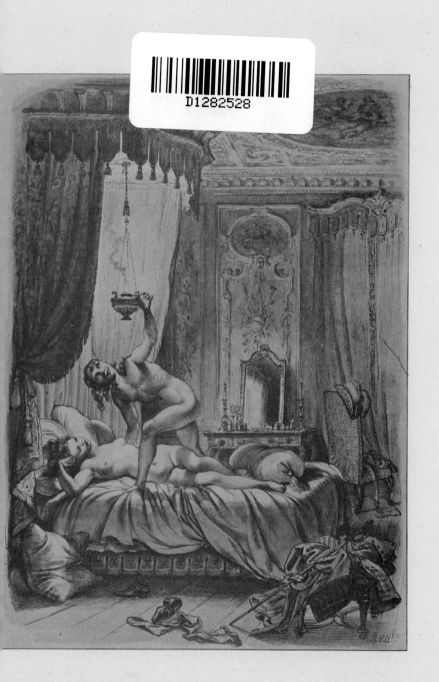

SOPHIE DOROTHEA

SOPHIE DOROTHEA

Sophie
Dorothea

RUTH JORDAN

GEORGE BRAZILLER
NEW YORK

Published in the United States in 1972 by George Braziller, Inc.
Copyright © 1971 by Ruth Jordan
Originally published in England by Constable Publishers

Standard Book Number: 8076–0626–x
Library of Congress Catalog Card Number: 73–178741

First Printing
Printed in Great Britain

CONTENTS

CONTENTS

ILLUSTRATIONS

The endpapers are taken from the illustrations by Rex Whistler to *Königsmarck*, by A. E. W. Mason, of which the originals are in the Tate Gallery, London.

THE SUCCESSION TO THE THRONE OF GREAT BRITAIN

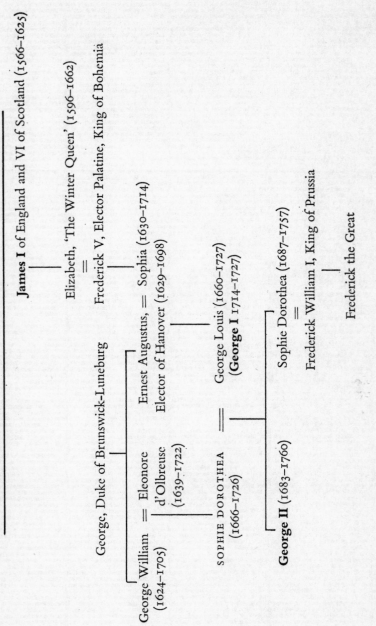

James I of England and VI of Scotland (1566–1625)

Elizabeth, 'The Winter Queen' (1596–1662)
=
Frederick V, Elector Palatine, King of Bohemia

George, Duke of Brunswick-Luneburg

Ernest Augustus, = Sophia (1630–1714)
Elector of Hanover (1629–1698)

George William = Eleonore
(1624–1705)   d'Olbreuse
(1639–1722)

George Louis (1660–1727)
(George I 1714–1727)

SOPHIE DOROTHEA
(1666–1726)
==

Sophie Dorothea (1687–1757)
=
Frederick William I, King of Prussia

George II (1683–1760)

Frederick the Great

PREFACE

The eighteenth century, which gave Great Britain a new royal dynasty from Germany, also gave her a succession of German-born queen-consorts. Sophie Dorothea of Celle would have been the first of them, had she not been divorced from George Louis of Hanover long before he went to England to become king. She was married to the future George I for twelve years and bore him the son who was to succeed him as George II. Although she never set foot on English soil, it was her direct descendants who ascended the throne. Biologically and genealogically, she is a true ancestress of the Royal House, and as such deserves to be better known.

The exact course of her life has been much obscured through the ages by an abundance of semi-fictitious works which have professed to tell her true history, but instead confused fact with fiction to a very considerable degree. The first romanticised account of her unhappy love was published within a year of Königsmarck's disappearance by a writer using the pseudonym Cassandro, purporting to tell the true life story of a well-known cavalry officer and his end. Another romantic account by a writer calling himself Menantes appeared in 1705, some ten years after Sophie Dorothea's removal to Ahlden. But it was Duke Anthony Ulric of Wolfenbüttel who provided the wide basis for what became the accepted version of her history. In 1707 he brought out the sixth volume of his *roman-à-clef The Roman Octavia*, where he told the story of the Princess's enforced marriage and her cruel imprisonment. A few years later he produced a second version of the story, with more dramatic details. This version served as an inspiration to later writers, possibly influencing the Memoirs of Aurora Königsmarck and even of her son Maurice Saxe. In 1732 the *Histoire Secrette* by Baron Poelnitz set the seal on a version that remained in favour throughout Europe until the late nineteenth century.

It was only then that serious scholars, German mostly, began to take a critical interest in the life of Sophie Dorothea and her association with Count Philip Christopher Königsmarck. By that time part of their correspondence had been bequeathed to the University Library of Lund, and there was much speculation as to its authenticity.

The first person in this country to apply herself to an analytical study of the letters was Mrs Everett Green, who had them copied for her use in their original French, her copy, with her annotations, being preserved in the British Museum. She did not, however, complete her work, and it fell to W. H. Wilkins, in 1900, to publish the first full-length biography of Sophie Dorothea in English, together with his translation of the Lund correspondence. A remarkable contribution was made a few years later by A. W. Ward, who brought to the attention of the world another part of the correspondence preserved in the Royal Secret State Archives of Berlin, and who did much towards dispelling some of the romanticised notions that still prevailed.

But it is mainly thanks to research carried out in our own times in Germany that a brighter light has been shed on a course of life which had eluded biographers for more than two hundred and fifty years. For a clearer conception of the past, I am greatly indebted to Professor Georg Schnath and Dr. Luise Gilde, whose separate researches into the life of Königsmarck and his correspondence with Sophie Dorothea have at long last made it possible to tear away some of the cobwebs of fiction.

The spelling of proper names raises a slight problem. Fearing a possible confusion between the Electress of Hanover and her daughter-in-law, I have followed W. H. Wilkins's example in spelling the one as Sophia, the other as Sophie (Dorothea). In general I have kept to the English spelling of German proper names.

Finally, may I thank H.R.H. Prince Ernest Augustus, the present Duke of Brunswick-Luneburg, for his kind permission to have photographs taken of his family portraits preserved in the Bomann-Museum at Celle, and in other museums in Hanover, and the directors and staff of the museums for their courteous and efficient cooperation in providing the illustrations.

The bartered bride

Of all statesmen-negotiated matches within the petty courts of seventeenth-century Germany, none was less likely to mature into a workable marriage than that of Sophie Dorothea of Celle to her cousin George Louis of Hanover, later King George I of England. Their subsequent separation surprised nobody. It was the culmination of a prolonged state of discord between two totally incompatible partners.

Basically there should have been nothing disastrous about a marriage which had been arranged between unsuited and even unwilling candidates for no other reason than dynastic or political aggrandisement. It need not have been foredoomed. Custom, which sanctioned the practice, also provided the remedy. A husband could console himself with mistresses. If indeed he found one who pleased him well enough to warrant a permanent liaison, he could raise her to the dignity of *maîtresse-en-titre*, forcing his wife to turn a blind eye. More rarely, even a wife could depart from the narrow path with impunity, particularly if her lover happened to be the sovereign. Her deviation would then not only be accepted, but regarded with envy and rewarded with obsequiousness. This unwritten law of convenience was practised all the way down the aristocratic ladder, and many an ill-assorted couple

I

managed to jog along and present the world with a tolerable façade. A complete and flagrant breakdown of the pattern was the exception rather than the rule.

With Sophie Dorothea and George Louis the chances of a tolerable façade were thin from the start. From their very childhood the cousins had been conditioned to regard each other's family with mistrust and dislike. George Louis, six years older than his beautiful wife, was quite impervious to her charms, for he had learnt to see her only through his mother's eyes, as the self-willed daughter of a French upstart; while Sophie Dorothea, under the influence of her French mother, thought Cousin George sullen, boorish, and insufferably proud of his untarnished pedigree. The estrangement between the two young people was the inevitable result of a union contracted against a background of mutual ill-will. If ever a negotiated marriage was doomed to failure, theirs was; for the rot that brought it crumbling down had set in long before their wedding-day, long before either of them was born or even thought of. It began many years earlier, when a pleasure-loving duke passed on his jilted bride to a younger brother, for a consideration.

After the Thirty Years War and the Treaty of Westphalia in 1648, the German house of Brunswick was divided into two independent lines, the Wolfenbüttels and the Luneburgs. Sometimes they consulted and acted together; more often they intrigued against one another and indulged in political rivalries.

The Luneburg line was represented by four brothers: Christian Louis; George William, the future father of Sophie Dorothea; John Frederick; and Ernest Augustus, the future father of George I. All four held the title of Duke, but only the two elder ones had inherited.

George William, the second of the four brothers, was born in 1624, and became Duke of Hanover at the age of seventeen. Taking advantage of his independence, he immediately went abroad in search of adventures and excitement, visiting England, France, Spain, Holland and Italy. Venice, with its carnivals and its numerous opportunities for a fast life, suited him best. He returned there as often as he could. During one of his visits he formed a liaison with a Venetian lady called Signora Buccolini, and had a son by her. Although in due course he tired of the mother, he showed himself generous to the son. He took him back to

Hanover, clipped his name to Buccow to make it German-sounding, and made it possible for the boy, when he grew up, to become Master of the Horse, and later a colonel of dragoons.

When George William first embarked on his chosen career of pleasure seeking, his youngest brother Ernest Augustus, born in 1629, was only twelve. From a tender age there had been a strong link of affection between them, and as soon as Ernest Augustus showed himself ready, his elder brother took him on his travels. Shared adventures forged their early tenderness into real devotion. They became boon companions, inseparable and irrepressible. It was characteristic of their relationship that the elder Duke paid all the expenses, while the landless one accepted his brother's generosity as a matter of fact.

George William was perhaps the most attractive of the four Luneburg brothers. Of medium height, with lively eyes and regular features, he combined in his personality distinction of appearance with simplicity of manner. To his friends he was generous; to his subjects, when he happened to be amongst them, he was benevolent. He never sought responsibility when he could avoid it, but he was brave in war. He was light-hearted and easy-going, and most gallant with the ladies.

Ernest Augustus too was noted for his charm and social accomplishments. But unlike his easy-going brother, he had a strong will of his own which manifested itself more and more as the years went by. Of all the four brothers he was perhaps the only born politician, always keeping a watchful eye for a chance to improve his position in the world. He was flexible and shrewd, tactful where tact was called for and hard where his own interest was concerned. He exercised a considerable influence over his elder brother, but his affection for him was unswerving, and withstood the many trials and tribulations which clouded their old age.

Years of money-spending abroad had not endeared George William to his Hanover subjects, at whose expense he was leading his life of idleness. His frequent absences made them restive, and they had little hesitation in making their displeasure known. In 1656, when George William was thirty-two, things came to a head. The loyal subjects demanded that their Duke should settle down at his court and attend to his duties, which included, among other things, getting married and begetting an heir. They threatened to cut down his allowance if he refused, while promising to increase it handsomely if he complied. The Duke saw the wisdom of their demand and decided to capitulate. His Chancellor cast about for a suitable bride, and eventually came up with a suggestion that seemed acceptable from every point of view. True, the bride-to-be did not have much of a dowry, but she was of a most noble descent, every bit as good as a Brunswick, and attractive to boot. George William had heard a great deal about her beauty and her accomplishments, and agreed with his Chancellor that Princess Sophia would be a most suitable lady for him to marry, if marry he must.

Princess Sophia was born in 1630, the twelfth child of Elizabeth and Frederick V, the Elector Palatine. A grand-daughter of King James I of England through her mother, Sophia was very conscious of her Stuart blood and her connection with the throne of England. At the time of her birth, however, glory and position were things of the past. Her father and mother were already the ex-King and Queen of Bohemia, and were living at The Hague in straitened circumstances. When Sophia was two her father died, leaving her to the mercies of elder brothers and sisters. She had to learn to fend for herself, and soon made the valuable discovery that tact and shrewdness were a poor heiress's best friends.

When the first approaches were being made from Hanover, Sophia was living at Heidelberg, at the court of her brother Charles Louis, the Elector Palatine. She had been sought in marriage several times before, but somehow nothing had worked out right. Yet she was attractive, with a pleasant speaking voice and a dignified manner. She spoke German, Dutch, French, Italian and English like a native, to go by what a contemporary wrote of her; and she had more than a little Latin. She took great interest in intellectual subjects, and in years to come formed a close friendship with the philosopher Leibnitz. Altogether she might have seemed a bit of a blue-stocking, but for her basic good sense, which taught her not to assert herself prematurely with people she was dependent on. She had a good opinion of herself, as her memoirs, written many years later, seem to indicate:

I had light brown hair, naturally wavy, a gay and easy manner, a good though not a very tall figure, and the bearing of a Princess.[1]

4

What she omitted to record was that at the age of twenty-one an attack of smallpox had left her otherwise pretty face slightly marked. Perhaps she felt that her noble bearing made up for what was after all not an uncommon blemish in those days. For her, pedigree came first. She took an inordinate pride in her royal ancestry and never let anybody forget it. If she ever felt an inclination for any of her suitors, she was careful not to show it. Her guiding principle in her choice of a future partner was his ability to provide her with the station her high birth entitled her to. It dictated her relations with the penniless Duke Ernest Augustus, who stopped at Heidelberg on the way back from one of his visits to Venice. In her memoirs Sophia explained why she had not encouraged his attentions:

His good looks have become even more striking since I first met him as a very young man in Holland, and everybody liked him. But as he was the youngest of his brothers, he could not possibly be considered a suitable match. We played the guitar together, which served to show off his exquisite hands. He was also a marvellous dancer. He offered to send me some of Corbetti's guitar music and began writing to me on the subject. I was the first to break off the correspondence, fearing that people might say that my friendship for him was too strong.[2]

George William's address was a different matter. His position and wealth, added to his considerable charm, were great assets as far as Sophia was concerned. As she frankly admitted in her memoirs, she accepted with alacrity. He therefore followed his Chancellor to Heidelberg, officially asked for the Princess's hand in marriage, was accepted by the family, and then took himself off to Venice for a last fling of bachelor pleasures. Allowing him to go back to the scene of so much past revelling was a tactical mistake, as Sophia soon found out to her mortification:

No sooner had the Duke of Hanover arrived in Venice than he attached himself to the first courtesan he met, a Greek woman who had no other claim to beauty except the clothes she wore. She put him in a frame of mind most unsuitable for marriage. He stopped thinking of me, and the loose morals of Venice took an unshakable hold of him. His subjects were slow to agree on the increase of his married allowance. All these things made him regret the promise he had given me, by word of mouth as well as in writing. His letters grew colder, and he failed to return on the appointed date. My brother the Elector became worried; as for me, I was too proud to be touched in any way.[3]

The situation was unprecedented. When previous projected matches had fallen through, it was usually due to failure to reach agreement between the negotiating parties on some material point. Any such unfulfilled match could be regarded as a business proposition which had failed to materialise. There was no disgrace attached. The present case was altogether different. An official fiancé, who had ceremoniously pledged his word, showed his preference for a cheap courtesan to the extent of breaking off his engagement. It was an insult no woman was likely to forget. Sophia might have actually fallen for the easy charm of the debonair George William; but it was the affront to her pride she must have minded most. Although the engagement was supposed to be kept a secret, the story of the gay duke who went a-whoring while his fiancée was crying her eyes out must have leaked out and fallen like manna from heaven into the hands of avid court gossips. Princess Sophia was no mere child to be trifled with, but a mature and self-assured woman of twenty-six who could not forgive and forget. Outwardly she might smile and put a brave face on it, but inwardly she smarted. That undeserved slight to her pride must have sown the first seeds of bitterness, which in the years to come, would grow into an ever-increasing resentment against any woman who might temporarily engage George William's affections, and particularly against the woman who succeeded in making him voluntarily renounce his bachelor state for ever.

For the time being she put on pride like a shield and pretended not to mind. Still, she would not give up without a struggle. In a typically feminine way, she calculated that the news of a new suitor might bring the old one running back. To avenge herself, as she candidly admitted many years later, she lent a willing ear to an offer of marriage from the Duke of Parma. The news failed to move George William if it ever reached his ears, and the offer from the Duke of Parma fizzled out. But an honourable solution was at hand.

The Duke of Hanover had no reason to dislike Princess Sophia. On the contrary, he liked and respected her, and his decision to opt out of marriage was due entirely to his love of freedom and bachelor delights. Now his conscience was troubling him. He felt that by letting his fiancée down, he had not behaved as befitted a prince, and he sought to make amends. While he was discussing his problem with his brother and boon companion, a happy idea suddenly struck him. Ernest Augustus had met Sophia and had got on well with her; he was handsome, attractive and about the same age as the Princess. If George William were to offer him a large regular allowance, he would be a very desirable match, whom Sophia might be tempted to accept. As for Ernest Augustus, he would be marrying a distinguished lady, and by presenting the good people of Hanover with an heir, he would be securing the duchy for his own descendants.

Ernest Augustus was quick to grasp the advantages of the offer. Tradition has it that while the two brothers were haggling over the size of the revenue George William would have to offer his substitute for his services, John Frederick, the other impecunious brother, burst into the room and fell into a rage because nobody had thought of offering him first refusal. In the end he was appeased, Ernest Augustus agreed to marry Sophia instead of George William, and a Chancellor was dispatched from Venice to Heidelberg to acquaint the lady with the terms of the honourable peace. The astute Sophia decided to cut her losses and accept with good grace:

My answer was that all I cared for was a good establishment, and that if it could be provided by the younger Duke, it would be no hardship for me to give up one brother for another. I would be only too happy to do anything considered advantageous to my interest.[4]

The negotiations for the new match went on for two whole years. The Elector Charles Louis had to be reassured that his sister was not being fobbed off with a cheap substitute. The Hanoverian subjects had to be persuaded that the switch was in their favour and that Ernest Augustus would try to give them the Luneberg heir they had set their hearts on, and George William had to promise his substitute a handsome allowance and undertake never to marry, so that on his death his duchy would pass into the hands of his brother and his descendants. In her memoirs, which Sophia wrote in French, she included George William's Declaration of Renunciation in its original German, coyly remarking that as she was writing solely for her own pleasure, there was no need for her to translate the document. The main clauses ran as follows:

> Having carefully considered how our Houses of this line may be best provided with heirs and be perpetuated in the future, yet being unwilling and unable to engage in any marriage contract, I have persuaded my brother Ernest Augustus to declare that provided he receives from me a Renunciation of Marriage for myself, he will forthwith enter into holy matrimony.
>
> Whereas my brother Ernest Augustus has agreed to enter into holy matrimony with Her Highness Princess Sophia, so do I, on my side, pledge my word, of my own free will, to ratify the above mentioned undertaking. As long as the said Princess and my brother are alive and continue in the bonds of matrimony, or, if after their decease they leave any male issue, I will not enter into a marriage contract with any person, so that the male heirs of the above mentioned Princess and my brother, in whose favour this Renunciation is made, may succeed to the sovereignty of one or both our duchies. To witness these undertakings, I have written and signed this Renunciation with my own hand and sealed it with my own seal, and thereafter handed it over to my brother's safe keeping.
>
> George William,
> Duke of Brunswick and Luneburg

11 April, 1658.[5]

George William's undertaking never to marry was by no means unprecedented. There had been at least six Brunswick uncles who had taken a similar step in previous years, to suit some scheme of their own. And of course it did not condemn anybody to celibacy. On the contrary, it opened up before the pleasure-loving Duke undreamed-of prospects of pursuing his amorous inclinations with impunity, for now he could never be expected to pay the price of love with matrimony. He was protected by the Renunciation. It never occurred to him he might live to regret such a pleasant arrangement. He felt he had acquitted himself with honour of a rather delicate affair.

In the autumn of 1658 the wedding of Princess Sophia and Duke Ernest Augustus was celebrated at the court of Heidelberg, where the bride was given away by her brother, the Elector Charles Louis. More than twenty years later, when already a mother of seven, she was still dwelling with pleasure on the pomp and circumstance of the occasion:

On my wedding day I was dressed in a white dress with silver brocade, according to the German fashion. My hair was combed loose, and a large crown studded with the family diamonds was placed on it. Four maids of honour carried my train, which was of prodigious length, and twenty-four gentlemen marched before us with lighted torches bedecked with ribbons matching the colours of our coats of arms; blue and white for me, red and yellow for the Duke. The moment the clergyman united us, a salvo of cannons was heard. . . . In the evening there was a banquet followed by a ball. The Princes danced in the traditional German way, all around us, carrying lighted torches in their hands.[6]

The journey from Heidelberg to Hanover, where the couple were to take up residence, was one long triumphant procession. At every stopping-place Brunswick dukes and their wives came to pay their respects to the new bride. George William went out of his way to see that his sister-in-law should have homage paid to her all along the route. The climax of the splendid journey was reached before the gates of Hanover:

The four ducal brothers honoured me by coming out to meet me, followed by their enormous retinues. I alighted in order to greet them, and then the four of them joined me in my carriage. I entered the city of Hanover to the sound of cannons. My mother-in-law the Dowager Duchess of Celle, and the Duchess of Wolfenbüttel, came out to meet me in their carriages and offered me their welcome.[7]

It was an auspicious beginning. Professing herself satisfied with the marks of honour which had been showered on her, Duchess Sophia as she had now become, was determined more than ever to make a success of a marriage that a twist of fate had thrust upon her. Always a stickler for etiquette, she now proceeded with great firmness to take up her duties as the first lady of the court of Hanover, where she and her husband were acknowledged as prospective heirs, while the actual lord and master was the light-hearted bachelor Duke George William.

An anti-contract

The affection between the two brothers did not diminish in the least after the marriage; if possible it became warmer. Now that they were living under the same roof, they became practically inseparable. George William might have been genuinely touched by his younger brother's readiness to save a situation which had been created solely through the elder one's selfishness; while Ernest Augustus, now that he was legally tied down by a marriage of convenience, was perhaps anxious to prove he was still his own master. Whatever the reason, they spent much of their time together, hunting, walking or playing cards; and soon the Duchess realised that to please her husband she must reconcile herself to the constant presence of her brother-in-law.

This innocent *ménage-à-trois* may have suited the two men, but it certainly did not suit Sophia. It was mortifying to see George William so blatantly enjoying his lucky escape from matrimony. The wound he had inflicted on her pride had not yet healed, and his lack of sensitivity only helped to keep it festering. Two years earlier she had tried to avenge herself by encouraging the Duke of Parma, hoping to revive George William's interest. Now she had recourse to other feminine wiles. She went out of her way to be sweet to him, hoping to make him regret his error of judgment. George William saw in it no more than the courtesy expected from a sister-in-law. She tried to pique his pride by treating him with extreme coolness. The only one who noticed her untoward lack of civility was her husband. Still she persevered, and in the end succeeded in persuading herself that George William had fallen in love with her. It would have been a sweet revenge, had it been true. Unfortunately the facts did not bear her out. While she was fondly pretending to herself that the two brothers were getting madly jealous of one another because of her, they were in fact discussing another trip to their beloved Italy. Unwilling to be left behind so shortly after her wedding, the Duchess expressed a desire to accompany them. She did not foresee that the two seasoned travellers would expect her to travel like them, in an open carriage in the midst of winter. Twenty years later she could still vividly recall the frustration that resulted:

> When we had gone but one day's journey from Hanover, I realised I could not possibly go any further. I was obliged to return home alone, while the two Dukes continued their journey together. I was inconsolable, and could not restrain my tears.[1]

No tears were shed by the brothers, for the following winter they arranged to go away again, while Sophia was encouraged to go and stay at her mother's court at The Hague. By then Sophia was expecting her first child, which must have caused her some anxiety as well as joy, for she was already in her thirtieth year. But underneath the excitement that surrounded the expected arrival of the much-desired heir, the old wound still throbbed, and would continue to do so for many years to come, subconsciously dictating her reactions to every new fluctuation in her brother-in-law's private life. Any inclination he might show for another woman was yet another blow to her ego, and instinctively she would try either to nip the affair or pretend it did not exist.

Two years after she became the first lady of Hanover, Sophia noticed that George William was paying marked attention to a young lady called Mlle Wattinsvain. She persuaded herself that he was doing it only to console himself for his unrequited love for his one-time fiancée. It was more difficult to keep up this self-delusion in the face of George

William's next attachment, which soon developed into an open love affair and became the talk of the court:

> The Duke of Hanover, when he saw how I discouraged his advances, attached himself to one of my ladies named Landas. I was of course thankful to be rid of his attentions, but it soon turned out that his fire was but of straw, and the attachment did not last long.[2]

In fact it lasted more than a year. It is not known how the final rupture between the lovers came about, but Sophia almost certainly had a hand in it. In the midst of the double excitement caused by the birth of her second son and by Ernest Augustus's succeeding to the bishopric of Osnabrück, which meant setting up a court of her own for the first time in her life, she found time to give the *coup de grâce* to George William's dying flame:

> The first thing we did at the court of Osnabrück was to marry off Mlle Landas. The affair she had with the Duke of Hanover somewhat tarnished her good name, and to make amends my husband married her to a former attendant of his, a M. Lente, who proved to be a real gentleman, if a bit stupid. Mlle Landas professed herself perfectly satisfied with the arrangement, and in due course became an excellent wife, giving the lie to those who had spoken ill of her and showing the world she had been misjudged. My husband invited the Duke of Hanover to attend the wedding, which he did without the slightest show of regret.[3]

That was the last time Sophia was able to interfere successfully with George William's love life. His next love, which was also his last, dramatically changed him from an amorous adventurer into a faithful and loyal companion. This voluntary transformation, perhaps more than anything else, hardened Sophia's original humiliation into a permanent sense of injury, which warped all her dealings with Eleonore d'Olbreuse, the woman she never ceased to regard as a usurper and a nobody.

The accession to the bishopric of Osnabrück had been anticipated for some time. The Treaty of Westphalia had stipulated that it should be held alternately by a Catholic priest and a Protestant prince from the Luneburg line of the house of Brunswick. In 1661, when the Catholic incumbent died, Ernest Augustus, who had long been designated as a successor, became the secular bishop of Osnabrück. His wife, after the German fashion, became Madam Bishop. Immediately the succession was confirmed, he and Sophia left the court of Hanover, where they had been no more than guests, and set up their own court at the episcopal palace in their new domain. As it did not meet with the new bishop's luxurious requirements, extensive alterations were needed, which were planned on a grand scale and took several years to complete. The old palace was transformed into a beautiful court, and the portal was piously inscribed with the motto *Sola Bona Quae Honesta* under Ernest Augustus' name. The gardens were re-designed by a French landscape architect from the school of Lenôtre, designer of Versailles. A *maître d'hôtel* was imported from Paris, and nearly every year the Duke's personal valet was sent to France, to purchase for Sophia and her ladies the latest in French fashion and refinement.

The household moved constantly between the palace of Osnabrück and the castle of Iburg, which was less pretentious, and therefore more of a home. In one of her letters to her niece Elizabeth Charlotte, later Duchess of Orléans and sister-in-law to Louis XIV, Sophia described her nearly idyllic life at the castle:

> We play at nine-pins, breed young ducks, amuse ourselves with backgammon and talk every year of paying a visit to Italy. In the meantime things go as well as can be expected for a petty bishop who is able to live in peace, and who, in case of war, can depend on the help of his brothers.[4]

While Madam Bishop was finding her life in her court quite pleasing, her restless husband was beginning to hanker again after Italy. He assured his wife it would give him great pleasure if she were to join him there, and so the matter was settled. Ernest Augustus went ahead with George William, arranging for Sophia to follow them a few months later.

This time there was no question of travelling in mid-winter in an open carriage. The tour was carefully planned with an eye to the

Duchess's utmost comfort and pleasure. Her entire household accompanied her, including ladies-in-waiting, equerries and even a band of musicians. Her ladies and women alone filled four carriages, while she was carried in a litter, with her gentlemen escorting her on horseback. The servants followed in numerous carts. It was a huge caravan, numbering some two hundred people, and the Duchess noted with satisfaction that its splendour far exceeded that of some of the princes who came out to meet her on the way. The itinerary included Verona, Vicenza, Venice, Milan, Rome, Loretto, Parma, Siena, Florence and Bologna, and took nearly a whole year to complete. The Duchess made the acquaintance of the Italian nobility and remarked with relief that their women were not half as attractive as her husband had led her to believe; in fact she considered most of them quite repellent. Venice too failed to please her; it had too much water about and was altogether too gloomy. Yet it was in Venice she agreed to do as the Venetians did. For once she put aloofness aside and danced with her husband out-of-doors, to everybody's delight and approval. On the whole however she felt at odds with the general air of light-heartedness and frivolity, and pronounced Italian morals too lax.

The happy mood induced by the Italian tour, the only one she ever made, was marred by the news that awaited Duke Ernest Augustus on their return to Germany. Christian Louis, the eldest of the four Luneburg brothers, had died, and John Frederick had taken advantage of the absence of the other two to help himself to the dead man's estate. For a while it looked as if civil war would break out, and troops were being hurriedly recruited on all sides. In the end wise counsels prevailed, and in the summer of 1665, after lengthy negotiations, the three brothers jointly agreed on a new distribution of their lands. George William, now the eldest, took the best and became Duke of Celle. John Frederick became Duke of Hanover; and Ernest Augustus, who had shown much ardour on behalf of the new Duke of Celle, was rewarded by him with the small domain of Diepholz. Peace was restored.

All the time the negotiations were going on, another family trouble was looming ahead. The incorrigible George William had fallen in love again. He was so infatuated with his new lady, that it took several desperate appeals from his brother to make him detach himself from Breda, in Holland, where the lady was living, and return to Brunswick to take part in the battle for his lands. Both Sophia and Ernest Augustus were shocked to see the change in him. He was depressed beyond words, and tears would fill his eyes at the slightest vexation. Ernest Augustus reassured him as best he could and promised him goodwill and troops, but he soon realised that his brother's depression had little to do with the conflict over his property. If George William was downcast it was not because his claim to a dukedom was in danger—he was quite willing to leave the battle in the capable hands of his loyal younger brother—but because for the first time in his life he was really and truly in love, and he was desperately afraid of losing a woman who would not yield her virtue without honour. Her name was Eleonore d'Olbreuse.

Eleonore Desmier d'Olbreuse was born in France in 1639. Daughter to the Huguenot Marquis d'Olbreuse, descendant of a distinguished Poitou family, she was taken as a young girl to the court of Louis XIV and was immediately acknowledged a beauty. She had a majestic figure, with dark brown hair, laughing dark eyes, rosy cheeks and flashing white teeth. She was well versed in the social arts, was a graceful dancer and had a touch of sprightliness that won her many admirers. Her career at court was cut short when her father's estates were confiscated because of his Huguenoterie. They left France and found refuge in the Dutch town of Breda.

Breda was in those days the chosen home of many political exiles. Charles II had stayed there with his loyal Cavaliers; Elizabeth, mother of Duchess Sophia, lived there for a while after she had lost the Kingdom of Bohemia; and so did many Huguenots. It became a gay little town, with feasts, masquerades, plays and balls. Its community of exiles was hospitable, and soon Eleonore became a lady-in-waiting to the Princess of Tarente, a Hesse-Cassel by birth, and an aunt to Duchess Sophia. It was during a family visit to that princess, in the winter of 1663–4, that George William first met Eleonore.

That he fell in love at first sight was by no means an unusual occurrence with him. But Eleonore d'Olbreuse was no Signora Buccolini or Mlle Landas. She held on to her virtue, and soon the bewildered Duke had to realise that the only way to win her favour was to offer her love with honour. Perhaps it was not only her resistance that brought about the fundamental change in his outlook on married life.

He was forty now, he had sown his wild oats, and the idea of a respectable relationship did not put him off as it had done in the past. Unfortunately marriage was out of the question because of his Declaration of Renunciation of eight years ago; but apart from marriage he was promising Eleonore everything he had in his power to offer, his eternal devotion and a handsome allowance. While Eleonore was still considering the risks of following her heart, for she too was in love, George William was recalled to Hanover, leaving his affair unsettled.

After the dynastic storm had blown over, the new Duke of Celle did not dare risk his position at home by another lengthy absence. He was dejected. He desperately wanted Eleonore to leave Breda and come to join him in Germany, although he knew her scruples would not allow her to do so. As usual, he took his problem to his younger brother.

It was a measure of Ernest Augustus's trust that he agreed to help without fearing that the new involvement might prejudice his claim to his brother's inheritance. It was he who suggested that a good way to throw a mantle of respectability over the impending affair, was to ask Duchess Sophia to extend a formal invitation to Eleonore d'Olbreuse to be her guest at the castle of Iburg. Neither brother could suspect that they were appealing for help to the only woman whom it hurt most to offer it. Sophia was indeed in a quandary. Refusing her husband's request would be ungracious; complying with it would bring nearer another rival. In the end she decided that the best way to gauge the danger was to face it. Self-deception helped to keep up her morale:

> My husband knew of his brother's inclination for Mlle d'Olbreuse, and was anxious to do everything in his power to help him. As for me, I was only too glad to be able to provide the Duke of Celle with some divertissement which would take his mind off me.[5]

Eleonore too was in a quandary. Her trump card had been her virtue, but her love for George William was weakening her resolution. Circumstances seemed to conspire to make her change her mind. Her mistress, the Princess of Tarente, had returned to France, leaving Eleonore with a companion of her own age at the Dutch town of Hertogenbosch, or Bois-le-Duc. Her closest friends and relatives painted in glowing colours the advantages to a penniless girl of an association with the Duke of Celle, and suggested that a recognised liaison did not fall far short of a legal marriage. Duchess Sophia's invitation tipped the scales. Eleonore felt she was not involving herself in a disreputable attachment, but, on the contrary, was about to be formally received by those who were going to be, to all intents and purposes, her future in-laws. She accepted. The ducal coach-and-six was sent to fetch her from Bois-le-Duc, and in due course she arrived at Osnabrück. The Duchess herself received her ceremoniously at the foot of the grand staircase of the castle of Iburg, then took her up to her chamber to partake of coffee and salt biscuits. Eleonore was overawed and grateful. She went out of her way to be sweet and deferential to the great lady, while the great lady was relieved to find in Eleonore such a docile spirit. Sophia was beginning to feel she could handle this situation as adroitly as the previous ones. She allowed herself to be generous, although her intuitive malice manifested itself even when she was appearing to praise:

Mlle d'Olbreuse had been described to me as high-spirited and gay, given to such tricks as pinching and nudging in order to attract attention. I found her the very opposite. She was grave and dignified, spoke little and behaved pleasantly. She was very beautiful and tall. Altogether I found her amiable. My husband, who was in Hanover with his brother, had written urging me to give her a cordial welcome at Iburg, for reasons he was going to explain when he should join us. I found no difficulty in obeying his instructions, for the young lady made herself agreeable to me. I believed her to be what she appeared, and put down as idle talk all I had heard against her.[6]

Soon after Eleonore's arrival at the castle, George William came to stay too. Sophia's complacency changed to alarm when she realised that with so much opportunity for sin, Eleonore was not going to succumb to temptation. She was obviously a dangerous schemer:

I noticed at once the understanding between the Duke of Celle and Mlle d'Olbreuse by the looks they exchanged, and realised that she was determined to lead him far. She kept him well in hand, impressing on him the warmth of her supposed affection for him on the one hand, and the strict propriety of her conduct on the other.[7]

There was a great deal of heart-searching between the lovers, until an acceptable formula was finally reached. It happened during the funeral of the late Duke Christian Louis at Celle. It was a grand family occasion, where the widow was present, the three surviving brothers, Duchess Sophia and her ladies, and Eleonore, in her capacity of prospective member of the family. On 11 November 1665 the seal was set on the future relationship between Duke George William of Celle and Mlle Eleonore d'Olbreuse, whom he could never marry. Writing from Celle to her brother, the Elector Palatine Charles Louis, Sophia dismissed this important event in a few words:

The funeral took place yesterday ... the marriage of conscience between Duke George William and the Olbreuse was made public, although the consecration was done secretly, without candles or witnesses. This is all I have time to say.[8]

Many years later, when writing her memoirs, the Duchess was able to fill in the details of this much-resented act of union, whose consequences were to be far more significant than any of the people present at the time could have ever imagined:

To bring matters to a conclusion, the Duke of Celle made an anti-contract of marriage with Mlle d'Olbreuse, which was drawn up by La Motthe [a lady-in-waiting] instead of a notary. The terms were as follows: 'As the affection I bear for my brother made me resolve never to marry, for his advantage and his children's; and as I shall never desist from this resolution; and as Mlle d'Olbreuse has decided to come and live with me, I hereby promise never to leave her. I undertake to give her two thousand crowns a year during my lifetime, and six thousand crowns a year after my death; while she, on her part, will promise to be as satisfied with this arrangement as I am. Having taken this decision with my brother's agreement, he has promised to sign it.' That was the contents of the anti-contract of marriage which the four of us signed, the Duke of Celle and the

Olbreuse, my husband and myself. After that the two lovers went to bed together without further ado.[9]

From Celle the family returned to the castle of Iburg, where George William and his bride stayed on for several months. Sophia was eagerly watching for any signs of cooling off between the lovers, and four weeks after the wedding was wishfully informing her brother that the relationship was bound to end soon:

All of us here watch with great interest the mutual caresses of Duke George William and his Signora. They are pretty violent, and I fear it cannot last long. Venus seems to be more in command over the Duke than Pallas Athena or Mars, of whom he has much more need these days.[10]

In spite of the Duke's ardent manifestations of love, Eleonore was not happy. She was not treated as a wife, and was never allowed to forget that she was of inferior rank. At meal times she was present only as a spectator, seated on a low stool, at a respectable distance from the diners, who included Duchess Sophia, Duke Ernest Augustus, and her own lord and master, Duke George William. Her own meals were taken later in her dressing room, in the company of her sister who had come to stay with her at the castle. After a few months of this regime Eleonore succeeded in persuading George William to bid farewell to their hosts and take her to his own castle of Celle, well away from Duchess Sophia and her scornful treatment. From there she was soon writing to an old friend of her father's like any young bride:

I was confident that you would approve of my marriage, and for me that was all that mattered, for the approval of someone like you is enough in a case like this. Though it will be said that I have dispensed with standing in a church before a priest, I feel no regret. I am the happiest woman in the world, for it is good faith that makes a marriage. The Duke has pledged his word to me before his whole family, who also signed the contract in which he bound himself not to take any other wife but me. . . . And he did not stop short at that, but went on to do so much for me that I am in a position to stand up to all my

ELEONORE D'OLBREUSE
by H. Gascar

GEORGE WILLIAM, DUKE OF CELLE

enemies, if I had a mind to. But all I can think of is how to please my Duke. You would like to see our home, it is the happiest in the world.

d'Olbreuse, Mme de Harburg[11]

The title of Mme de Harburg, after a small domain in the duchy of Celle, was given to Eleonore immediately after the consummation of the contract, as a sort of face-saver in view of her unwedded state. It was by this name that Duchess Sophia contemptuously referred to her for the next ten years, except when she was calling her 'that creature' in her letters to her niece Elizabeth Charlotte, Duchess of Orléans.

The same week that Eleonore was writing ecstatically to her old family friend, Duchess Sophia was writing spitefully to her brother the Elector:

The Duke my husband has paid a visit to Hanover and reports that John Frederick's court is very beautiful and well ordered, with lots of honest people in it. As for the court of Celle, the less said about it the better. It has nothing good about it except its table; and Mme de Harburg is pregnant.[12]

On 15 September 1666, ten months after the anti-contract of marriage, Mme de Harburg gave birth to her first and only surviving child, Sophie Dorothea.

Legitimisation

The castle of Celle was built on an elevation overlooking one of the fertile bends of the river Ahler, surrounded by woods and streams. Basically a fine and spacious building, it had become grim and cheerless through long years of neglect. But its foreboding appearance did not deter Eleonore. Frenchwoman that she was, she set her mind on transforming the bleak halls into an elegant court. She re-arranged the furniture, ordered new hangings, checked the linen, inspected the kitchens and let it be known that nothing was too good for the Duke, now that he was permanently in residence. With the household staff she was both firm and gracious. She soon became the acknowledged mistress of the castle. She did not seek to dazzle curious neighbours with her newly-acquired splendour, and put all her energy into making the Duke comfortable. Her charmed lover was finding his domestic evenings at home far more enjoyable than anything he had experienced in the past. Under Eleonore's influence, a steady pattern of life was established.

In the mornings the Duke would see his ministers and attend to his duties, so long neglected. In the evenings he would join Mme de Harburg and her ladies. When he went hunting, he would take Eleonore with him. He was a keen hunter and kept no less than three hundred and seventy horses, mostly English, and a large number of dogs, also of English breed. What with looking after his domains, hunting, and being attentive to Eleonore, his days were full. Neighbouring courts remarked with astonishment on the change in his way of life, and the French-born Countess of Aldenburg wrote that Eleonore's influence on his character was so great, that from the most inconstant man on earth it had turned him into a paragon of fidelity.

Only the Bishop and Madam Bishop of Osnabrück were perturbed by the untoward change in the old roué. A reformed George William was a threat to their peace of mind, for it was proof that he was slipping away from old friends and allies. The festivities which were held at Celle after Sophie Dorothea's christening, were seen at Osnabrück as a bad omen. Ernest Augustus angrily remarked that had the baby been a real princess instead of just the daughter of his brother's *Madame*, no greater fuss could have been made of her. And Duchess Sophia, irked by regular reports about George William's devotion to Mme de Harburg and her daughter, vented her contempt for them in a letter to her brother, where, in the midst of her idiomatic French, she had to have recourse to an English expression, to indicate the full extent of her disapproval:

As for *the sweet family* of George William's, it is not of my doing. I had judged it politic not to oppose the union so as not to antagonise someone who is going to make my children his heirs one day. I am told the most devout consider it as a marriage before God; as for me, I prefer it to be a marriage before God than before men.[1]

The Duchess's premonitions were not unfounded. In her heart of hearts Eleonore d'Olbreuse had never accepted the terms on which she was brought to live in the castle of Celle. The birth of a daughter, which had endangered her life and brought the Duke even more under her influence, strengthened her determination to legalise her position. The first step was to secure the loyalty of the Duke's subjects. Dressed in all her finery, radiantly beautiful and holding the pretty baby in her arms, Eleonore would go for drives through the village of Celle, smiling graciously to the local people who lined the narrow streets to see her. She had already endeared herself to them by making their wandering Duke take up his residence in his ancestral home. The touching picture of the young mother and her baby won their hearts completely. Eleonore felt sufficiently emboldened to ask one of her brothers from Poitou to come and stay at the castle, and it was no doubt at her instigation that he approached the Duke on the subject of a legal marriage. He pointed out that Eleonore d'Olbreuse had the good name of her family in France to consider, and in all fairness to her the Duke should marry her in church. But the Duke, however enamoured of his lady, was not yet prepared to go back on his word to his brother; on the contrary, he was most anxious to prove that he was a man of honour. A few months after the birth of his daughter, he invited Duchess Sophia and her two eldest sons to stay with him at Luneburg, where he devised all kinds of entertainment for them. For his young nephews he recruited a company of sons of the local burghers, to enable them to play at real soldiers. For the Duchess he arranged games of cards, plays, balls and fêtes, professing all the time his intention of leaving his duchy to his brother's offspring. Sophia was temporarily placated. She reported to her brother that George William's friendship towards her family had not cooled in any way, in spite of Mme de Harburg's interference. Still, the show of goodwill did not allay her fears altogether, and for the next ten years she kept a watchful eye on any new move on the part of the Duke of Celle towards the improvement of the material estate of his *Madame* and her daughter.

Within the next few years Eleonore gave birth to three more daughters, none of whom survived. Although she felt secure in her husband's love—for so she regarded him—she genuinely feared for her safety should he die and leave her to the mercies of the Bishop of Osnabrück and his Duchess. In her search for a future haven for herself and her daughter in case of emergency, she turned her eyes to France.

George William, like so many other princes of his day, had always admired the glory France achieved under Louis XIV. He had been to the court of Versailles, and was much impressed by its splendour. Even before he met Eleonore d'Olbreuse he emulated French dress and manners and liked to surround himself with Frenchmen who, mostly for religious reasons, had emigrated to Protestant Germany. In this he was not exceptional, for the courts of Hanover and Osnabrück also welcomed French noblemen and promoted them to posts of importance. At Celle however, with a Frenchwoman acting as the lady of the castle, the tendency was more pronounced. Some of the highest dignities in George William's court were held by Frenchmen. There were Beauregards, Villiers, Malorties, Boucoeurs, Boisclairs, Launays and Desmiers, the last being relatives of Eleonore's. Her own household was entirely French. It included Samuel Chappuzeau, a man of letters, and his son Christophe, who later became private secretary to George William and proved a staunch friend to Eleonore and to Sohpie Dorothea until her dying day. From Versailles came reports that Louis XIV favourably viewed this French infiltration through a liaison with a Poitevin lady. Celle became significant as a potential ally, and a French envoy was appointed to it. He was so delighted with the French atmosphere he found there that, when first dining at the Duke's table, he openly complimented him on it. 'Monseigneur,' he exclaimed with more candour than tact, 'What a charming gathering you have here. There are no foreigners here except you'.

Through the mediation of this envoy, and with George William's approval, Eleonore cultivated her French connections in Versailles and petitioned Louis XIV to issue her daughter Sophie Dorothea, French through her mother, with a Certificate of Naturalisation. Hoping to gain some future concession from the influential Duke of Celle, probably in the form of troops, the Sun King graciously granted the request:

Louis, by the grace of God King of France and Navarre. To those present and those to come, greetings. Having regard to the very humble request which has been presented to us on behalf of the lady Sophie Dorothea of Brunswick and Luneburg, who is of the Protestant faith, asking for permission to come and live permanently in France, we declare that, apart from the goodwill we have always had for those who bear this name, we are pleased to bestow on her, in her individual capacity, this mark of our esteem and our benevolence. For these reasons and others, of our own special grace, powers and royal authority, we have recognised, accepted and approved the said lady Sophie Dorothea of Brunswick and Luneburg and signed this document in our own hand. We desire that in her capacity of a French subject she should be allowed to abide in any town or place in our Kingdom which might please her, and that she be allowed such privileges, franchise and liberties as are enjoyed by French subjects by birth. She should be allowed to own property and furniture, provided she ends her days in our Kingdom. . . . This is our pleasure, and in order to perpetuate it we have caused our seal to be affixed unto these instruments.

Given at Lille, in the month of May, in the year of grace one thousand six hundred and seventy one, and the twenty ninth of our reign; also signed,

Louis[2]

Having thus secured a place of refuge for his daughter in case of need, the Duke of Celle set about assuring her future in her own homeland. With little or no pressure from Eleonore, he bought Sophie Dorothea, round about her fifth birthday, five small domains, which were to go to her after his death. Although they were not part of the duchy, and their presentation to Sophie Dorothea did not detract from the integrity of Celle, Ernest Augustus raised all manner of objection. He had to be placated with a large sum of money, and thus a precedent was created. Whenever George William bought more land to bequeath to his daughter, an appropriate compensation had to be paid to his brother. Ernest Augustus grumbled every time, but in actual fact he was much pleased with the arrangement. Not only did it replenish his ever-dwindling coffers, but it was proof that the Duke of Celle, by making separate provisions for his daughter, had no thought of depriving his nephews of their promised inheritance. Only Duchess Sophia foresaw the worst. She could quote at least two examples from German history of Dukes who, having legally bound themselves never to marry in order to bequeath their lands to brothers and nephews, later broke their word and had their Renunciations abrogated. Soon she had fresh cause for alarm.

Great things were taking place at Celle. With the introduction of so much French elegance and taste, the old castle seemed to be in need of total renovation and improvements. A renowned architect was brought over from Italy, and, with the help of local workmen recruited at Eleonore's tactful suggestion, he had the old castle transformed within five years into one of the most attractive residences in Germany. Following a renaissance design, it was divided into four wings, with large interior courts and a forecourt. It had one hundred and eighty rooms, with ornate ceilings and high mantelpieces, and four hundred windows to let the light in. The little theatre in the old part of the castle was renovated, fitted with a large stage, boxes for guests and a royal box for the ducal family. There were plays and concerts by Italian and French troupes, to which Eleonore invited the local dignitaries, seating them according to rank. The Duke was pleased and gratified at her popularity. He was anxious for neighbouring courts to accept her, as guests to his own court did, as his true lady.

In the summer of 1671, shortly after Louis XIV had shown his acceptance of the liaison by conferring a Certificate of Naturalisation on its issue, an opportunity occurred to have Eleonore officially received in the highest quarters. In August of that year, King Frederick III of Denmark and his Queen, sister to George William and Ernest Augustus, came to Germany to arrange a suitable match for their daughter, Princess Wilhelmina. When they made a stay at Altona, George William asked his sister to receive his consort. Duchess Sophia recorded the story of the meeting in her own inimitable way:

The Duke of Celle was anxious to present his mistress to the Queen. At first Her Majesty made some difficulty, but my husband, who wanted to please his brother, used so much persuasion that Her Majesty at last agreed to see her. Accordingly Mme de Harburg came to Altona. She saluted the Queen, who avoided kissing her, but all the same invited her to dinner. Piqued by this reception, the lady revenged herself by making derogatory remarks about the poor quality of the food served at the Queen's table. Her mind was too vulgar to understand that the gods of the land are sustained by higher things than ragouts, and that food to them is a means to exist, not an end in itself.[3]

There was a return of hospitality, and some of the royal party travelled to Celle to spend the day there. The two Dukes shared a carriage with Duchess Sophia and Princess Wilhelmina, while Mme de Harburg was relegated to another, sharing it with her ladies and the French envoy. During the journey Eleonore, who was pregnant, confided to her travelling companions that if she gave birth to a son, the Duke would surely marry her. Her bragging was duly reported to Duchess Sophia, who was greatly upset. Wisely, she did not make an issue of it on the spot, but waited two whole months for a suitable opportunity to tackle George William on the unforgivable presumptuousness of the woman who was, after all, a French nobody. George William was most understanding, to judge by Sophia's memoirs:

> With the approach of winter, the Duke of Celle invited us to pass the cold season at his castle. He had also invited the Princess of East Friesland, who is so entertaining, that it is a pleasure to be in her company. By that time the Duke's love for me had mellowed into friendship, and that was why I hesitated for some time before complaining to him about Mme de Harburg's boast to Princess Wilhelmina that he would marry her if she gave birth to a son. The Duke of Celle was most annoyed and said he could not believe that she could have spoken such utter nonsense. He added that if she did have a son there would be all the more reason for him not to marry her. He assured me he would never marry her in any event, and wanted to oblige me by reprimanding her in my presence for having given me cause for grievance. I instantly begged of him not to make an issue of it and assured him I was fully satisfied with the promises he had made me.[4]

As it happened, Eleonore gave birth to yet another daughter who did not live. By that time Sophia must have given up all pretence that George William was pining for her, or that his fire for Mme de Harburg, like his previous flames, was but of straw. The realisation made her dislike Eleonore all the more. But the real cause of her hostility had deeper roots. Duchess Sophia was a fierce believer in pedigree. A marriage between a Brunswick duke and the daughter of an obscure French count would have been a *mésalliance*, whatever the circumstances. Equality of rank was all-important, and adherence to it virtually an article of faith. That it was thicker than blood Sophia proved years earlier, long before she ever met George William and Eleonore d'Olbreuse.

Charles Louis, the Elector Palatine, at whose Heidelberg court Sophia lived as a young girl, had married Princess Charlotte, daughter of William V of Cassel. After seven unhappy years, he issued a statement in which he formally claimed that throughout their married life his wife had been cantankerous, contrary, moody and rebellious, and that he was therefore obliged to separate from her. At the same time he made known his intention of marrying Baroness Louise Degenfelt, a former maid-of-honour to the Electress. He consulted churchmen and lawyers, and after the divorce was authorised, married Louise in January of 1658. Nine months later she gave birth to a son, the first of their thirteen children, all of whom were created *Raugrafs* and *Raugräfins*.

Some three years after the marriage was sanctioned, Duchess Sophia, who had just borne her first son George Louis, came to spend the winter at her brother's court. In spite of her very real affection for him, she could not bring herself to condone what to her must have seemed a shameful departure from the family code of geneaological parity. She went to see the Electress, who although divorced was still living at Heidelberg, and definitely refused to call on Baroness Degenfelt. She explained to her brother that a formal call might be interpreted as approval on her part of his divorce. Charles Louis, who was very anxious for his sister to meet his wife and the mother of his children, then organised a casual meeting, which the etiquette-bound Duchess could attend, without in any way seeming to approve. She recorded it very carefully in her memoirs:

On March 1, which the English in general and the Royal Family in particular observe by eating in the evening a leek which they have been wearing in their hats throughout the day, in memory of a Prince of Wales who won a battle while wearing this ornament, my brother arranged to send leeks to all the English residents, to Mme Degenfelt, to her children, and to me. He invited me to come and eat my leek in his rooms, and there I met his mistress with the prettiest son and daughter in the world. I greeted all and patted the children, but avoided any further contact, for fear of annoying the Electress Charlotte and bringing upon me the displeasure of my husband. For that lady had not yet attained the position she ultimately held, nor had the Electress entirely given up her claims, which she did in the end, when she went back to her native Cassel.[5]

Many years later, when Charles Louis was long dead, the elderly Duchess Sophia showed much kindness to his children by his second marriage, but she could never bring herself to forgive Baroness Degenfelt for having overstepped her rank. Small wonder she could not forgive Eleonore d'Olbreuse, who had committed the same heinous offence, in much less mitigating circumstances.

Unaware of the forces working for and against her, little Sophie Dorothea was growing up, basking in the love of her parents and the admiration of their court. She was brought up after the fashion of the day, trained in all the accomplishments expected of a young lady of rank. She could sing, dance, embroider and make pretty conversation. She spoke German and French, and as her correspondence later showed, could express herself with clarity and feeling. If she could not compete in book-learning with her cousin Sophie Charlotte, who, like her mother Duchess Sophia, had a bent for philosophy and was reputed to be able to hold her own against Leibnitz himself, she was no different in that respect from the rest of her female Brunswick relatives. She had a lively mind and a quick wit, and more than a touch of French vivacity. She had an instinctive flair for clothes and elegance, which was encouraged and guided by her mother. She was allowed to attend court entertainments, and no doubt was delighted to find herself a growing centre of attraction. There were not many restrictions at the court of Celle, but there was no laxity either. The perfect harmony between the Duke and Mme de Harburg set a high moral tone, and Celle, unlike Osnabrück and Hanover, became known for its virtue and decorum. Duchess Sophia contemptuously called it a mock-court; she may well have envied it its moral stability.

Thanks to her father's purchases of land, Sophie Dorothea, at the age of five or six, was a rich heiress. None was more attracted to her dowry than Duke Anthony Ulric, of the Wolfenbüttel line of the house of Brunswick. He was a man of culture, a writer of some merit, and religious to the point of turning Catholic towards the end of his days;

but above all he was hard up. The upkeep of his court which, like those of Celle and Hanover, was one of the most splendid in Europe, required vast sums of money that far exceeded his revenues. He calculated that a match between his eldest son, Prince Augustus Frederick, and wealthy Sophie Dorothea, would bring in a handsome dowry which would ease his financial difficulties. Accordingly he made a tenative proposal to George William, and had a most encouraging response, for it was deemed a great honour for Sophie Dorothea to be sought in marriage by the son of a Brunswick duke. Then Anthony Ulric produced his one and only condition. He demanded the legitimisation of Sophie Dorothea. A future Duke of Wolfenbüttel, he argued, impoverished as he might be, could never bring home a bride who had no recognised status at her father's court. The condition was welcomed by Eleonore; indeed, she may well have suggested it, as the price of her support. But in all probability it was Anthony Ulric himself who had thought of it. He was just as conscious of his high birth as any other Brunswick. It was hardly surprising that he should point out that no dowry could be acceptable without the backing of a recognised pedigree.

The Duke of Celle was quick to see how important it was to give his daughter a suitable background. A German genealogist was dispatched to France to study the d'Olbreuse family tree. He brought back a genealogy which traced Eleonore's ancestry, through the distaff line, all the way back to Charlemagne. Leibnitz, historiographer to the house of Guelf, from which all the Brunswicks were descended, wrote after examining the genealogy that it was not far removed from reason or credibility. Some of the most illustrious families of France had been known to mingle their blood with lesser, if equally honourable ones. But beyond that statement he remained noncommital, and the Osnabrück court, now really provoked at the prospect of Eleonore's advancement, exposed the whole thing as pure fabrication. Duchess Sophia's niece, the Duchess of Orléans, drew a caricature of her own head cook, with a mock family tree, claiming that he too was descended of an ancient King of France.

All this time the Duke of Celle was moving away from a political alliance with France, in spite of occasional gestures to the contrary. After a period of vacillation, both he and his brother decided to throw in their lot with the Emperor Leopold. In 1672, when the French invaded the United Provinces of the Netherlands, George William ranged his troops against the invaders and commanded the Brunswick-Luneburg troops which formed part of the Imperial army. Ernest Augustus followed suit, and later they both achieved a brilliant military success which led to the recovery of Treves. At that battle the fifteen-year-old George Louis, eldest son of Duchess Sophia and Ernest Augustus, took part. The proud father wrote a detailed letter to his wife, telling her of her son's prowess and of the victory in general. The Duchess recorded in her memoirs how she shared the good news with Mme de Harburg.

I was so pleased with the news, that I at once communicated it to Mme de Harburg, pointing out however that all the Osnabrück men fought valiantly, but not so the men of Celle, who were to blame for Melleville's and Hoxthausen's wounds. . . . That malicious woman, who could not withhold her poison, misinterpreted my letter to mean that I attributed the whole glory of the battle to my husband, whose good fortune made her envious. She was annoyed I said nothing about her Duke, but it was for her to give me his news. She tried to pick a quarrel with me and wrote back some very nasty things. I sent her letter to the Duke of Celle, in order to anticipate any mischief she might try to make between us. He told her to write and apologise to me; but as she had already misconstrued one of my letters to her, I thought it best not to send a reply, and from then on ceased writing to her altogether, to avoid any further misunderstanding.[6]

Whatever Duchess Sophia felt about the performance of the Celle troops on the battlefield, the Emperor Leopold thought highly of it. In Duke George William he saw a loyal and desirable ally, and he was well disposed to reward him in accordance with his proved merit. An opportunity to do so was shortly brought to his notice.

Not having succeeded in making Eleonore d'Olbreuse a scion of French royalty, George William decided to try and obtain for her an hereditary German title. He bought her, with a provision that on her death it would go to Sophie Dorothea, the beautiful island of Wilhelmsburg, on the Elbe, halfway between Harburg and Hamburg. As before, a peace offering had to be sent to Ernest Augustus, in the form of a large sum of money. The purchase of the island was only a first step. The next was to petition the Emperor to confer a German title of nobility on Mme de Harburg, now owner of German land, in consideration of services rendered to His Imperial Majesty by the Duke of Celle on the field of battle. In July 1674 a patent was issued from the Vienna Chancery, granting Eleonore d'Olbreuse the hereditary title of *Reichsgräfin*, Countess of the Empire. At the same time the Empress conferred on the new Countess of Wilhelmsburg the Order of the Female Slaves of Virtue, which was reserved for princesses. Then the right was secured for Sophie Dorothea, daughter and heiress to the Countess of Wilhelmsburg, of bearing the arms of the house of Brunswick, should she marry the young Wolfenbüttel Prince.

All this was gratifying to Eleonore, and pleasing to George William, who felt he was guaranteeing the future of the daughter through the elevation of the mother. The only one who remained dissatisfied was Duke Anthony Ulric. He pointed out, perhaps goaded again by Eleonore, that Sophie Dorothea's birth was still under a cloud. The surest way of securing her incontrovertible legitimisation would be for her father to marry her mother. This was of course what George William would have willingly done years ago, had he not been bound by his Declaration of Renunciation. But now a powerful and persuasive côterie, consisting of Duke Anthony Ulric, Chancellor Schütz and Eleonore, was artfully suggesting that the Duke would not be breaking his obligations if he contracted a morganatic marriage, that is, a marriage which although legal, would not give the right of succession to its issue. George William was willingly persuaded, and authorised Chancellor Schütz to start negotiating with Ernest Augustus to obtain his consent.

This proved a most onerous task. Ernest Augustus had to be reassured every inch of the way. If his brother were to marry, a new foolproof Renunciation had to be made. Men of law, historians and councillors were consulted. Long documents were carefully drawn up, checked, altered and recast. The Emperor's chancery had to be kept informed. No loopholes were to be left. The marriage, if it had to take place, would not be allowed to divert the duchy of Celle from its rightful successors, the Osnabrück nephews.

Halfway through the negotiations the official engagement was announced between Prince Augustus Frederick of Wolfenbüttel, aged eighteen, and Sophie Dorothea, aged nine. Rings were exchanged. Duke Anthony Ulric, impatient for the dowry, thought he might expedite matters by appealing to Duchess Sophia's reported common sense. He wrote her a charming letter, in his best literary style, asking her to tell everybody that to the best of her knowledge Mme de Harburg and the Duke of Celle had legally married in Holland years ago. The Duchess coldly replied that she was not in the habit of telling lies. Instead she wrote to George William upbraiding him for his lack of constancy. He sent back a most reassuring reply.

Madam,
I have received your two letters, but I believe it would be sufficient for me to answer the second only, as both are concerned with the same subject. It is true I am on the point of accomplishing the business which came under discussion at Brockhausen, but it will be done in a manner which will certainly not do you any injustice, and which will leave both you and your children in absolute security. After all I have personally done towards that end, it seems to me, Madam, that you have nothing to fear. Even if Mme de Harburg wishes for the title of Princess, it will be granted to her in a manner which will not affect your children's right of succession. . . . Let this set your mind at rest. May I assure you again that I shall have your interest at heart as long as I live, and that more than anybody else in the world I am your most humble, most obedient,
George William[7]

The negotiations lasted the best part of two years, but at long last legal matters were settled to Ernest Augustus' satisfaction, with the Emperor's approval. In April 1676 a morganatic marriage was contracted between George William, Duke of Celle, and Eleonore d'Olbreuse, Countess of Wilhelmsburg, in the presence of courtiers, local dignitaries, foreign envoys and the Wolfenbüttel family. Duchess Sophia wrote later to her brother that the marriage was celebrated in secret; but that only meant that she had chosen not to be informed of its exact date, in order to have a reasonable excuse not to attend it. In fact the ceremony was given much publicity, with the express purpose of vindicating the omissions of the past. Church bells rang out all over Celle, and the whole court watched their Duke lead to the altar the lady with whom he had been living for the past eleven years. Within a few days the Emperor's envoy came to pay his respects and addressed the Duke's wife as Highness. In church her name was joined in prayers with his, as if she were a reigning Duchess. To Duchess Sophia, daughter and grand-daughter of kings and queens, that must have seemed sacrilege. Two months after the morganatic marriage she wrote venomously to her brother:

Lise Lotte [the Duchess of Orléans] tells me that George William has become the laughing-stock of the French court, for having married a creature who is known to have used all her wiles at one time in order to try and marry the father of the first valet of Monsieur Colin. I have not heard the story before, but it can certainly serve as material to embellish the fine romances which Duke Anthony Ulric embroiders. . . .[8]

At the courts of Celle and Wolfenbüttel there was much jubilation. Eleonore had achieved her ambition of becoming the legal wife of the Duke. George William succeeded in doing the right thing by the woman he loved, without defrauding his younger brother of his promised inheritance. Ten-year-old Sophie Dorothea, fully legitimised, was officially engaged to a Brunswick prince. Duke Anthony Ulric had secured for his son a wealthy heiress and a titled one; and Chancellor Schütz was congratulated all round for having brought off this diplomatic coup, for which, it was rumoured, he was very handsomely and ungrudgingly rewarded.

In August of the same year, barely four months after the happy conclusion of the long drawn-out negotiations, news reached the courts of Brunswick that nineteen-year-old Prince Augustus Frederick of Wolfenbüttel, Sophie Dorothea's fiancé, had died of wounds received in the siege of Philipsburg. To all intents and purposes, he had been no more than a catalyst.

A marriage has been arranged

In the summer of 1665, after a near civil war, the three surviving Luneburg brothers re-distributed their lands according to seniority. George William became Duke of Celle; John Frederick became Duke of Hanover; and Ernest Augustus retained his position as secular bishop of Osnabrück and his right to inherit George William's duchy, as specified in the Declaration of Renunciation.

With the immediate dynastic and matrimonial complications sorted out, the three brothers turned their attention to the glorification of their courts. Each one tried to outshine the other two, and all three modelled their style on Versailles.

The court of Celle, after the alterations and improvements to the castle, was full of splendour. The concessions made to numerous French noblemen fleeing from Catholic France, to settle and worship freely in the duchy, made it easy for the Duke and his wife to keep up the style of their court in the best Versailles tradition. Although George William was rumoured to give the best welcome to those fond of hunting, he also encouraged the arts. He had not frequented Italy in vain. He encouraged musicians, actors and men of letters. Writers dedicated their work to him, while Eleonore took an intelligent interest in literature, history and religious polemics, and found time to read Bossuet's *Histoire des Variations*, specially sent to her from France.

Entertainment served to show off the cultural standard of the court. During the winter season there were plays, balls, concerts and ballets. Italian and French troupes presented their repertoires. A French company of twenty-four was engaged to appear in Celle for four months a year, while John Frederick of Hanover and Ernest Augustus of Osnabrück supported it in their turn, also for four months a year each. During the summer the same entertainments continued in the beautiful castle gardens, where ladies strolled among the trees in grand Parisian dresses. Masquerades were just beginning to become the fashion, and George William gave the lead by appearing as a Spaniard, with Eleonore as a shepherdess. Every year the court went to take the waters at Pyrmont or Wiesbaden; to accommodate the large household sumptuous tents were pitched for the duration of the stay.

The court of Hanover was just as magnificent as Celle. Although John Frederick's subjects looked askance at a Luneburg Duke who had been to Rome and embraced Catholicism, they approved of his exertions to make Hanover a political and cultural centre of importance. Like his brothers, he was widely travelled and had profited by his visits to Italy, Vienna, and above all to the shrine of the splendour-loving German princes of his day—Versailles. He introduced improvements to the ducal palace, and planned a summer residence at nearby Herrenhausen. He imported French actors and actresses, dancers and a whole Italian opera troupe. Like the Duke of Celle, he kept five hundred guards, mounted or on foot, fifty lackeys and twenty-five pages, all in rich liveries. His stables, like George William's, were full, and his coaches were superb. His most outstanding contribution to the name of Hanover, however, was his founding of a magnificent library, at the head of which he put the twenty-six-year-old Leibnitz, already an acclaimed philosopher and mathematician, and a Fellow of the London Royal Society. Leibnitz was also appointed historiographer to the house of Guelf, from which the Brunswicks were descended, and was entrusted with political missions. For the next forty years Hanover basked in his glory.

The court of Osnabrück, although smaller in size and importance, did not lag far behind when it came to spending. Ernest Augustus indulged his taste for luxury, while Duchess Sophia elevated it by insisting on etiquette. Already accomplished as a young woman, she now became a real *grande dame*. As her husband did not let her take part in state affairs, she found an outlet for her intellectual gifts in her patronage of the arts and her large correspondence with the learned, Leibnitz first amongst them. But most of her time was taken up with the bearing and bringing up of her family. In fourteen years she bore Ernest Augustus six boys and a girl.

The eldest, George Louis, destined to become King George I, was born on 28 May 1660 (O.S.). His education was directed towards a military career, for which he showed great promise. When invited as a young boy to visit his uncle, Duke George William, at his Luneburg castle, nothing pleased him more than playing at real soldiers, being put in charge of a company of young boys specially recruited from among the sons of the local people. At fifteen he was already accompanying his father on his campaigns. After the victory of Treves, Duke Ernest Augustus wrote to his wife that 'her Benjamin', as he was wont to call her favourite son, had never left his side throughout the battle, and had proved himself worthy of his mother. This must have been a tribute to the way she brought her children up, for she was a strict disciplinarian and tried to instill both valour and virtue into them. But virtue could never be a characteristic of a court ruled by the pleasure-loving Ernest Augustus. Behind the facade of strict etiquette, there was much licence. Early in his married life the Duke took a mistress called Susanne de la Manselière, who was later succeeded by a chambermaid named Esther. The Duchess had to accept her husband's infidelities, while the young princes tried to emulate the paternal example.

George Louis inherited some of his father's appetites, without his charm. He was short, fair-skinned, with bright blue eyes, which were said to reflect the irascible expression of the Guelfs. His manner was rough and ready. Brought up as a soldier, he carried into court some of the habits of the field. Not even a spell at Versailles could improve his manners. By nature cold and reserved, he was accused of being stupid and lazy. He certainly had no interest in the arts, but was fond of music, particularly of opera. He spoke and wrote both German and French. Rude and brutal he might have been, but not a seeker of intrigues. It was said that he never told a lie.

With the passing of years, Duke Ernest Augustus, a mere life-bishop of Osnabrück, was beginning to cast about for a suitable bride for his eldest son, who would bring him a welcome dowry. Not unnaturally, his thoughts turned to the rich heiress in nearby Celle. Duke Anthony Ulric had done all the spadework. Thanks to his efforts, so unwelcome at the time, Sophie Dorothea was now the legitimate child of Duke George William and his legally-wedded wife; a future Countess of Wilhelmsburg, and an heiress in her own right. If a match were to be arranged between George Louis and his cousin, the whole vexed question of the Celle succession would be settled once and for all, for George Louis would inherit the duchy not only on the strength of the original Renunciation, still in danger of being revoked through some fresh intrigue, but also on the strength of a matrimonial alliance. Ernest Augustus had always been fond of his elder brother, and no doubt regretted the hostility that had grown between the two families. He never disliked Eleonore d'Olbreuse as a person, and certainly had nothing against her daughter, whose charm and beauty must have reached his ears. Altogether it seemed to him a shrewd way both of making his peace with his brother and of looking after his family's interests.

By that time Sophie Dorothea had several suitors: the French Count Soisson; the Hereditary Prince of Sweden; Prince Henry Casimir of Nassau-Dietz; and Prince George of Denmark (later the husband of Queen Anne). At the top of list, however, there was another young Wolfenbüttel.

Having once had the prize within his grasp, Duke Anthony Ulric was loth to let go of Sophie Dorothea's dowry. He therefore suggested a match with his second son, only a year younger than the bride. Eleonore, his grateful ally of previous years, was all for it; but George William was in no hurry to accept. Now he could afford to bide his time. When Ernest Augustus broached the subject of marriage between the two young cousins, he listened with interest. He too felt the time had come to bury the hatchet, and uniting the two houses in matrimony was the best way of doing it. Weighing the advantages of one match against the other, George William decided to play safe. He made a gentleman's agreement with Anthony Ulric, accepting his suit on behalf of his son, on the understanding that the engagement would be kept secret until Sophie Dorothea's sixteenth birthday. That gave him some three or four years to look around and to consider his brother's proposition at leisure.

The main obstacle was of course the feud between the women of the two families. Even if the brothers could see the need for a *rapprochement*, the wives still had to be won over. George William tackled his side of the problem by allowing Eleonore to think that the matter was settled with the Wolfenbüttels, and that the overtures from Osnabrück were not to be taken too seriously. She was not therefore unduly worried. But Duchess Sophia, when told of the project, was horrified. She had never ceased to regard the Frenchwoman as an upstart, and the idea of allowing her 'Benjamin' to marry the daughter of a nobody must have been galling. On the other hand she was a practical woman. She had proved it years ago when she accepted one husband as a substitute for another; and she could be relied on to prove it again when it came to the material well-being of her children. In June 1679 she wrote to her brother for advice:

Ernest Augustus often feels that, as he is not well and might die before his brothers, his children would be left unprovided for. Now for some time there have been overtures from Celle, offering him an annual allowance of 50,000 crowns as well as 100,000 in cash, if he agrees to the marriage of my eldest son and George William's daughter. The boy has an aversion for the marriage and so have we for an alliance with d'Olbreuse, although Mr Hyde [father of Anne Hyde, wife of James II] was not better descended; but his daughter at least was twice legitimate. In view of these considerations I feel I ought to ask them to raise the sum offered. What would you say if they offered 80,000 by way of annual allowance? Would you consider it a sufficient inducement? .... Though even this will not make the proposition pleasant to me, becoming related to a *scoupette* [?][1]

An entry in Duchess Sophia's diary, made later that summer, tried to strengthen the impression conveyed to her brother, that the proposal had not originated from Ernest Augustus who could have never conceived of such a shameful plan, but from outside:

Some genuinely or professedly well-meaning persons tried to reconcile the two brothers. But it was not easy to forget the step the Duke of Celle had taken, and my husband could not come towards him without prejudicing his own interests. A marriage was suggested between the Duke of Celle's daughter and my eldest son, but my husband found it so much beneath his son's dignity, that he decided never to accept it, unless it was to his definite advantage, and unless it guaranteed him finally against any evil machinations, should Mme de Harburg give birth to a son. My husband therefore demanded two fortresses and an annual allowance of 100,000 crowns, and deliberately took a very long time over the negotiations without coming to any definite arrangement.[2]

The gradual increase of the annual allowance from 50,000 to 80,000, and finally to 100,000 crowns, indicated that both sides were keen on the bargain. However, Eleonore put a temporary spoke in the wheels when she snubbed the Duchess of Mecklenburg, who tried to act as a mediator between the two parties. Duchess Sophia accused Eleonore of being haughty. Perhaps she was; or perhaps she just entered into the spirit of the game and proved a hard bargainer. Whatever the reason, the negotiations came to a temporary halt.

The respite gave Duchess Sophia a chance to fulfil a cherished dream of hers. It was nearly thirty years since she had last seen her sister Louise, now the Abbess of Maubuisson; and she was missing her niece Lise Lotte, Duchess of Orléans. She decided to visit them. Ernest Augustus readily agreed to let his wife go to Versailles, for pleasure could be combined with a diplomatic mission. Relations with France had been rather strained since the two Brunswick Dukes openly espoused the cause of the Emperor, and Madam Bishop's visit could be used as an unofficial gesture of reconciliation. At the same time it was decided that eleven-year-old Sophie Charlotte, the Duchess's fourth child, would accompany her mother on the trip, with an eye to a possible French match. The ambitious Duchess set her sights high, hoping to carry off no lesser a prize than the Dauphin himself. She travelled incognito, calling herself Mme d'Osnabrück, and arrived in France in time to witness the engagement, by proxy, of young Marie Louise, a niece of Louis XIV's, to Charles II of Spain.

Although it was not a state visit, Mme d'Osnabrück was lodged in the palace. She recorded in her diary that the two rooms allotted to her were rather small and poor, as the best ones were occupied by Mme de Montespan, the King's *maîtresse-en-titre*. After the engagement ceremony was over, she had an unofficial meeting with the Sun King, in the presence of the Duchess of Orléans, her husband the Duke of Orléans, or Monsieur, as he was called as brother to the King, and the Dauphin. Louis XIV treated Duchess Sophia as if she was an accredited envoy, and it was to her credit that she never set a foot wrong and knew how to ward off his attack with tact and firmness. She described the meeting in great detail:

The King was announced. Madame ran forward to salute him, and so did I. He said aloud: 'I have not come to see you, Madame, but Mme d'Osnabrück'. He asked at once if the Queen had come, giving me to understand that he had wished her to do so in my honour. But her Spanish pride would not let her come.

The King neglected nothing in his manner and conversation that could show him the most courteous of princes. Monsieur tried to whisper something in his ear, but His Majesty said aloud: 'It is not polite to whisper in the presence of Madame d'Osnabrück.' Monsieur raised his voice to make me see how anxious the King was to please me. Indeed His Majesty omitted nothing that could prove it to me, and he made every imaginable agreeable speech, even mentioning to me one of the battles that the Dukes had won against him, saying that he realised they were his enemies. I replied that as they had not had the good fortune to win his favour, at least they had tried to win his esteem. The King said there had been a time when he dared not ask for their friendship. I said I was pleased that such a time was a thing of the past, and that I had since seen him swear to peace. He said there was indeed a clause about peace, but it was binding only as long as it was for the good of his country. I expressed the hope it would be for long. He retorted, raising his head: 'I do not think the German princes will go to war against me again.' He then spoke of his troops, of the number he had dismissed, and the strong numbers he still had. Monsieur followed his example by exaggerating likewise. Then the King complimented me on my daughter, whom he said he thought pretty, and added he heard she was also intelligent. He asked whether she should be addressed as Mademoiselle or Madame, explaining he believed that Madame was the German customary form. After some further small talk he took his leave, absolutely forbidding me to accompany him.[3]

There was no immediate political outcome of that visit. The hoped-for match with the Dauphin never got off the ground. The Sun King however showed his friendship and esteem by sending both Duchess Sophia and her daughter two large boxes set with jewels. On examination, the Duchess pronounced them poor in quality, and Louis XIV, to placate her, sent her another present consisting of a set of twelve diamond buttons.

Duchess Sophia was no sooner home than the unpleasant prospect of a Celle marriage came up again. In November 1679 she wrote to her brother:

I have talked to M. Coppensten of the proposition made to us from Celle. This is a bitter pill to swallow, but when it is gilded with an annual allowance of 100,000 crowns, I shall close my eyes and take it . . . . Ernest Augustus says he is a sick man and wants to see my children well established when they grow up and the business of the succession settled, to set his mind at rest. As for me, I find this business most disagreeable, and I would sooner have John Frederick's girl for a daughter-in-law, with only 30,000 crowns annual allowance . . . .[4]

At this stage, a most dramatic change occurred in the fortunes of the Osnabrück family. In December 1679 Duke John Frederick of Hanover, always a heavy drinker, suddenly died, without leaving an heir. On hearing the news, Sophia merely remarked that 'he died like a true German, a glass in hand'. Ernest Augustus, not any more grief-stricken than his wife, simply shrugged his shoulders and said he was well pleased it was not himself who had died. He had every reason to be pleased, for he was next in the line of succession. Overnight he found himself a Duke not only in name, but in practice. His status became equal to Celle and Wolfenbüttel. His standing with the Emperor, and indeed with any other sovereign, was no more conditioned by Celle's leadership. At long last he became a power in the land, to be reckoned with in his own right. He lost no time in moving his court from Osnabrück to Hanover, where, twenty years earlier, he had started life as a married man.

On his coronation as Duke of Hanover, in October 1680, a few months after his brother's death, Ernest Augustus set about improving his new court. He seized upon his predecessor's plan to build a summer residence at Herrenhausen, and elaborated it. The gardens were laid out by Lenôtre himself. The orangery, with its glass panels, was a sensation at a time when glass houses were still a rarity. It provided the ducal table with oranges, apples and pineapples out of season, and in later years became a favourite retreat of the ageing Duchess. The stables were put at a suitable distance from the residence, with room for six hundred horses and many carriages.

The same grand scale was applied to improvements at the Hanover palace on the Leine river, in the heart of the city. It was renovated and redecorated. Pictures and tapestries were imported from Holland. The interior of the palace chapel was gilded from top to bottom. An entirely new opera house was built, and an Italian opera established under the Venetian composer Steffani. Like George William, Ernest Augustus now employed hundreds of guards, lackeys and pages. There were ministers, equerries, stewards, officers, valets, maids of honour, ladies-in-waiting, and chamber maids. The arts were encouraged. The Duchess invited French artists to weave a Gobelin tapestry, depicting scenes from the life of Duke George, ancestor of the Luneburgs, and that of her mother, the Queen of Bohemia. There were frequent plays and concerts. On Sundays the court would assemble in chapel for the service, in the afternoon watch the French comedians. A contemporary foreign visitor wrote that there were few courts in Europe which could outshine those of the two Luneburg brothers, at Hanover and Celle.

In the midst of all this excitement, Sophia lost one of the few people she really loved and trusted, her brother Charles Louis, Elector

Palatine. He was carried off by an eight-day fever, in the summer of 1680, and thus did not live to see his little sister, whom he once married off to a landless Duke, crowned as Duchess of Hanover. Sophia felt his loss deeply. He had been like a father to her—he was thirteen years her senior—and she had always sought and trusted his advice. They used to correspond by every post, and his letters were one of her chief pleasures in life. With his death, she suddenly felt that she too was an old woman. She was nearly fifty, she suffered from an affection of the spleen, and for a time she thought it would not be long before she would follow her brother to the grave. However, it was not like her to be despondent. Family affairs were demanding her attention, and with her new status, exciting new possibilities were opening up. Her thoughts turned to matrimonial projects.

Duchess Sophia had always set much store by her Stuart ancestry, and never tired of pointing out that her mother was Elizabeth, Queen of Bohemia, and her grandfather King James I. Nor was it hollow pride on her part. For her it was a factor that had to be taken into account when looking at the future. Although many degrees removed from the English throne, she knew that each death among her numerous relatives in England brought her a step nearer. To strengthen her links with the royal family, she now suggested that George Louis should go to London, to ask for the hand of Princess Anne of York, whose sister Mary was the wife of William of Orange. Ernest Augustus did not think much of the idea, but allowed himself to be persuaded and equipped his son for the journey.

George Louis, an awkward youth of twenty, set out on his way, paying a courtesy call on William of Orange at The Hague. William had maintained cordial relations with both Luneburg Dukes, and exchanged letters with both Sophia and Eleonore. On Ernest Augustus's accession to the Duchy of Hanover, he persuaded him to make the final gesture of peace towards Celle, by recognising Eleonore's right to the title of Duchess. Sophia pretended to herself that her husband did it out of kindness to his last surviving brother, but the truth was that Ernest Augustus agreed to call Eleonore Duchess in the hope of winning her over to his pet idea of a match between the two houses.

George Louis reached England in December 1680. His barque anchored in the mud off Greenwich with no court officials to welcome him, although his visit must have been expected. He sent word to his uncle Rupert, who immediately sorted things out and had his nephew installed at Whitehall. Early in the new year, George Louis reported to his mother on his progress:

After wishing Your Serene Highness a very Happy New Year, I will not delay in telling you that I arrived here on December 6, having remained one day at anchor at Greenwich till M. Beck went on shore to take a house for me. He looked up Uncle Rupert and let him know of my arrival, and he, on his part, informed King Charles at once. His Majesty immediately allotted me an apartment at Whitehall. M. Beck requested Uncle Rupert to excuse me; but King Charles insisted that I should be treated like a cousin, and after that no more could be said. On the following day M. Cotterel came to Greenwich with a royal barque and took me to Whitehall. I had not been there more than two hours when Milord Hamilton came to take me to the King, who received me most kindly. Uncle Rupert had gone there before me, and was at court when I saluted King Charles. When making my obeisance to the King, I took the opportunity of giving him your letter. He then spoke of Your Serene Highness and said that he 'remembered you well'. After he had talked with me for a while he left to join the Queen [Catherine of Braganza]. When I was taken to them he made me kiss her skirt. The next day I saw the Princess of York, and I greeted her with a kiss, with the consent of the King. The day after I went to see Uncle Rupert, who received me in bed, for he has an ailment in his leg which often keeps him to his bed. He has to take care of himself. All the Milords came to see me without discussing matrimonial projects. Milord Grey came to see me very often indeed. They cut off the head of Lord Stafford yesterday, and made no more ado about it than if they had chopped off the head of a chicken. I have no more to tell Your Serene Highness, and therefore conclude, remaining your very humble son and servant,

George Louis[5]

The courting was not successful. Princess Anne, seventeen and attractive, did not think much of her unprepossessing German relative, who could not speak a word of English. Other forces were also working against him. William of Orange, married to Mary of York, used secret diplomacy to prevent the match between Anne and George Louis, in order to have one less obstacle on his slow progress towards the throne of England. His allies discreetly whispered in Anne's ear that George Louis disliked her on sight, and that if he did not press his suit, it was chiefly because he considered that the daughter of Anne Hyde was not good enough for a Brunswick. After that Anne would have nothing to do with him, and to the end of her life treated him with extreme coolness.

Neither King Charles nor his brother the Duke of York, later King James II, were keen on the match, and soon George Louis realised he was wasting his time. But as he had come such a long way, he took the opportunity of paying a visit to Cambridge, where an honorary degree of Doctor of Laws was conferred on him. In the spring of 1681 he returned home, empty-handed.

His father had not thought much of the English plan in the first place. Its failure gave him an added argument in favour of his own. By that time he had an influential ally at Celle. Chancellor Schütz, who had sided with Eleonore, was mercifully dead, and his place was taken by his son-in-law Bernstorff. The new Chancellor continued the negotiations between the two courts, and proved more of service to Ernest Augustus, with whom he was supposed to bargain, than to George William, whom he represented. Through his mediation, relations between the two courts became more cordial, outwardly at least, and eventually the time came when the Duke and Duchess of Celle were invited to visit Hanover.

It must have been a trial for both Duchesses, but both apparently played their parts well. Sophia was gracious to the woman she still despised, but to whom she now accorded the full title of Duchess; and Eleonore, received at last by her haughty relatives on equal terms, must have known better than to rake up old quarrels. She was flattered and grateful and spoke, for the first time in years, of the civility and kindness shown her by the Duke and Duchess of Hanover. By then she must have also weighed up the advantages to her daughter of marrying George Louis. Barred from becoming Duchess of Celle through her father, Sophie Dorothea was being offered a chance of obtaining that title, and more, through her future husband. It was a prize that Eleonore d'Olbreuse, woman of the world as she was, could not dismiss off hand.

The visit went off without a hitch. There were receptions and festivities, and much haggling behind the scenes. The brothers were inseparable again. They spent long hours talking to one another as of old, and Leibnitz dubbed their frequent tête-à-têtes 'the princely debates'. Mostly they were debating the size of Sophie Dorothea's marriage settlement, which one brother considered too large, the other too small. Other visits followed. The Duchess of Celle was in two minds about the whole scheme, and kept her eyes and ears open for other proposals. In August 1682, a few weeks before Sophie Dorothea's sixteenth birthday, Eleonore and George William went to Hanover for yet another round of talks. M. d'Arcy, the French envoy to Celle, their constant companion, sent a detailed report to Louis XIV, who had been kept closely informed of the progress of the negotiations, as he hoped that an alliance between the French-orientated court of Celle and that of Hanover would be advantageous to him. The envoy wrote:

On our way back to Celle, two days later than anticipated, the Duchess told me of the main points of the negotiations. She confided to me that the Duke of Hanover talked to the Duke of Celle some five or six hours every day, trying to obtain his consent to his conditions. . . . The Duke and Duchess of Hanover talked to her too, and also to her sister the Countess of Reus. Their ardour to consummate this business was so great that the Duchess of Hanover got out of her bed as many as three times in one night, in order to come and talk to the Duchess of Celle. . . . Her Highness is apprehensive of this marriage, which would make her dependent on the house of Hanover, who are no friends of hers, and which could diminish her influence over her husband. . . . She did not conceal from me that she had done, and would go on doing, all she could to stop the conclusion of the negotiations. . . . She indicated that the contract should be either concluded or totally abandoned within the next eight or ten days.[6]

The time-limit of eight or ten days was an allusion to Sophie Dorothea's approaching sixteenth birthday, on 15 September, when, if the Hanover deal fell through, the Wolfenbüttel suit would be made public. By that time the 'secret' understanding must have been a known factor in court circles, and quick action was taken accordingly. Count Platen, Ernest Augustus's minister, drew up a final draft, withdrawing some of his master's most exorbitant demands, and took it to Celle. After some further modifications the financial terms were acceptable to both parties. On 14 September, the French envoy D'Arcy sent the following despatch to Louis XIV:

Sire,
The marriage between the Princess of Celle and the eldest Prince of Hanover was agreed upon the day before yesterday. Monsieur Platen arrived here two days ago, having been preceded by three messengers, and spent all day working with the ministers of the Duke of Celle. In the evening, noting that his court was anxious to be informed of the progress of the marriage negotiations, the Duke took me aside together with his wife the Duchess and told me that the marriage had been agreed upon, and that he was telling me that in confidence, in my capacity of minister to Your Majesty, and also because I was a personal friend, for they were not going to announce it publicly for some time yet. . . . The Duchess later admitted that what decided her to give up her opposition to the marriage was the realisation that the Prince of Nassau [on whom she had pinned her hopes] was not going to be able to meet the demands that the Duke of Celle had made as a condition for the hand of his daughter.[7]

Once the agreement was signed and sealed, Eleonore put a brave face on it, silencing her maternal fears for the happiness of her daughter under a show of enforced gaiety. On 8 October she wrote to her brother in France:

At last, dear brother, my daughter has been settled with the most pleasant prince in Germany, and the richest. He is the heir of this house, Prince of Hanover, and my husband's nephew. As nothing more advantageous could have ever happened to my daughter, I am sure you will share the joy that this arrangement gives me.[8]

It was a pure business transaction, without any regard for the feelings of the two persons most concerned. But both knew what to expect.

Three years of negotiations could not have left them in ignorance of what was going on. If the long period of suspense did not help to endear the cousins to one another, it at least took away the element of shock. That the choice finally fell on the person each liked least was unfortunate, but it was certainly not unexpected.

This fact cannot be stressed enough, in view of the many accounts that the match was arranged at the eleventh hour, descending on the Princess and her mother out of a clear sky. Sophie Dorothea's later unhappiness won her a host of apologists, who clung to a highly-dramatised version of the match-making, in order to excuse her subsequent deviation from the narrow path. Foremost among them was Duke Anthony Ulric, who, in 1707, twenty-five years after the event, brought out a sixth volume of his *roman-à-clef* entitled *The Roman Octavia*, in which he dramatically embroidered on the happenings preceding Sophie Dorothea's marriage. He had of course an axe to grind, as the father of the unsuccessful suitor; and he was a staunch friend of Duchess Eleonore, in spite of the failure of their mutual matrimonial projects. His story was a clever mixture of fact and fiction, that so caught the imagination of later generations, that it was repeated and rehashed throughout the eighteenth, nineteenth and even the twentieth century. The lack of factual evidence was made up for by the story's emotional impact.

According to this version, both the Duke and the Duchess of Celle were very much in favour of the secret agreement with the young Prince of Wolfenbüttel, and had no thought of entering into negotiations with any other suitors. The Duchess was happily ticking off the days left until Sophie Dorothea's sixteenth birthday, when the secret engagement was to be made public. As 15 September 1682 approached, the castle was alive with preparations for the great occasion. Chancellor Bernstorff, a minister to George William but a despicable spy for the court of Hanover, suddenly became alert. Perhaps his suspicions were aroused by the festive preparations which seemed far too elaborate for a mere birthday party; or perhaps the Duchess herself, bubbling over with excitement, let slip something about the surprise announcement to be made at the banquet. Bernstorff was quick to put two and two together. He immediately sent word to Hanover that Celle was about to be united to Wolfenbüttel, and that if Duke Ernest Augustus wanted to take steps to secure his inheritance, there was not a moment to lose.

Greatly alarmed at the news, the Duke summoned his wife for a council of war. He told her of the impending engagement, and explained how it might undermine the Succession agreement, about the validity of which he had never felt quite happy. He suggested that to avoid future complications, it would be best for their eldest son George Louis to marry Sophie Dorothea. He then proceeded to discuss ways and means of carrying out his idea. He cunningly pointed out to the Duchess that, as she was the one who had most shown contempt for the future in-laws, it was up to her to take the first step towards reconciliation. He flattered her on her tact and powers of persuasion, and hinted that George Willian was still fond of her and would sooner listen to her good sense than to the wailing of his wife.

Horrified as the Duchess was at the prospect of entering into matrimonial relations with the family of 'that creature', she soon realised how much her son stood to gain from it. She also realised the tremendous urgency of the situation. It was late evening on 14 September. The engagement with the young Prince of Wolfenbüttel was due to be announced the following morning. There was only the space of one night left for action.

Once her mind was made up, she knew exactly what to do. The ducal coach and the fine Mecklenburg horses were ordered out, outriders were ready in no time, and the Duchess was on her way. There are twenty miles between Hanover and Celle. The autumn rain had made the road muddy, and the heavy coach rumbled all night before it came to a halt outside the gates of the castle. The heavy-eyed guards, stung into action at the unaccustomed sight of the red and blue liveries of the house of Hanover, instantly lowered the drawbridge. The morning sun had just risen. Once in the forecourt, the Duchess heaved a sigh of relief. There were no carriages there. The Wolfenbüttels had not yet arrived. Barely waiting to be announced, pushing footmen and pages out of her way, she charged in and demanded to be taken immediately to His Serene Highness the Duke of Celle. When told that he had just woken up, she had herself conducted to his suite without ceremony.

The astounded George William was at his dressing-table. His

wife was at hers, in the adjoining room, with the door half-open. Duchess Sophia loudly explained that she had come all the way from Hanover to be the first to offer her congratulations on the occasion of Sophie Dorothea's sixteenth birthday. She then produced her very special birthday present, a miniature of cousin George Louis, set in diamonds.

Glancing disapprovingly at the half-open door, behind which Duchess Eleonore was obviously listening, Sophia switched from French into Dutch, or Low Dutch, or even to what one version called 'the Teutonic language', with none of which the Duchess of Celle was sufficiently conversant. In one of those languages Duchess Sophia disclosed to her brother-in-law the real purpose of her visit.

As she expected, he was first taken aback, then charmed. By breakfast-time he had made up his mind. He summoned his wife and his daughter and informed them that a better match had just been arranged. A few minutes later, when the Duke of Wolfenbüttel's carriages rolled into the courtyard, he went out to greet them with the same announcement. The Duke and his son did not wait to be further insulted and drove out straight away, leaving the field clear to the Duchess of Hanover.

It was no use pleading with the Duke of Celle. The serpent's logic of his sister-in-law clouded his judgment, and he turned a deaf ear to his wife's entreaties and his daughter's sobbing. Sophie Dorothea shut herself up in her rooms and refused to go down and greet her future mother-in-law. When Duchess Sophia's birthday present was sent up to her, she so vehemently flung it against the wall, that all the precious diamonds were scattered on the floor. But she could not hold out long against paternal authority. In the evening she went down to the banqueting hall and presided over her birthday feast, attended by Duke Ernest Augustus and Prince George Louis, who had come post-haste from Hanover, as soon as Duchess Sophia's triumphant message reached them. The whole court heard with astonishment the announcement of an engagement they had not expected. The bride and bridegroom sat scowling at one another, while the Duke and Duchess of Hanover gloated over their victory. A contract was speedily prepared, making all Sophie Dorothea's property over to her future husband. The marriage was celebrated almost immediately, 'with as much pomp as the little

THE ELECTRESS SOPHIA
by Hannemann

ERNEST AUGUSTUS, ELECTOR OF HANOVER
by Vaillant

THE CASTLE AT CELLE

time they had to prepare would admit'. The bride was beautifully dressed, but all the ornaments in the world could not conceal her unhappiness. 'As for the bridegroom, he was by nature sullen, reserved, haughty and selfish. He considered the Princess as the title deed to the duchy of Celle.... and though he gave his hand to his bride, his heart still remained in the bosom of his mistress.'⁹

A few days later George Louis took his young bride home to Hanover. As he was helping her out of her carriage, in the forecourt of the ducal palace, she happened to look up at one of the windows. A richly dressed woman was insolently staring at her full in the face. It was George Louis's mistress. Sophie Dorothea's slim chance of happiness vanished for ever.

Even without the highly-coloured elements of this traditional version of the union, Sophie Dorothea's chances of happiness could not have looked very bright in the autumn of 1682. Her dislike for her boorish cousin must have far outweighed the charm of becoming Princess, and in due course Duchess, of Hanover. Nor could she delude herself about the reception the court was going to mete out to the daughter of the woman until recently so openly resented. Unfortunately there was nothing a young princess could do against the wisdom of politicians. Her best course was to resign herself to the marriage, and dissemble her fears and repugnance as best she could. And so, guided by her mother, Sophie Dorothea penned a stilted letter to her future mother-in-law, hiding her unhappiness behind well-chosen words of submission:

Madam,

I have so much respect for my lord the Duke your husband, and for my lord my own father, that in whatever manner they may act on my behalf I shall always be content. Your Highness will do me, I know, the justice to believe that no one can be more sensible than I am of the many marks of your kindness. As long as I live I shall strive to deserve it, and I hope to make it evident by my respect and my very humble service, that Your Highness could not have chosen as daughter one who knows better than myself how to pay you what is due. In which duty I shall feel very great pleasure, and also in showing you by my submission that I am,

>Madam,

>>Your Highness's very humble and very
>>obedient servant,

>>>Sophie Dorothea[10]

Celle, 21 October 1682.

Three days later she put her signature to the marriage settlement agreement drawn up by the court ministers. Her property was made over to her husband, leaving her without any private income of her own. This arrangement did not strike anybody as either unfair or incautious, for it was taken for granted that the Prince of Hanover would keep his wife in a state that befitted her rank. Duke George William put his signature next to his daughter's, while Duke Ernest Augustus and his son signed in their turn. There was nothing left to it but to prepare the wedding festivities. The preparations progressed with all possible speed, and the marriage was consecrated on 21 November 1682. The French envoy d'Arcy dutifully reported the details to Louis XIV:

The marriage was consecrated yesterday without any ceremony and without anybody's knowledge, as we had indeed imagined it would. In the evening, after Their Highnesses of Celle and Hanover had supped in the usual way, with the same people as on previous evenings, they retired to their apartments round ten o'clock at night. Then they went to the Princess of Celle's suite, where a minister was already waiting. The marriage was consecrated in the presence of Their Highnesses of Celle and Hanover, M. de Podewils and M. de Chauvet, their lieutenant-generals, and some of the chief officers of the two Dukes, who had been secretely warned to be present. . . . The following evening there was a small opera and ballet combined, to celebrate the occasion, and tonight I believe there is going to be quite a beautiful display of fireworks.[11]

It was a far cry from the ceremony that marked the wedding of Duchess Sophia twenty years earlier. There were no bridesmaids holding a train of prodigious length, no cannons, and no German princes dancing round the young couple with lighted torches in their hands. All the same, the village of Celle was bedecked with flags, and visitors from other courts drove in their splendid carriages to offer their congratulations and their presents. Ten days after the wedding the bride and bridegroom drove to Hanover, escorted by a cavalry regiment and an elaborate procession of trumpeters, pages, officers and ministers, with both ducal families following in their state coaches. In Hanover festivities were organised on a scale which far outshone the relatively modest ones offered at Celle. The court dutifully paid its respects to the new Princess, while Leibnitz commemorated the occasion with a specially composed epithalamium, in which he lavished fulsome praise on the bride and bridegroom like any fashionable versifier:

O Prince, whose valour and whose lofty thought
Dazzle an age where Love holds court,
Win all thy fame, then givest to passion
What Mars and Venus each ask in their fashion;
Thy heart so bold in war's alarms
Admits a victor and lays down its arms . . .

The Heavenly Fair who conquered thy heart
Returneth thy love and shared joys doth impart,
While the people, entranced by the cause of thy capture,
Kiss the ground where she walks, fair goddess, in rapture.
Like a present from Heaven devoid of all spot,
That binds you together, puts the seal on the knot.
We owe after all our best thanks to fair France
Who sent us this lady our lives to enhance.
Adorable Duchess, raised now to this sphere,
Where virtue adorns even those without peer.
All Europe expects of this noble alliance
The product of beauty and proud defiance.
Prince, fair is thy fortune, for whom Heaven is so zealous,
Thou makest the gods, let alone kings, jealous.[12]

The reign of mistresses

Early in her married life Duchess Sophia had to admit that the state of holy matrimony had not changed what she discreetly referred to as 'the Duke's gay character'. She observed that he was restless, easily bored, contemptuous of what he possessed and hankering after what he did not. She was too sensible and too much of a lady to make any jealous scenes. She hid her grief behind a mask of dignity, and professed to be content with the outward marks of honour that the Duke meticulously paid her. Indeed, her resignation to her husband's infidelities was so misleading that many took it for indifference and criticised her apparent friendliness towards her husband's mistresses. Only to her diary could she confide how lonely she was during his frequent absences from home and how happy she was whenever he came back. The very writing of her diary was a task she undertook to take her mind off her loneliness during one of his long Italian tours.

The visits to Italy afforded the Duke all the latitude he wanted, and continued for many years. When they had to be spaced out for reasons of state, consolation was found nearer home. The Duke's early extra-marital affairs were of little significance and made no noticeable impact on court life. But the situation changed radically with the arrival at Osnabrück of Clara Elizabeth von Meissenburg.

Clara Elizabeth was the eldest daughter of Count Meissenburg from Hesse, who had lost his fortune and who was, according to some accounts, no better than a military adventurer. When his second daughter, Catherine Marie, came of age he took both sisters to Versailles, to give them the final social polish, and perhaps to find them French husbands. As his hopes did not materialise, he took them back to Germany and cast about for a suitable court to introduce them into. Osnabrück, under its gay Bishop, had already made a name for itself as a centre of elegance and pleasure. The three Meissenburgs decided to try their luck there, and in due course had themselves presented.

The sisters could not have chosen a more propitious time to show off their accomplishments. The year was 1673. Duchess Sophia's two eldest sons, aged thirteen and twelve, had just returned with their governors from an educational tour abroad, and many festivities were being held in their honour. The two sisters, fresh from Versailles, obtained permission to contribute a short French entertainment, of their own composition, in which they both appeared as shepherdesses. They described it as 'a pastoral play to entertain their Highnesses the young Princes of Brunswick-Luneburg on the occasion of their return to Osnabrück, devised by the *demoiselles* Meissenburg'. They must have been quite clever with their words and rendering, for the sophisticated court pronounced their play the best entertainment of all. They were much sought out and their popularity was assured. Clara Elizabeth was twenty-five, Catherine Marie eighteen.

In view of their later careers as accomplished court mistresses, it was alleged that even at that early stage the sisters were out to capture the hearts of the two young Princes. This might be taken with a pinch of salt, for both Princes were mere boys at the time, and had not yet embarked on the military career that was to make men out of them. It is more likely that the sisters genuinely tried to make a favourable impression, with the legitimate aim of finding suitable husbands. This they were soon able to do. Clara Elizabeth married Frank Ernest Platen, governor to Prince George Louis, while her younger and prettier sister married John Busche, governor to the younger Prince. Both husbands were coming men. Platen, when no longer required as governor to an adolescent prince, was offered another post of distinction at court, and gradually became Ernest Augustus's trusted minister. His wife was made Mistress of the Robes in Duchess Sophia's household. The Busches did equally well, and when the Osnabrück court moved to Hanover, the two families moved with it. By that time it had become clear that marriage, for both sisters, was only the first rung in the ladder.

Clara Elizabeth Platen was described by her biographers as the epitome of all evil. She was dishonest, vicious, mean, jealous and wicked, while her lust for power was exceeded only by her lust for men. She may well have been all that, but the key to her character was her ambition. Above all she wanted power and the privileges that went with it, and, in common with so many women of her age, she believed that the surest way to achieve both was through the sovereign's bed. In that she was no more reprehensible than any other courtesan of her time. She was perhaps less delicate than Mme de Montespan in her technique; she was certainly less scrupulous then her French counterpart in her methods of removing obstacles from her way. But basically she was no worse than any other royal mistress who was determined to defend her equivocal status as best she could.

It is not certain when exactly she became Ernest Augustus's mistress. It could not have been immediately after her marriage, for no doubt was ever cast on the paternity of her first child, a boy, who was ingratiatingly named Ernest Augustus, after the Duke. It must have been after his birth that the young matron found a way to draw her sovereign's attentions to herself; and if contemporary gossip is to be believed, she had her husband's full cooperation in that. Apparently Platen, in his daily conferences with his master, discreetly hinted that some of his best political suggestions emanated from his wife. The Duke, who must have already noticed the handsome lady in the Duchess's entourage, professed a desire to confer with her in person. The rest followed quite naturally. Mme Platen, at that time at the height of her beauty, intimated she was willing to serve the Duke in whatever capacity he would desire her to. Ernest Augustus was a most willing prey, and Mme Platen conquered without an effort.

That she conquered so smoothly was hardly an achievement; many women before her had found the lecherous Duke equally obliging. Her distinction was that she retained her power over him long after her sexual charms had gone. She ruled him and moulded him to her will for nearly twenty-five years, and her influence over him hardly diminished even when they had both grown old and decrepit. She pressed her advantage to the full, and saw to it that her position became official. It did not take her long to establish herself as the unchallenged *maîtresse-en-titre*. The whole court deferred to her and fawned on her. Even the Duchess treated her with forbearance and acknowledged her status. Mme Platen became, if not in name, at least in practice, the first lady of Hanover. Together with her husband she controlled all the strings of power.

At Ernest Augustus's expense, she had herself installed in a much embellished residence half-way between the ducal palace in town and the summer house at Herrenhausen. Monplaisir became another ducal court. Mme Platen had her own days for giving audiences and listening to petitions. Anybody who hoped to gain favour with the Duke, came to her first. She acepted homage and presents, and distributed promises and reprimands. She frequently gave banquets which were more lavish than those given at the Palace, and were marked by heavy drinking, cards and lustful interludes. Her princely entertainments included every luxury that could attract the courtiers and the young bloods of Hanover. Her liveries and equipages rivalled the sovereign's, while her dresses and jewels far outshone those of the Duchess. Her husband, first elevated to the rank of Baron and then to that of Count, condoned her useful association with the Duke, or indeed with any person of her choice. It was said that he often entertained to dinner two, and sometimes even three of his wife's current lovers, all at the same table.

Although the Countess forgave laxity in herself, she kept a watchful eye over the Duke's female entourage, particularly when she was getting older and beginning to lose her florid looks. No method was too reprehensible. When she once caught the Duke flirting with one of her pretty attendants, she immediately had the girl thrown into prison on a trumped-up charge, and none of the girl's relatives dared uphold the cause of justice against the powerful first lady. The girl was released only after she had undertaken to leave court and never set foot in Hanover again.

The birth of a daughter, to be named Sophie Charlotte, further consolidated the Countess's position. Considering that the father was known to be Ernest Augustus, it was a bold gesture to give the girl the same name as his legitimate daughter's. This second childbirth, Countess Platen's last, left her health much impaired. She contracted a mysterious disease which gradually marred her beauty and rotted away her limbs. It was openly suggested that the cause of her ailment was 'a long course of profligacy', at the end of which 'the once beautiful favourite was a loathsome object to herself and to all those who approached her'. It was stated that Duke Ernest Augustus also contracted it and that they both died, the Countess two years after the Duke, in a semi-debilitated state, of the same malady. It might well have been syphilis. In the meantime, while still in her heyday, Countess Platen tried all manner of medicine, and took to having daily baths of milk; and as she hated seeing good food go to waste, she had the milk carefully distributed after use to the poor of the town.

Possibly to disguise the progress of her illness, she was always very heavily made up. Nobody ever saw the face behind the painted mask. Young Prince Maximilian, one of Duchess Sophia's most unruly sons, once mischievously spilled some pea-water over her face, hoping to see the paint come off. It did not. When Tsar Peter the Great visited Hanover in 1697 and seemed much taken with her, Duchess Sophia resentfully remarked that the Countess appealed to him only because of her 'painted face', which reminded him of the heavily painted Russian favourites at his own court. Her make-up must have been far cruder than any of the other Hanoverian ladies, whom Lady Mary Wortley Montagu so vividly described later on:

All the women have literally rosy cheeks, snowy foreheads and bosoms, jet eyebrows and scarlet lips, to which they generally add coal black hair. These perfections never leave them until the hour of their deaths and have a very fine effect by candle light, but I could wish they were handsome with a little more variety. They resemble one another as much as Mrs Salmon's [waxwork] court of Great Britain and are in as much danger of melting away by too near approaching the fire, which they for that reason carefully avoid, though it is now such excessive cold weather, that I believe they suffer extremely by that piece of self-denial.[1]

Assuring herself of her influence over Ernest Augustus was not enough for the far-sighted Countess Platen. Although he was only in his mid-forties when he first made her his reigning mistress, he was not considered robust, and the thought that he might die and leave her unprotected was constantly in her mind. It was necessary to ingratiate herself with his son and heir, who would one day succeed to the seat of power. Prince George Louis was no longer the thirteen-year-old boy in whose honour she and her younger sister had once acted in a pastoral play. He was now in his late teens, a young man matured by military service and used to the ways of the world. It was essential to secure his goodwill and bind him through a cooperative mistress. To Countess Platen's way of thinking, no one was more suitable for the part than her pretty sister, Catherine Marie Busche.

Catherine Marie Busche, who, like her sister, was blessed with an acquiescent husband, had many admirers at court, and had the distinction of having set the fashion of 'drinking tobacco' among the ladies of Hanover. She was only too willing to fall in with her sister's plan, and soon found her way into the young prince's heart and bed. The liaison was common knowledge at court and was regarded as a natural milestone in George Louis's career. It did not stand in the way of any matrimonial plans that were being visualised for him. When, in September 1682, Duchess Sophia informed the French envoy Abbé Balati of her son's forthcoming marriage to Sophie Dorothea of Celle, she added in a matter-of-fact way: 'At the moment George Louis is with his mistress.'[2]

The prospect of George Louis's marriage did not worry the ambitious Countess Platen. Marriage was a state duty which a prince of the blood had to perform, but which was not expected to interfere with the course of pleasure. The Countess therefore did not frown on the negotiations with Celle, and as her husband was instrumental in their satisfactory conclusion, it is more than likely that she knew and approved of them. Through her sister she was hoping for long mutual domination over father and heir, wives notwithstanding. She little expected what actually happened.

When Duchess Eleonore realised that her daughter's marriage to George Louis was inevitable, she courageously made one condition. She demanded that Sophie Dorothea's future husband should dismiss his mistress and start his married life on an honourable footing. Accustomed as she was to her husband's fidelity, it was only natural that she should want to secure the same happy state for her daughter. She must have discussed this delicate matter with Duchess Sophia during the last stages of the negotiations, and the Duchess for once saw her point. In her turn she mentioned the matter to Duke Ernest Augustus, who failed to see the importance of it, but agreed to leave it in his wife's hands. Accordingly the Duchess conveyed to her son that the continuation of his affair with Mme Busche was prejudicial to the success of his future marriage, on which the peace between Hanover and Celle depended, and suggested it would be politic to break it off. At the same time she instructed Mme Busche to leave court.

Tradition has it that Mme Busche, sure of her lover's protection, openly defied the order and stayed on to confront the young bride who was trying to supplant her. According to some accounts her liaison with George Louis continued uninterrupted for some time; according to others she hurriedly left court when Duchess Sophia unequivocally repeated her command. From lack of evidence to the contrary, it would seem that the affair did come to an end. George Louis might indeed have been persuaded that a marriage of such political importance was well worth a show of respect, at least at the beginning; or he might have had enough of a mistress much older than himself, whose charms seemed to pall against the radiant youth of his bride. Whatever his reasoning, the association with Mme Busche fizzled out with no evidence of regret on his part, and what little influence she might have had over him as an adolescent, disappeared without a trace.

Countess Platen felt out-manoeuvred and outraged. With her sister out of favour, her own influence over the Hereditary Prince of Hanover was non-existent. She knew only too well there was no question of controlling the young man through his father. Suddenly she realised that the bride from Celle was not the nonentity she had expected her to be. She obviously had a will of her own. Her mother had already extracted from Duchess Sophia an unprecedented concession, and the girl might take it into her head to assert herself further. In her innocence and inexperience of court conventions she might upset the whole power structure which had taken so many years to build up. Even before she made her first obeisance to the new Princess of Hanover, Countess Platen regarded her as a rival and a potential enemy.

Life at court

The young bride who arrived at the court of Hanover to take up her place as wife to the Hereditary Prince was not ignorant of the demands that her new position was to make on her. Nature and upbringing had sufficiently prepared her to fit into a society which expected a wife to provide her husband with heirs, and be a gracious hostess to his visitors, without ever meddling in state affairs. In fact, Sophie Dorothea had more than her fair share of the social graces. Shortly after her arrival at court, the fashionable Paris paper *Mercure Galant* published a pen portrait of the new Princess of Hanover, as she was styled:

She is very well made. Her hair is light brown and her face is oval with a pretty little dimple on the chin. Her complexion is beautifully smooth and her neck is lovely. She dances very well, plays the clavicord and sings to match. She has a great deal of wit, is very vivacious, has a happy imagination, and has much benefitted from her reading of books. She has a naturally good taste, which has increased thanks to the care which has been taken over her education. If a man were as knowledgeable as she is, he might well be pleased with himself and content himself with staying as he is. She is well informed on all subjects, and has much to contribute to any conversation held in her presence.[1]

The young couple were installed in a wing of the Old Palace, in the middle of the town. Although it could not boast such a magnificent castle as Celle, Hanover had three palaces instead of one. Apart from the Old Palace there was the main one on the Leine, where the ducal family resided, where state functions were held, and where the Princess was later allocated a suite as well. And there was the lovely country residence of Herrenhausen, about half an hour's drive outside town. Sophie Dorothea must have been impressed, if not overawed.

The court of Celle, with all its elegance and its splendour, was far less pretentious than Hanover. The ambitious Ernest Augustus had inflated his household beyond all proportion to the importance of his domain, and his Duchess imposed a protocol whose strictness did not lag far behind Versailles. Court society was rigidly divided into classes.

Towering above all others was the ducal family, which consisted, in order of precedence, of Duke Ernest Augustus, Duchess Sophia, Prince George Louis and his wife, then all the younger brothers and the one sister.

The second class consisted of the Field-Marshal of the army, who was a class unto himself, lower than the family, but higher than the rest. Then came the third class, which included the military and civil authorities, the privy councillors and ministers, and the generals of the army. The fourth class was made up of the High Chamberlain and the marshals of the court, noblemen and noblewomen who held various posts on the ducal household, such as pages, maids of honour and ladies-in-waiting.

Last came those court officials who were not noble by birth, but respected for their services; gentlemen ushers, physicians, musicians, scholars, all in their graduated order, down to footmen, coachmen, cooks and grooms.

Sophie Dorothea, as Princess of Hanover, was officially near the top of the pyramid. She was given her own household, with her own chamberlain, ladies-in-waiting and pages. When she went out she drove in her own coach, an enormous gilt one, with postillions and running footmen.

She soon noticed that although as Prince George Louis's wife she was second lady of the court after Duchess Sophia, she was tacitly relegated to the position of third, having to cede precedence to Countess Platen. Sophie Dorothea was well aware of her mother's past struggle to assert her rank among the Hanoverians, and in the court's attitude to her own status, she might have felt a concealed attempt to slight her. She must have felt it was of paramount importance to insist on the rank that was hers. Continuous brushes with Countess Platen made her ever more jealous of her rights. She became over-sensitive. When the Dowager Duchess of East Friesland came to visit at the Leine Palace, Sophie Dorothea openly refused to cede precedence, and disputed her place at table, to the great consternation of Duchess Sophia, who was under instructions from her husband to woo the elderly Duchess in order to win East Friesland as a political ally. Sophie Dorothea, with what seemed like childish obstinacy, spoiled the game. Inexperienced as she was in the intricate byways of court politics, she adhered to a rigid slide-rule code of precedence, not realising that compromise sometimes paid better than insistence on the letter of the law. That was her first mistake.

Her second was her impatience with court etiquette, which she found bewildering, and after a while, quite irritating. It was hard to put up with all the formalities and restrictions that seemed inseparable from rank. Sophie Dorothea could not quite master all the minutiae of court protocol the Duchess Sophia imposed. After a while she stopped trying and went her own way. Young and impetuous, she sometimes greeted effusively someone whose rank entitled him or her only to an acknowledgement; and much worse, she sometimes only distantly acknowledged someone who should have been singled out for royal favour. When the company of a stolid court circle bored her, she would take her leave without troubling to disguise her reason for doing so. Sometimes she would stay away from a gathering organised by Duchess Sophia, and convey her lame excuses by messenger. The court was scandalised and looked out for fresh proof of the young wife's unorthodox behaviour. Duchess Sophia shook her head knowingly and wrote to the Duchess of Orléans that Sophie Dorothea had been badly brought up, and had no idea how a Princess should conduct herself.

In spite of the grandeur of the court, Sophie Dorothea's days

dragged on in a monotonous routine. Her mornings were spent
lazing in bed, getting up late to write a few letters or to put a stitch or
two to her needlework. If the weather was fine, she might take a stroll
in the palace gardens. Occasionally, but apparently not too frequently,
a change of routine would occur with the taking of a bath. This luxury,
which was preceded by lengthy preparations, necessitated her staying
indoors for most of the day, for fear of catching a cold.

A great part of the day would be agreeably passed in being dressed
and trying on new fashions and jewels. Sophie Dorothea loved self-
adornment, and even in her later days of solitude and misery, never
went out without being splendidly dressed, with rich diamonds
gleaming in her hair. Her constant concern with her clothes and
appearance made Duchess Sophia pronounce her shallow, while Countess Platen, until then the most extravagantly dressed woman at court,
raged at the young Princess's greater show of elegance.

The midday meal was a grand family affair. Sophie Dorothea
would go down in style, preceded by a page and attended by a lady-in-
waiting, usually Mlle Knesebeck, one of the three she had been
allowed to take with her from Celle. Duke Ernest Augustus would
descend from his own apartment, and so would Duchess Sophia with
her daughter Sophie Charlotte, two years younger than Sophie
Dorothea and deemed a desirable companion for her. Prince George
Louis would also attend, if he was not away with his regiment. Then
all the younger brothers would appear, assembling in the great hall,
taking their seats in order of precedence, after much bowing and
curtsying. The German food, washed down with quantities of beer and
wine, must have seemed gross to the daughter of French Eleonore
d'Olbreuse. After the heavy fare Their Highnesses would retire to their
respective apartments, when Sophie Dorothea would often indulge in
an afternoon nap, to digest the meal.

Later in the afternoon some social life was indicated. Sometimes
Sophie Dorothea would go out for a drive in her gilded coach. Sometimes she would pay a call on some distinguished ladies whom etiquette
demanded she should honour with a visit, the duration of which had
been prescribed in advance. Some afternoon she would hold court and
receive visitors, amongst whom Prince Charles, a young brother-in-
law, was a frequent one. Sophie Dorothea was known for her gaiety

and sprightliness, and many courtiers came willingly to her public days. But soon she noticed, with growing vexation, that if Countess Platen's social gatherings happened to coincide with hers, the flower of the nobility would stream to Monplaisir rather than to the Old Palace, leaving her to entertain some dull courtiers, under the ever-watchful eye of a lady-in-waiting.

The evening meal was again an occasion for great ceremony, when rich costumes and dazzling jewels were displayed. Again Duke and Duchess, Princes and Princesses would repair to the great hall, again they would formally greet one another, bow and curtsy, finally taking their seats in strict order of precedence. After supper the family would mingle with the general circle of the nobility. There would be conversations, some music making, and games of cards, during which large sums of money would be won and lost. This would go until the Duchess would signal her readiness to retire, and the Princess would follow suit.

When foreign princes and envoys came on visits, they would be entertained by frequent plays, supervised by no less a person than the chief minister himself, Count Platen. His critical remarks, presented in a report to Ernest Augustus, throw an interesting light on the standard of acting offered at the court theatre:

M. de Prefleury: very good for kings and fathers and queer characters. Unfortunately his tendency to drink is a hindrance to his study of new parts.... Mme A. is unintelligible because she is so old and has lost all her teeth. The *prima donna*, though very good in scenes of love-making, is so difficult she cannot be managed, and should be dismissed if any discipline is to be maintained.[2]

A year of married life had passed in this fashion, when, on 30 October 1683, Sophie Dorothea gave birth to a son, who was named George Augustus, and who, forty-four years later, ascended the throne of Great Britain as George II. The happy event set the seal on the reconciliation between the families of Hanover and Celle. The two Duchesses, now that they had a grandson in common, took great care not to hint at past misunderstandings. The Duke and Duchess of Celle became frequent visitors at Hanover. Duke Ernest Augustus and his son George

Louis sometimes returned the courtesy and visited Celle, or went to stay with George William and Eleonore at their hunting lodges at Brockhausen, Ghörde and Wienhausen. Occasionally Sophie Dorothea would be allowed to visit her parents at Celle, although the court of Hanover regarded this as an unnecessary extravagance. Duchess Sophia alone kept her reconciliation cool, and although she often played hostess to George William and Eleonore, she rarely, if ever, returned to Celle, after her first visit necessitated by the wedding of her son.

But now she moderated her criticisms of Sophie Dorothea's behaviour. She appreciated that her daughter-in-law was quick to present the house of Brunswick-Luneburg with an heir, and was willing to show her more forbearance. She went as far as to undertake to improve what she considered Sophie Dorothea's neglected education, and treated her to long lectures about her pet subject, the history of England. Sophie Dorothea listened politely, never failing to ask intelligent questions and thank her mother-in-law for her interesting discourse.

All this time Countess Platen had been watching Sophie Dorothea's progress with great concern. Her initial premonitions against the young bride seemed to be justified when the Princess, immediately on her arrival at court, tried to put her in her place and refused to acknowledge her unofficial status as the most deferred-to lady at court. Duchess Sophia, the long-suffering wife, might well have preached tolerance by example; the intolerant Sophie Dorothea saw no reason to cede anything to a mere countess who had no legal claim to the power she exercised. There were constant brushes which the young Princess won and quickly forgot, but which the obsequious older woman rancorously harboured against a day of reckoning.

With the birth of a son, Sophie Dorothea became more immune than ever to the machinations of the Countess. Moreover, Duke Ernest Augustus had openly fallen for the charms of his attractive daughter-in-law. He was the first to treat her with friendliness, later mingled with some jocular flirtatiousness, permissible in a father-in-law. For a while it looked as if the young Princess of Hanover was going to develop into a personality with whom court intriguers would have to reckon. Such misgivings were soon dispelled.

The initial incompatibility between George Louis and Sophie Dorothea had not diminished after their marriage. On the contrary, the first few months of married life made it more pronounced. The young Princess was quick-witted and fond of a good repartee. The Prince was generally sullen and slow to respond to facetious baits. His wife's *esprit*, so brilliantly displayed in the presence of others, gave him the uncomfortable feeling he was being made fun of, when no more than social badinage was intended. Her lightness and vivacity, instead of winning him over, strengthened him in his earlier prejudices against her. A few months of bed-sharing for the glory of the Hanover-Celle alliance did not make communication any pleasanter. Having disliked her before he ever met her, George Louis now disliked her for having got to know her. She was not obsequious like a dependent mistress. There was nothing comforting about her. She seemed to expect devotion as of right. She was self-assertive, and was not content to stay in the shadow. As soon as it became obvious that he had done his duty by her, George Louis announced his intention of rejoining the Imperial army.

By that time the French côterie of Celle had lost most of its influence, to Duchess Eleonore's great disappointment. Baron Bernstorff, George William's chief minister, tended to see things Ernest Augustus's way, and was instrumental in persuading his master to break with France in favour of the Emperor, whom Ernest Augustus had been courting for some time. Having once before thrown in his lot with the imperial fortunes, George William did not need much persuasion. In view of the future unification of Celle and Hanover, he agreed to regard the current Hanoverian foreign policy as his own. Duke Anthony Ulric of Wolfenbüttel was also persuaded to join. Together, the three Brunswick Dukes equipped troops and put them at the service of the Emperor, who at that time was fighting desperately against the growing power of the Turks.

George Louis, already a seasoned warrior, threw himself heart and soul into the campaigns of the time. Not waiting to see his wife safely delivered of her first baby, he went with the Imperial army to fight the Turks in Hungary, and in September 1683 took part in the relief of Vienna. From one of his campaigns he brought back two young Turkish captives, who were a nine-day wonder in Hanover.

Mustapha and Muhammed became his faithful servants, never left his side, guessed his every wish and became such an integral part of his entourage, that when, many years later, he went to England to become King, they went with him as his influential stewards and distributors of his favour.

Sophie Dorothea was left very much alone. A royal baby, tended by a host of nurses and handmaids, could hardly fill the tedium of her days. Once however, a grand circle of festivities, in honour of Sophia Charlotte's marriage to the Elector of Brandenburg, temporarily brightened up the daily routine. Duke Ernest Augustus gave a masquerade in which everybody had to take part. Duchess Sophia came in as 'a lady of ancient times'; her husband appeared as Harlequin; George Louis, back for his sister's wedding, as Scaramouche; Countess Platen as a lawyer; and Sophie Dorothea with Sophie Charlotte as young Turks. Fully disguised, they all piled into the ducal coaches and drove to the gardens of Herrenhausen for games and pranks. In the evening, still in their masquerade costumes, they drove back to the Leine Palace, waving cheerfully to the gaping Hanoverian burghers in the cobbled streets. After supper the whole court took part in a dance that lasted until dawn.

The wedding took place in the autumn of 1684. For a whole week there were military displays, concerts and suppers; and to crown it all, there was the traditional German torch dance of the princes. It is not difficult to imagine what Sophie Dorothea's thoughts must have been when comparing this beautiful and flattering ritual with the perfunctory celebrations that had marked her own wedding day only two years earlier. She was not sorry to see Sophie Charlotte leave for her new court at Brandenburg. For Duchess Sophia the parting from her only daughter was a wrench; for Sophie Dorothea, who had been constantly, and unfavourably, compared with her erudite sister-in-law, her departure was no loss. At the end of the festivities she resumed her lonely routine, languishing in her rooms and indifferently waiting for news from the front.

As soon as his daughter was safely off his hands, Duke Ernest Augustus set out for Italy. As if anticipating it was going to be his last visit, he made it his longest. He left towards the end of 1684, and stayed away for two whole years, making Venice his headquarters. His temporary court included his indispensable chief minister Count Platen, who, for appearances sake, had to follow wherever the Countess went. The Countess openly played the part of first lady of the court, and had the additional pleasure of having her sister Mme Busche near her, with her docile husband.

Life in Venice was one long round of pleasure. Ernest Augustus entertained lavishly, and some of his banquets cost as much as seven or eight thousand crowns at a time. In a way he was buying the good-will of the Venetians. He had persuaded them to let him recruit for them two thousand Hanoverian soldiers, for whose services large subsidies were being paid. His extravagance in Venice helped to redress the balance.

While Ernest Augustus was thus enjoying himself, George Louis was commanding a contingent of Hanoverian and Celle troops in the Hungarian campaign against the Turks. When it was over, he betook himself to Italy to have a holiday, without first calling at Hanover to salute his long-neglected wife. He had not seen her since his sister's wedding.

Duke Ernest Augustus thought it might be a good idea to bring the young couple together again. As soon as he heard that his son was coming to Italy, he sent word to Sophie Dorothea inviting her to join him at his temporary court in Venice. Sophie Dorothea did not wait to be asked twice. With Duchess Sophia's approval, she set off on her way with the escort the Duke had provided, accompanied by her faithful lady-in-waiting, Mlle Eleonore Knesebeck, and the Mistress of the Robes.

Sophie Dorothea was now in her nineteenth year, a wife and a mother, but with no experience of foreign parts. Her arrival in Venice coincided with carnival time, and she threw herself into its gaiety with all the zest of her youth. Her lack of inhibition somewhat alarmed her Mistress of the Robes, but more than delighted Ernest Augustus, who was gratified to see his hospitality so keenly appreciated.

Unfortunately the meeting with George Louis was not as successful. His wife's vivacity and spontaneity irked him more than ever. The more people praised her social charms to him, the more he withdrew from her; and he certainly resented his father's benevolent meddling in his domestic life. A whole year with Sophie Dorothea in Italy, under the paternal supervision, was not George Louis's idea of a holiday. When Ernest Augustus decided to spend Easter of 1686 in Rome, George Louis let his wife go with his father, while he went to Naples on his own, content in the knowledge that he had again done his duty by her. When the ducal party returned to Hanover, Sophie Dorothea was pregnant, for the second and last time.

The contrast between the gay and carefree life in Italy, and the constant neglect in which she lived throughout the last months of her pregnancy, was most marked. She was lonely, bored, and clearly avoided by her husband. The courtiers, quick to leave a sinking ship, shunned her *levées* and her afternoon receptions. Duke Ernest Augustus, well-disposed as he was, was too absorbed in his own pleasures and duties to mind his daughter-in-law's grievances; and Duchess Sophia, correct but never over-sympathetic, seemed immersed more than ever in her voluminous correspondence with the Duchess of Orléans, Leibnitz, and numerous German relatives.

At this juncture Countess Platen stepped forward.

It was common knowledge at court that the Prince of Hanover was not merely indifferent to his wife, but openly hostile. It was noticed with relish that he did not come near her very much, and speculation was rife as to who would fill the vacancy in his bed. Countess Platen, always anxious to increase her power and secure the future, fell back on her old plan of winning George Louis through her sister. She had her recalled and threw her again into the Prince's arms. To the sisters' joint disappointment, George Louis remained cold. Mme Busche's time was decidedly over. Countess Platen was quick to change her tactics. If she could not ingratiate herself with him through her sister, she could supply him with a younger and prettier mistress, equally docile to her benefactress, and win the Prince's gratitude through her thoughtful ministration to his needs.

Her choice fell on a young lady called Ermengarda Melusina Schulenburg, who had only recently arrived with her father at Hanover, and had stayed at Monplaisir. She was well descended, but poor, and Countess Platen took her under her wing. She presented her at court, obtained for her the post of lady-in-waiting, and introduced her to George Louis.

In looks and disposition Ermengarda, only a year younger than the Princess, was her very opposite. She was purely Germanic in type, with fair hair and large blue eyes, generously shaped, and unusually tall. She had an unassuming simplicity about her and a slowness of speech which must have been a relief from Sophie Dorothea's pride and over-quick wit. Ermengarda was not a natural intriguer, and might well have preferred an honourable marriage to the life of a mistress. But she was poor, and the prospect of a wealthy marriage was remote. Ermengarda had too much good sense to refuse an opportunity that fate and Countess Platen were conspiring to offer her. She agreed.

George Louis liked her enormously. He took her riding and hunting, had her seated next to him at the court theatre, and led her at dances. In due course he installed her in a beautiful house, visited her every day when he was not away, and spent most of his time with her. Duchess Sophia shrugged her shoulders at her son's attachment to a woman so much taller than him. To an English lady visiting the court she remarked: 'Look at that malkin; and to think that she is my son's passion.' The liaison became official.

As her influence over George Louis increased, Mlle Schulenburg shed Countess Platen and used the Prince to satisfy her own ambition. Under her slowness she was shrewd, and in spite of her simplicity she was quick to seize her opportunities. She stayed with George Louis as his resident mistress, if by no means his only one, until the end of his life. As an old and unattractive woman, already nicknamed 'the beanpole' for her leanness and described as 'rapacious' for her greed, she followed him to England to see him crowned and share his glory. In 1719, as George I, he created her Duchess of Kendal. After his death she lived in semi-retirement at Kendal House, near Twickenham, and died at the ripe old age of eighty-five.

The news of her husband's attachment to the 'malkin' did not take long to reach Sophie Dorothea's ears. She must have heard rumours long before it became a recognised affair. Certainly Countess Platen was not one to enjoy her enemy's discomfiture in secret. She was the first to drop hints in Sophie Dorothea's presence, and under the guise of well-wishing imparted the information in a manner calculated to hurt most. What made the hurt even deeper was Sophie Dorothea's unrealistic approach to court morals, which was based on the unusual example of her parents' constancy. She could not and would not resign herself to a husband's deviation, as other wives did, notably her mother-in-law. She was too proud to accept his infidelity, even though there was no love on her part to make her jealous. Nor did she neglect any opportunity to make her feelings known to George Louis. Their rare meetings were marked by constant quarrels, with Sophie Dorothea upbraiding her husband for his infidelity, and George Louis contrasting his wife's querulousness with his mistress's even temperament.

Towards the end of her pregnancy, Sophie Dorothea followed George Louis one day into his study, in his own apartments, and tried to plead with him. Baron Poelnitz tells us in his *Histoire Secrette* that she implored her husband to tell her how she had incurred his displeasure and begged him to instruct her how she might win back his esteem.

It is difficult to imagine how a proud and indignant princess could bring herself to use such humble language to a man she never liked, and whose company she must have required mostly as a matter of prestige. Not blessed with her mother-in-law's self-restraint, nor yet mellowed by age and experience, it is more likely she used impetuous language and angrily demanded to be treated, publicly at least, with the respect due to the wife of the Prince of Hanover and the mother of his son and heir. George Louis, cornered in his own study, told her to 'hold her peace', which must have been the chronicler's euphemistic way of reporting that the Prince told his wife to shut up. He then strode out of the room.

On another occasion, when Sophie Dorothea reproached him more sharply than ever, George Louis could not contain himself any longer. He shook her violently, nearly strangling her, then rushed out of her presence. The scene so upset Sophie Dorothea that she was taken ill, and for a time it was feared she might miscarry. Duchess Sophia found it necessary to intervene in order to avoid an open scandal. She used what little influence she had with her son, and induced him to visit his wife's sickroom every day for a few minutes, until the danger was over. George Louis sat there sullen and wordless, reluctantly holding his wife's hand, for as long as he thought required by courtesy. In March 1687 the Princess gave birth to a daughter, who was also called Sophie Dorothea, and who later became Queen of Prussia. The arrival of the baby was welcome to George Louis, if not for itself, at least for relieving him of his tedious duty towards his wife.

After the lying-in, it was thought necessary to offer the Princess some consolation for her sufferings. Again Duchess Sophia found the tactful solution. She invited a large house-party to her beautiful summer residence at Herrenhausen, which, although not far from Hanover, was a haven of peace. Apart from its gardens and wood, it boasted a lake, a grotto and a moat. No efforts were spared to make the visitors' stay as agreeable as possible, to judge by an eighteenth-century account:

> Magnificent gondolas, rowed by gondoliers, lightly habited, were seen on the great canal which terminated the garden, for the use of those who chose to amuse themselves on the water. Carriages were ready every evening for those who wished to ride in the park, and they afterwards assembled in an elegant saloon which formed part of the orangery. Here they found a table decorated with every luxury, and the Duchess permitted her suite of both sexes to sup with her. After the repast, they amused themselves at play, and walking in a gallery which led into a room adorned with the most choice and delicate paintings.[3]

George Louis was not one of the party, but his mother went out of her way to show kindness to his wife. Her own daughter had left home to be the wife of the Elector of Brandenburg, a widower eleven years older than his bride, who had been chosen not for his charms but for his political usefulness. The knowledge that Sophie Charlotte was not having an easy time at her new court, might have tended to make her mother more understanding of Sophie Dorothea's situation. She renewed her efforts to broaden her outlook and interest her in world affairs, which to her meant the domestic policy of England. She carefully explained her own right to the English throne, as granddaughter of James I, and expressed her hope to outlive all other claimants. She indicated that, thanks to her marriage with George Louis, Sophie Dorothea might find herself one day Queen of England. Sophie Dorothea was too engrossed in her immediate present to take much interest in what seemed a very remote possibility. To do her justice, she was no more indifferent to Duchess Sophia's English hopes than Duke Ernest Augustus or George Louis, both of whom considered them at that time no more than a dream.

The Duchess never neglected an opportunity to hold forth on her pet subjects. They were strolling together in the picture gallery one day, when Sophie Dorothea paused to admire a recent acquisition, a portrait of a beautiful lady, representing Venus and Cupid. The Duchess pointed out that it was a real portrait and, with an upsurge of her old prejudice against the enormity of unequal marriages, gave the daughter of Eleonore d'Olbreuse the true story behind the picture:

Charles Louis, my brother, being smitten with the incomparable beauty of the Baroness Dengenfelt, whose picture you have just seen, married her privately, in the lifetime of his first wife, from whom he was divorced. Although he had several children by her, this separation was so fatal to our house, that it occasioned the total extinction of it; and I have had the misfortune to see our dominions in the possession of a foreign power. [France].[4]

To accelerate Sophie Dorothea's recovery, Duchess Sophia went as far as to invite her parents over, and gave one of her most sumptuous balls in their honour at the Leine Palace. As she did not dance herself— she was in her mid-fifties—the honour of opening the ball fell to the Duke of Celle, who led it with his daughter. George Louis danced with her next. Ernest Augustus watched benignly. It looked as if appearances had been saved. It was all good manners, smiles and affability. But behind it Sophie Dorothea's marriage was rapidly disintegrating.

*An equal mixture
of
Mars and Adonis*

The name Königsmarck was first taken notice of during the Thirty Years War, when a hitherto obscure Swedish nobleman distinguished himself in battle and rose to the rank of general. After the Peace of Westphalia he was made governor of Bremen and Verden, which had been ceded to Sweden by the Emperor of Austria. He was created Count and settled in Stade, where he built himself a large castle which he named Agathenburg, after his wife Agatha. He died wealthy and dreaded.

His surviving heir, the second Count Königsmarck, also had a distinguished military career and further enhanced the family name for gallantry. He married a general's daughter, and when he died in battle in 1673, left behind a wealthy widow with four young children: Charles John, Marie Aurora, Amelia Wilhelmina and Philip Christopher.

Charles John, the heir to the title, began his travels early. He visited France, Italy, Spain, Malta and England, sometimes indulging in amorous adventures, sometimes temporarily putting them aside to participate in one of the battles of war-ridden Europe. During a visit to Venice he made the acquaintance of the Duchess of Southampton and cultivated an affair with her. When he left for France, she accompanied him, discreetly disguised as a page. Their ruse did not deceive the Duchess of Orléans, who, with her ears open to malicious gossip and her pen ready to spread it about, was quick to regale her friends with the juicy details of their progress:

> It is apparently customary for English ladies of rank to accompany their lovers on their travels. I have known a Count Königsmarck whom an English lady accompanied disguised as a page. She was with him at Chambord. . . . I have never seen a figure as beautiful as hers. After a time he found her lodgings at an inn. One day, while he was taking a walk in the woods, the landlady rushed out to find him, shouting: 'Sir, your page is having a baby.'[1]

This was only one of Charles John's numerous affairs, which seemed to follow one another with enviable rapidity. At the same time he was thinking seriously of marriage and was always on the lookout for a suitable bride. His choice eventually fell on Lady Ogle, an heiress and a widow, whose brief marriage had not been consummated. She was eleven years old.

Charles John had met her during one of his visits to London. In 1680, armed with a letter of introduction from the King of Sweden, and accompanied by his young brother Philip Christopher, he felt emboldened to ask for her hand in marriage. Her guardians refused, and married her instead to the wealthy master of Longleat, nicknamed for his vast yearly income 'Tom of Ten Thousand'. One day, as this Thomas Thynne was driving in his coach along Pall Mall, three mounted men seized his horses, knocked down the postillion, and shot him with a blunderbuss. A few hours later he died of his wounds. His three assailants were arrested immediately, and so was Charles John, who was suspected of having instigated the murder.

The trial which followed was one of the most sensational of King Charles II's reign. It was recorded by Evelyn and reported by foreign envoys. Court circles were in a quandary. The murdered man had been a friend of the Duke of Monmouth, while Count Charles John was obviously a protégé of the King of Sweden. The course of justice was not clear. In the end Charles John succeeded in establishing an alibi which proved his non-complicity and was freed, while the other three were all found guilty of murder and were hanged in chains.

Although he was officially acquitted, Count Königsmarck had become *persona non grata* in England. He left as soon as he could, throwing himself again into military service. He died in 1686, aged twenty-seven, fighting the Turks in the Morea, leaving his title and his wealth to his younger brother.

Philip Christopher, the next and last Count Königsmarck, was born at Agathenburg Castle in the spring of 1665, between five and six in the morning, as his mother carefully recorded. He too was destined for a military career, and when he reached the age of twelve or thirteen, his widowed mother looked around for a suitable court where he could receive his initial training. Celle was a natural choice. It was relatively near home; it had a splendid reputation for military discipline; and Eleonore d'Olbreuse was a friend. In fact, she was a relative of some of the Königsmarck French connections. The young boy was duly sent to Celle, where he made the acquaintance of Sophie Dorothea, only a year younger than himself.

At that time Sophie Dorothea had not yet been raised to princely rank, and the Dowager Countess Königsmarck entertained some hopes of a matrimonial alliance with the daughter of the Duke of Celle. The son she had in mind for the match was Charles John, the heir to the Königsmarck lands, who at that time was having a gay time somewhere in Europe. She actually mentioned her plan to Eleonore, but the scheme fell through with Sophie Dorothea's legitimisation, which put her well above such a modest proposal of marriage. Being a friend, Countess Königsmarck then acted as a mediator in Eleonore's negotiations with the Hereditary Prince of Sweden, who was for a while amongst Sophie Dorothea's suitors. Philip Christopher, who may have met Sophie Dorothea quite often at her parents' court, did not leave any evidence of having formed a particular attachment for her. After his period of military training, he returned to Agathenburg.

His education was by no means complete; and when Charles John returned home for one of his rare visits, a family council was held, during which it was decided that the elder brother would take the younger one to England, to continue his studies. They landed in Hull about the same time that young George Louis of Hanover was beginning to pay his court to Princess Anne of York.

Fifteen-year-old Philip Christopher was first sent to Oxford to acquire some English and Latin, and in the summer was taken on a tour of the main sea-ports of the south and west coasts of England. His mother must have enjoyed his dutiful letters of that period, written in careful French, no doubt checked by his Swedish tutor:

London, 2 September, 1681

Madam,

Your letter of 27 July reached me rather late, and if I had carried out my plan of visiting Scotland, I would not have received it even now. An accident with my foot and other reasons dissuaded me, and as it is late in the year, my brother feels it is better for me to start by training at M. Foubert's Academy, so that next spring I should be able either to go to Spain by sea, in a warship, or join the fighting with the French army, as I do not see a chance of a company in Holland. But as your wishes and your commands will always dictate all my moves, I am very careful not to undertake the smallest step without your approval, which I hope I have, when it concerns my welfare.

The trip I took in England was very enjoyable, and the King [Charles II] appeared to be satisfied with the account I gave him on my return. Next Monday I am going back to Oxford to take away my books so that I can set up here, hoping to prove on all occasions the respect and veneration I have for you, Madam,

> Your very humble
> Very obedient & very faithful
> Servant and son,
> P. C. Königsmarck.[2]

Foubert's Academy, where he registered that winter, was a fashionable school for young gentlemen, in the Haymarket. Königsmarck studied French, dancing, riding and fencing. His Swedish tutor, Frederick Adolf Hansen, was entrusted with the dual task of watching over the young man's moral behaviour and preparing him for higher studies at Oxford. Philip Christopher seemed to have had a heavy timetable.

Charles John however was free to pursue his own pleasures. Having presented his letters of recommendation at court, he had the entrée to the great houses of London, and was soon busily pressing his suit on young Lady Ogle. When he was brought to trial for the murder of Thomas Thynne, young Philip Christopher was called from his school to give evidence for his brother. Unfortunately all he was able to say in his brother's favour was that he had brought with him a vast sum of money, which he meant to spend on English horses.

The trial tarnished the name of Königsmarck to such an extent, that Philip Christopher could no longer prolong his stay in England any more than his brother could. Without much regret he abandoned the idea of going up to Oxford, and after fifteen months in England left for France. At Versailles he put the finishing touches to his education, perfecting his spoken French, but failing to improve his spelling, which to the end of his life remained wonderfully individual.

From France he went back to Agathenburg to see his mother, to whom he was very attached. Towards the end of 1682 he went with her to Celle, where they arrived shortly after the newlyweds, Sophie Dorothea and George Louis, had left for Hanover. After a few weeks' stay, Königsmarck went to the wars. At first he entered the services of the Prince of Baden, then joined the Imperial army which was fighting against the Ottoman Empire.

The siege of Vienna in 1683 kindled a crusading spirit in Europe against the Turks, and an alliance was formed against them, consisting of Austria and Germany, Venice, Poland, Russia, Malta and Tuscany. The Imperial army fought in Hungary, the Venetians in Greece, the Russians in the Crimea and the Poles in Podolia. For the next few years Königsmarck fought mostly in Hungary, but he must have gone as far as the Morea, one of the six Turkish *sanjaks* of Greece, and the most dreaded battlefield of the area. It was probably there that he caught malaria, which was to trouble him for several years to come. He was a keen and dauntless warrior, and at twenty-one was already a colonel of cavalry. He could look forward to a dazzling career.

His being a Swede in no way hindered his progress in the Imperial army. The courts of Germany were filled with noblemen of many nationalities who held important posts at court or in the army. They were mostly high-spirited young gentlemen who followed an exciting career half-way between that of a knight-errant and a mercenary. Their outlook was cosmopolitan, and their services much sought after and rewarded.

By the age of twenty Philip Christopher must have fully developed those qualities which made him one of the most attractive young gallants roaming the courts of Europe. He spoke and wrote excellent French and German—spelling apart—and had some English, Latin and Italian. He was familiar with the light music and literature of the day, and wrote verse. He could be witty, courteous and charming, as well as insolent and brutal. He would gamble and drink with the wildest, or take his place at the head of his regiment on the battlefield. Women found him irresistible. His sister Aurora, herself a connoisseur of men, described him in her memoirs as he then was:

He was a noble Swede, in the Flower of his Age, admirably well made, tall, handsome, with flowing hair and sprightly Eyes; in one Word, an equal mixture of Mars and Adonis.[3]

Towards the end of January 1687, while on leave, Königsmarck paid his first visit to Hanover, which thanks to the splendours of its carnival, had come to be known as 'The German Venice'.

Under Ernest Augustus, the Hanover carnival season started in December of each year and went on until Easter, with February being the gayest month of all. Visitors kept flocking to Hanover from all over Germany, and even from further afield. They were well looked after, to encourage them to spend their money in the capital. Distinguished parties were met outside town and escorted to their appointed lodgings with a guard of honour, its trumpets at full blast. Sometimes a whole court would come to take part in the carnival festivities. State visitors were lodged at the Leine Palace; others were found accommodation in town. All were invited to the ducal entertainments. There were plays, operas, ballets, and above all, gay masquerades. The revellers would drive madly from the Leine Palace to Monplaisir, from Monplaisir to Herrenhausen, from Herrenhausen back to the Palace. The burghers followed the example of their betters and emulated their style of dress and their kind of entertainment.

In the middle of the season the Brunswick Annual Fair was held, under the patronage of Duke Anthony Ulric of Wolfenbüttel. It was an occasion for a grand Brunswick reunion, with dukes and princes of distant branches coming together for further festivities and jollity. After the Fair, they would go to Hanover, if they had not been there already, for the second part of the season.

On his arrival, Königsmarck presented himself at court and paid his respects to the Duke and Duchess of Hanover. The court of Celle was there too, and he exchanged compliments with one or two of his past acquaintances. He did not however meet Sophie Dorothea, who was at that time near the end of her second pregnancy, and who was lying ill in her own quarters. Nor did he enjoy his stay as much as he had anticipated, for news had reached him that his cavalry regiment was about to be disbanded. He wrote to Marshal Bielke, his commanding officer in the Imperial army, to verify the rumour, and added by way of explanation:

I have come here for the carnival. As soon as I went to court, Their Highnesses inquired after you, and M. Chauvet and M. Boisdavid asked to be remembered to you.[4]

Establishing the date of Königsmarck's first visit to Hanover is of great importance, in view of his later intimacy with Sophie Dorothea. Attempts to put his arrival a year or two earlier resulted in a doubt over the paternity of her second child, the daughter called after her, who was destined to become Queen of Prussia and mother of Frederick the Great. The Prussian court was naturally contemptuous of any suggestion that touched the purity of their sovereign's genealogy, and dismissed it as evil gossip. It may well have been started by the *böse Platen*, the vindictive Countess, who on seeing one day the toddler Princess in Königsmarck's arms, hastened to make insinuations that Sophie Dorothea's enemies enjoyed repeating, without necessarily crediting. Königsmarck's letter to Marshal Bielke, dated 31 January 1687, and his earliest known one from Hanover, seems to settle the question. The following day he left for Hamburg.

At the beginning of 1688 his regiment was finally disbanded, and the young colonel found himself without a post. Writing to Marshal Bielke, he confided to him that he was worried about what people

COUNT PHILIP CHRISTOPHER KÖNIGSMARCK

might say if he did not get another commission soon. He was also out of pocket, for there was quite a lot of back pay due to him. As the Hanover carnival season was still on, he decided to go there again, not only to take part in the revelries, but to meet old comrades-at-arms and see if he could get a commission with the Hanoverian army. This time he was in no hurry. He arrived well-equipped and well-recommended, and was immediately invited to a masqued ball given by Duke Ernest Augustus.

The Hanover court records kept by Marshal Malortie gave a very full description of that ball, held on 2 March 1688. It was attended by Duke Ernest Augustus and Duchess Sophia, Prince George Louis and Princess Sophie Dorothea, Prince Maximilian, Prince Charles, the Duke and Duchess of Celle, Duke Anthony Ulric with his Duchess and one of two of their daughters. The guests included Countess Reus, sister to the Duchess of Celle, Count and Countess Platen, Count Montalban, and 'a young Count Königsmarck'. The ball started at four o'clock in the afternoon and went on to the small hours of the morning, by which time the guests had supped, danced, watched a comedy or a ballet and played cards.

It was at this ball that the Swedish Count was formally presented to the Princess of Hanover, now completely recovered from her childbirth a year earlier. The Duke and Duchess had retired early, and the supper-table was presided over by Sophie Dorothea, resplendent in the crimson robes of a cardinal, not at all put out by the fact that the Princess of Wolfenbüttel had also dressed as one. Philip Christopher courteously reminded his hostess of their earlier acquaintance at her father's court; but although Sophie Dorothea must have been charmed to discover in the dashing young cavalier a childhood friend, she was content to leave it at that. So was he. His thoughts were with another young lady, to whom he was about to get engaged. She was nineteen-year-old Charlotte Dorothea, daughter of the Danish Count Rantzau of Holstein, where Königsmarck had some property. Years later seven of her love letters were found in his desk. For some reason the engagement was broken off shortly after it was announced, and the young Countess, who had never enjoyed good health, died at the age of twenty.

In September 1688, after some six months' stay at Hanover, Königsmarck was called to Italy, to see to the funeral arrangements of his much-admired uncle Otto, who had died in the Morea, commanding the Venetian army of mercenaries against the Turks. It took a long time to transport the coffin to Venice, where the funeral was to take place. Philip Christopher, joined by his widowed aunt, stayed on until the beginning of the following year, when the splendid obsequies were at last held.

Having inherited his uncle's wealth as well as his brother's, some two years earlier, the young Count was in a position to live lavishly wherever he chose. He had not abandoned his plan of entering the Hanoverian service, and as soon as his business in Venice was concluded, he returned to Hanover. He set up house in a fashionable street near the Leine Palace, with practically adjoining gardens, and invited his unmarried sister Aurora to come and stay with him. His sister Amelia had married the Swedish Count Lewenhaupt, who then made use of his mother-in-law's connections with Duchess Eleonore to obtain the post of general in the Celle army. As there was much military traffic between Celle and Hanover, Amelia was a familiar figure at both courts.

The three Königsmarcks soon became much sought after at court entertainments. They were all good-looking, high-spirited and pleasure-loving. Young and gay, they often found themselves thrown together with Sophie Dorothea, who at court balls would forget her grievances and enjoy the dancing to the full. In Aurora particularly Sophie Dorothea found a kindred spirit, and when she was away, the Princess would sometimes write to her.

Königsmarck in the meantime acquired some land in Hamburg and frequently went there on business. He always travelled in great style, accompanied by a vast retinue. He had an insatiable urge to dazzle and attract attention. At court, at the opera, at the carnival, at the chase, he was always the most conspicuous and the most extravagant. He gambled, played and entertained most lavishly.

But he was no idler. He had come to Hanover to offer his services, and that he did. Duke Ernest Augustus was only too glad to recruit the wealthy young officer who had already proved his mettle in so many battles. In May 1689 he offered him a commission and put him in charge of the Palace Guards, who later became infantry regiments.

Königsmarck's joining the Hanoverian army coincided with the appointment of Sir William Dutton Colt to the post of first English envoy to the courts of Celle, Hanover and Wolfenbüttel. The new envoy presented his letters of credence in July 1689 and immediately wrote disparagingly of Celle:

The town is very poor, and all the country round nothing but a deep sand and wood of small fyr trees, full of all sorts of wild beasts which with the Duke's passion for hunting makes him reside constantly here and at some little houses he has in the neighbourhood. I fear to pass a very miserable winter here, in extreme cold and very ill houses.[5]

A week later he reported with relief from Hanover:

This place has much more the appearance of a court and the town much larger and finer, people laying out their money in building and furnishing their houses, besides abundance of strangers resorting constantly hither.[6]

Colt's main objective was to persuade the three Brunswick Dukes to join the recently-formed Grand Alliance, championed by William III, against Louis XIV. He made it his business to be pleasant to the Dukes and charming to their officers. Whatever opinion he must have formed of the Königsmarck brothers in England, he was careful not to voice it in Hanover, where the young colonel might be called upon to command a regiment in a campaign against a common enemy. He watched him travel between Hanover and Celle, the two military centres of the unified command, and when he first brought up his name in one of his dispatches, some two years later, it was to report that Königsmarck was marching at the head of his regiment towards the Elbe, to guarantee the safety of Hamburg, which was thought to be in danger of invasion at the time.

At first, however, Königsmarck's duties kept him at court. With his seemingly inexhaustible wealth and his position, he was considered a most eligible young man. Before he had been in the Hanoverian service for more than a few weeks there was talk of a match between him and Sophie Charlotte, the daughter of Countess Platen and Duke Ernest Augustus. It was an attractive proposition, for whoever married Sophie Charlotte was going to marry power. Königsmarck wrote to his mother to ask her advice, but somehow nothing came of it.

Although his duties required his frequent presence at the Leine Palace, his first contacts with Sophie Dorothea were confined to court functions. It was only through his friendship with young Prince Charles that he came to see her at her own quarters of the Palace, on days when she was at home to callers.

He was of course as aware as any other courtier of the state of affairs between the Princess and her husband. Their married life had taken on a set pattern. George Louis openly consorted with Mlle Schulenburg, and rumour had it that she had borne him two daughters, who were discreetly removed from court immediately after birth. Sophie Dorothea did not see much of him, and when she did, had nothing pleasant to say to him. At twenty-two, she was not the diffident young girl she had been at sixteen. Six years of married life, troubled as they were, had given her stature. She had formed her own circle of friends and had gathered round her a small côterie of her own.

Most assiduous among the Princess's visitors was her young brother-in-law Prince Charles, who from her earliest days at court had taken her part against her detractors. It was he who took Königsmarck along to her afternoon gatherings and prejudiced him in her favour. She, for her part, found in Königsmarck a sympathetic listener. She would readily tell him of her petty grievances, of Countess Platen's intrigues against her, or of Duchess Sophia's latest, and unjustified, reprimand. Gradually she came to regard the handsome young colonel, who was always so attentive, as a confidant and an ally, and when he happened to call on her one day immediately after a particularly painful scene with her husband, she poured out her heart to him and told him all the humiliating details of the quarrel. There was nothing inappropriate about her confidence, for she talked to him, as always, in the presence of a lady-in-waiting. Königsmarck was so deeply moved by what he heard, that when Charles joined them a little later, he was still unusually quiet. Charles was quick to sense something in the air and discreetly warned his friend not to involve himself with other people's marital problems. But Philip Christopher was not a person to follow sensible advice. His genuine sympathy for the distressed Princess, combined with his instinctive attraction to a beautiful unprotected woman, dictated another course of action. If he hesitated, it was not through common sense, but because he was not yet aware of his real feelings for her.

Hanover was then going through an exciting period in its history. For years Europe had been perturbed by the growing power of Louis XIV, until the League of Augsburg was formed against him, including the Emperor Leopold and other sovereigns anxious to check the French expansion. When in 1688 William of Orange came to the throne of England as William III, he became head of the anti-French coalition and used all his influence to close its ranks against the enemy of Protestantism. In 1689 the Grand Alliance was formed.

The three Brunswick Dukes were much sought after by William, but Ernest Augustus was in no hurry to indicate whether he was going to join the Grand Alliance against France, or Louis XIV against his enemies. William instructed his envoy to sway Ernest Augustus to his side; Louis XIV gave similar instructions to the French envoy. There resulted much diplomatic activity, which, according to the custom of the day, revolved round banquets and balls, the perfect setting for string-pulling and secret dealings. The English envoy, hoping to decide Ernest Augustus in favour of the Grand Alliance, gave a magnificent ball in his honour. The French envoy, hoping to achieve the opposite, retaliated with a more magnificent one, and expensive presents for the main guests. The Duke and Duchess of Celle, influential participants in Hanoverian foreign policy, came to stay at court and were lavishly entertained. The ball in their honour was nominally given by George Louis, but was presided over by the Duke and Duchess of Hanover. The two ducal families, with their parties, sat on a raised dais, acknowledging homage. There was a play, followed by a supper, culminating in a dance. Königsmarck, as a high-ranking officer and a budding diplomat, attended this function wearing an exquisite suit of pink and silver, while Sophie Dorothea, dressed as Flora, was all in white with no ornament except white flowers in her hair. After the official opening of the ball by the Duke of Celle and his daughter, she was handed to Königsmarck for the next dance. They made a splendid couple.

Among those who were keenly watching their dancing, was Countess Platen, whose predatory instincts must have been aroused at the sight of the attractive young nobleman lavishing his charm on her hated rival. Putting on her best manner, she went up to Königsmarck and complimented him before the whole company on the perfection of his dancing. He thanked her and repaid her with a compliment of his own. Their conversation continued with the usual pleasantries until the circle of courtiers round them melted away. Countess Platen then hinted that she could do much to further his career, and invited him to Monplaisir to discuss the matter further. She was about forty at the time, handsome in her florid way, and known to be far from satisfied with the attentions of the gout-ridden Duke. There was no mistaking her invitation. It was a command, but at the same time it was a highly flattering and exhilarating one. As soon as Ernest Augustus retired to his rooms, the Countess took her leave too. Königsmarck discreetly followed her to her residence, where he became her lover.

Perhaps Countess Platen's mature charms did not come up to his expectations, or perhaps he dimly realised that even in a mode of life that did not require him to be physically faithful to any particular woman, it was wrong of him to have become the lover of the Princess's worst enemy. He was smitten with remorse. The following morning, somewhat unsure of his next move, he presented himself as usual at Sophie Dorothea's apartment. The news of his conquest had preceded him, for the Hanoverian courtiers were quick to put two and two together, and could not have failed to put the correct explanation on Countess Platen's bold compliments the night of the ball. Sophie Dorothea, who had come to regard Königsmarck as her ally and her own personal acquisition, felt betrayed. But she played her hand very coolly.

Receiving him in her most gracious manner, she talked with her usual candour, telling him how much she had enjoyed having her parents in Hanover, and how lonely she was going to be now that they were going back to Celle. She also told him that she had requested permission to go over to Celle and spend some time with her family, but that her request was turned down on the advice of Count Platen, who regarded such a visit, which could not be effected without a large retinue for the Princess and costly presents for her hosts, as an unnecessary expense. Sophie Dorothea dwelt at some length on Count Platen's unkindness, and then innocently suggested that, as her good friend Königsmarck was known to be on such intimate terms with the Count, or rather with his wife, perhaps he could persuade them to stop intriguing against a lonely Princess who had no friends in the world. Königsmarck wished he had never succumbed to a temporary temptation. He vehemently assured Sophie Dorothea that his loyalties were entirely with her, that Countess Platen meant nothing to him, and that he would willingly stop seeing her altogether.

Giving up Countess Platen was more easily said than done. She had no intention of letting her young lover go, and he, for his part, knew that he could not possibly break with her without danger to himself. If she suspected that she was being dropped to suit a whim of Sophie Dorothea's, she might well take a leaf out of Potiphar's wife's book, and tell Duke Ernest Augustus that his young colonel had made an attempt on her virtue. Königsmarck found himself in a cleft stick. By day he continued his visits to the Princess, feeling more of a traitor then ever, while by night he attended Countess Platen's card-parties and bed. His love-making must have become quite unsatisfactory, for the Countess darkly hinted that his heart was obviously somewhere else. Königsmarck realised he was directing her suspicions against Sophie Dorothea; at the same time he feared for his own safety should the Duke find out that he was having an affair with his resident mistress. He decided to go away and let distance smooth out his difficulties. He volunteered for active service.

There were two main fronts where he could be expected to be sent. One was Hungary, the Balkans and the Morea, all traditional battle-grounds of the Imperial army against the Turks; the other was Germany, where Louis XIV had recently started a policy of aggression, partly in support of his claim to the Palatinate, the expected inheritance of his sister-in-law the Duchess of Orléans. As an old ally of the Emperor, Ernest Augustus was sending troops to both fronts.

Early in 1689 the French committed a deed which was to sow the first seeds of the bitter hatred that was to persist between Germany and France for many generations. Unable to hold the Palatinate, captured a few months earlier, they ruthlessly laid it to waste, retreating behind columns of smoke. Mannheim, Spires, Oppenheim and Worms were devastated, and, above all, beautiful Heidelberg, Duchess Sophia's childhood home. As the Imperial army, reinforced by the Grand Alliance, followed the French along the Rhine, Königsmarck was ordered to join it at the head of his infantry regiment.

About that time twenty-year-old Prince Charles was preparing to go to the Morea to gain his first experience of battle. Not aware that Königsmarck had already been ordered to the Rhine, he asked him to go with him, thus hoping to arrest the progress of his friend's growing attachment to the Princess. The court was greatly concerned when the two young men made their plans known. Duchess Sophia was afraid for her son; Countess Platen for her lover; and Sophie Dorothea for her two loyal friends.

As the day approached, Königsmarck became increasingly dejected, not acting in the least like a battle-loving officer who should be looking forward to active service. He managed to avoid Countess Platen's invitation to a private farewell meeting, and took his leave of her hurriedly and perfunctorily. His leave-taking of the Princess was more difficult. Under Charles's watchful eyes he had to be circumspect and cheerful, while she, unaware of his turbulent state of mind, openly bemoaned his departure and told him how much she was going to miss her only true friend in a hostile court.

In August Königsmarck and his regiment met up with the Grand Alliance troops marching along the Rhine. A month later he took part in the siege of Mainz and had the satisfaction of seeing it recovered by the Allies. At that siege he was wounded in the thigh. He went to Hamburg to recover, and by the end of the year returned to the front. Charles had left for the Morea.

The following winter was a hard one in Hanover, with thick layers of snow lying on the plains. To meet the cost of maintaining troops on two fronts, heavy taxes had to be levied. The burghers grumbled, the peasants died of cold and starvation, but the court was as extravagant as ever. No campaigns were allowed to interfere with the splendours of the carnival season. Countess Platen kept open house at the expense of the treasury, and thousands of crowns were spent nightly on keeping up the morale of the courtiers, who were fretting about their kinsmen's fate at the front.

The news from the Morea was disquieting. Prince Charles was somewhere in Albania, when rumours trickled through of a complete rout. It was said that the joint troops of the Dukes of Hanover, Celle and Wolfenbüttel had been almost annihilated, and that of Duke Anthony Ulric's eleven hundred men, only one hundred and thirty survived. Charles's fate was not known for certain. At first the court was still hoping that he had only been taken prisoner and could be ransomed from Constantinople; but later more accurate information came through. Charles had sustained multiple wounds and died on the battlefield. The English envoy Colt dutifully reported back to London:

> Hanover, 25 February, 1690
> We have received certain news that Prince Charles was killed on the spot where his body was found, with several of his officers and his servants round him dead. He had several cutts with a gymeker, and was run thro' the body with a lance. Their last hope of his being a prisoner has very much increased their sorrow here, and we are going into mourning.[7]

The gruesome details of Charles's death, arriving after a long period of suspense, were too much for Duchess Sophia. She had a nervous breakdown and her life was in danger. Her whole family rallied round her, and even the Duchess of Celle hurried over with her husband to try to comfort the bereaved mother. Sophia was ordered to Carlsbad to take the waters, but it was many months before she recovered. She never got over the death of her best-loved son, and although it was not to remain her only loss, it was by far the most cruel.

The disastrous news from the Morea must have reached Königsmarck while still on the Rhine. He returned to Hanover a much soberer man. He allowed Countess Platen to understand that their amorous interlude was over, and renewed his attendance on the Princess. Now that Charles was dead, his frequent unescorted calls began to invite comment. Countess Platen could not forgive the insult inflicted on her and constantly looked for a way to revenge herself on the man who jilted her and the woman who attracted him. She was the first to link their names and insinuate the worst, long before there were any grounds for doing so.

Love's labour

By the beginning of 1690 Duke Ernest Augustus was sufficiently committed to the Grand Alliance to equip troops against Louis XIV. The spring brought about what was to become the seasonal campaign against the French in Flanders, with the experienced George Louis as commander-in-chief of the Hanoverian army. His officer corps included young Prince Ernest, who was to see active service for the first time; and Count Königsmarck, who was ordered to the front at the head of his infantry regiment.

Königsmarck's friendship with the Princess had progressed no further. His imminent departure for the front, where he might die without ever having made his feelings known to her, encouraged him to take the plunge. He declared his love.

Sophie Dorothea was well versed in the ways of the world. It was not the first time that an attractive young man had made advances to her. Her brother-in-law Max often had, and there was some gossip about a French marquis who had tried to win her favours several years earlier, while she was staying with Duke Ernest Augustus in Venice. Nor could she find the declaration impudent. Many married ladies of rank had gallants who sought, and sometimes enjoyed, their favours.

The erudite Sophie Charlotte, her own sister-in-law, married off to the Elector of Brandenburg, was reputed to have consoled herself for the inadequacies of her much older husband with a number of young lovers; so did the Duchess of Saxe-Eisenach, the Princess of Etting, and several others.

Far from being offended, Sophie Dorothea must have been moved and excited. She was twenty-four, married for eight years, without ever having been loved or in love. Königsmarck was one of the most dashing young gallants at court, and a proven friend. The Princess must have reflected that it was to please her that he had broken off with the powerful Countess Platen, and that perhaps because of her he had not since formed a lasting liaison with any other woman. The thought of attaching him to her person as her permanent gallant must have been intoxicating.

Yet she was not Eleonore d'Olbreuse's daughter for nothing. Sophie Dorothea had been brought up to believe in virtue; she upheld a moral standard that her husband's infidelities enhanced rather than weakened. She was fully aware of the implications of Königsmarck's declaration, and did not let herself be carried away. The only concession she made was to grant him permission to write to her from the front, half-promising to send an occasional note of acknowledgement. There was however a fully-understood bond of complicity between them when it was arranged that his letters would not be addressed directly to her, but to Eleonore Knesebeck, her faithful lady-in-waiting and confidante.

The 1690 campaign brought about a resounding French victory at Fleurus, in the Netherlands. For Königsmarck it marked the beginning of his clandestine correspondence with the Princess. His first extant letter, written from Ath, near Hennegau in the Netherlands, had already the characteristics of the later ones. Its tone was intimate and direct, its style a mixture of elegance and colloquialisms, its spelling erratic; and in spite of a light attempt to disguise his passion under a mask of deference, there was no mistaking the ardour of a persistent lover:

Ath, 1 July [1690]
I have reached the end; and the only thing which can still save me is a few lines written in your own incomparable hand. If I were fortunate enough to hear from you I would be comforted. I hope you will

have the charity not to deny me this favour, and as it is you who are the cause of my suffering, it is only right that you should be the one to take it away. Only you can soothe the deadly pain I feel at being away from you, and only then shall I know if I could really believe the kind words you had said to me once or twice. If I were not writing to someone for whom my respect is as great as my love, I would find better words to express my feelings; but fearing to offend, I will end here, begging you to think of me sometimes and believe me your slave.[1]

For some time there was no reply. Königsmarck was in an agony of suspense. He kept wondering whether his letter had gone astray; or, if it were safely delivered, whether the Princess was going to reply or simply put the whole risky venture out of her mind. He was consumed with passion, torn between hope and despair. His longing and his uncertainty made him ill. He had indeed reached the end.

Not one of Sophie Dorothea's letters written during the first twenty months of their correspondence has come to light so far; most likely they were destroyed. But that she did write was evident from Königsmarck's answers. She must have taken some time to bring herself to do so; his first reaction to her reply was written about six months after his first letter from Ath. By that time the defeat of the allied troops at Fleurus was a thing of the past, and did not need referring to. Königsmarck was only concerned with his suit:

Today I received your answer. You can well imagine my suspense all this time. You must believe me when I tell you this is why my illness has lasted so long. I was in agony, thinking you have forgotten all about me. But now that I know this is not so, I feel so much better that I hope to see you soon. Really it is I who should complain of having to be careful, for this does hurt me. But I will bear my misery with fortitude, for I know the cause of it is the sweetest, loveliest person in the world. If there is anything to add to what I have already said, it is only that I shall never change, unless you force me to. I could be so happy. My happiness would be perfect, I would wish for nothing else in this world. These words mean much, and I do not know whether you have fully weighed them. If you would kindly write a few more lines, I should recover more quickly and would be better able to tell you face to face that I am indeed your most obedient servant.[2]

Sophie Dorothea did weigh his words fully and was horrified at her own audacity. Surrounded by unfriendly courtiers and spied on by Countess Platen's minions, she realised far better than Königsmarck the folly of indulging in an extra-marital friendship. When he returned from Flanders she went out of her way to treat him with indifference. A year earlier she might have welcomed him back with undisguised joy and drawn him to a window to hear all about his military exploits. Now she was very guarded. She received him surrounded by ladies-in-waiting and courtiers, avoided his overtures and all but ignored him. His hopes of seeing her alone and telling her of his undying love were frustrated. He could not reach her. After several days of vain attempts he sent her an agitated appeal, speaking of his feelings quite plainly:

I am desperate at having so very few opportunities to talk to you. I dare not even show my admiration for the eyes that give me life. I beg of you to give me a chance to see you and say just two words to you. What a price I have to pay for my love for you! The joy of speaking to you every now and then makes me stomach a lot of pain. I am leaving here the day after tomorrow. God knows when I shall see you again, my life and my goddess. The thought of it is like death to me, and when I think I shall not be seeing you for a whole week I feel so desperate I want to plunge a dagger in my heart. But since I must live, I beg you to let me live always for you.[3]

For the first and last time in the whole of her relationship with Königsmarck, Sophie Dorothea was firm. She did not grant him a tête-à-tête, and he was still prowling around in search of ways and means to see her privately, when, in January 1691, Duke Ernest Augustus ordered him to accompany him to The Hague, to meet William III of England and attend the congress of the allies.

Europe had seldom witnessed such a congress. The Elector of Brandenburg was there, the Elector of Bavaria, the Regent of Würtemburg, the Landgraves of Hesse-Cassel and Hesse-Darmstadt, the Princes

of Saxony, Holstein and Nassau, Duke Anthony Ulric of Wolfenbüttel
and the Duke of Hanover, representing also the Duke of Celle, who
was prevented from attending by an attack of gout. The Emperor
Leopold had sent an envoy, as did the Kings of Spain, Poland, Denmark,
Sweden, and the Duke of Savoy. The congress went into session and
decided to oppose Louis XIV with a grand army of two hundred
thousand men; but in April, before the participants had a chance to act
on their decision, Louis won his spectacular victory at Mons and
returned triumphant to Versailles. The congress broke up.

But while it lasted The Hague was transformed. Its quiet streets
were alive with gallants from Vienna, Berlin, London and Hanover.
Königsmarck swaggered, gambled and caroused with the best of them.
He was presented to William, and on an impulse offered him his services.
As it happened, Duke Ernest Augustus refused to release him. Instead
he gave him leave to go on temporary attachment to the English army
in Brabant. But Königsmarck could not bear to stay away for long.
After an absence of no more than a few weeks, he returned to Hanover.

What must have influenced his decision was a contrite letter from
Sophie Dorothea who apparently convinced herself that she had been
unnecessarily wary, and that her pretended coldness had gone too far.
Her half-apologetic note gave him fresh hope for a private meeting:

If you had not felt you were to blame, you would not have had the
grace to write. Why do I still worship you after the way you have
treated me? Still, your haughty airs made me decide to go away the
day after tomorrow. If you still want to comfort an unhappy heart
torn by jealousy, let me come and see you, you know where. This is
perhaps the only favour I shall ever ask of you, for I hope God
would take my life rather than let me suffer so. I beg you not to
refuse me this request, and although you want to force me to take
another decision, I shall never stop loving you.[4]

On his return Königsmarck gave a masked ball, to which several
members of the ducal family were invited. His guests included Prince
George Louis and young Prince Ernest; Prince Christian; Count and
Countess Platen; and of course Sophie Dorothea. It was a warm spring
evening, and the guests strolled about in the illuminated garden,

indulging their tastes for flirtation and intrigue. Countess Platen, outwardly all smiles but inwardly seething with revenge, concocted a plot to trap Sophie Dorothea. Apparently she stole an embroidered glove that George Louis had brought his wife back from Flanders, and planted it in a secluded pavilion, from which a loving couple was seen hastily departing. When questioned, Sophie Dorothea, like Desdemona, could neither produce the lost glove nor account for its being found in the pavilion. But George Louis, unlike Othello, was no gullible husband. He had no love for his father's mistress, and did not wish to be indebted to her. He let the incident pass.

Yet it was about that time that Sophie Dorothea's resistance broke down. From the tone of Königsmarck's letters during the spring of 1691, it must be assumed that it was then that their love was consummated. He began to write more intimately, plainly alluding to shared delights, complaining of inconstancy. He was impetuous and demanding, while the Princess was timid and easily frightened. Neither had any illusions about their chances of keeping their affair a secret for long; but they tried any subterfuge they could think of to divert attention from themselves. Because they did not trust themselves to hide their feelings in public, the Princess asked her lover to forgo her afternoon gatherings and avoid her company at court functions. When he obeyed, reluctantly, she would be seized with jealousy and accuse him of being unfaithful. If, on the other hand, he heard of a court entertainment from which he was banned, and at which she behaved with deliberate gaiety, he would fly into a rage and reproach her for her inconstancy. The opportunities to meet in private were few, and their rendezvous furtive and charged with tension. In between they exchanged letters, pouring out their love, their frustration, their jealousy and their longings. Königsmarck wrote nearly every day, sometimes twice a day, entrusting his letters to a messenger when he was in Hanover, or to the post if he was on his travels. He was away when he wrote the following one:

No mortal was ever as happy as I was when I found your letter waiting for me here on my arrival. I flatter myself that I am again in your favour and have already forgotten all the unfounded suspicions that had tormented me so. Do not doubt my love;

God is my witness that I have never loved anybody as I love you. If you believed me you would ask yourself: 'How could anybody be so depressed?' I can, because I am away from you. My noble companion [Prince Ernest] could tell you in what state he sees me everyday, though you may be sure I hide the real cause from him. You may not believe it, but on my word of honour, I have often been so out of sorts that I felt faint. Last night I was out for a walk and when I thought how many days must pass before I can see you again I had such palpitations that I had to return home, and I do not know what would have become of me if my servant had not fetched me some cordial. Even then it was a long time before I revived, and without your dear letter I should still be a broken man. It was excellent medicine for my sickness, and I beg you to send more of it, more often, for I need it so. You are wrong to reproach me for my inconstancy, I am never like that where you are concerned and never shall be. Do please give me an opportunity to deserve your love. I am ready to put my life, my name, my future and my fortune at your feet. As for women, I have already given them up for your sake; if you do not believe me, name those you wish me never to see again and I will do so with pleasure, because all women except you are repulsive to me. Goodbye, my lovely dark one. The post is about to leave, I must finish. I kiss your knees.[5]

Königsmarck had never made a secret of his past love-life; indeed he used to boast of it. It was only natural that Sophie Dorothea should fear that during their enforced separations he would find himself a new mistress. Her loneliness, her longing and the fear of being discovered made her tense and unreasonable. She imagined him surrounded by hordes of mistresses, all conspiring to make him forget the love he had sworn her. He wrote back reassuringly:

My mistresses are stopping me from thinking of you? Oh God, is it possible that you really believe such a thing? And even if I had not written to you about all I do (this is my fourth letter), you should have never had such thoughts. How could you possibly think I could love anyone but you? No, I protest that after you I shall never love again. It will not be difficult to keep my word, for once I have loved you, I can find no other woman pretty. You wrong yourself if you think such a thing. How can you compare yourself with others? And how could it be possible, after I have loved a goddess, to look at mortals? No, really, I have too good a taste for that, and I am not one of those people who cheapen themselves. I adore you, dark charmer, and I shall die with these feelings in my heart. If you do not forget me, I swear to you I shall love you as long as I live.

I do not expect to hear from you again because I shall soon be back, and then my only preoccupation will be to show you that I love you to distraction, and that nothing is so dear to me as your favour. Adieu.[6]

This letter, and the other three alluded to, might have been written from Brunswick, where Duke Ernest Augustus had gone to confer with Duke Anthony Ulric, taking his entourage with him. On his return to Hanover Königsmarck fell ill; this was no love sickness but a genuine fever, probably the recurrent malaria he had contracted during his early Turkish campaigns. While he was lying in his house, he sent Sophie Dorothea one note after another, begging her to come and see him. She was alarmed and suggested that, far from her coming to see him, it would be wiser if he left Hanover once and for all. He wrote back reproachfully, veering between despair and hope, at one moment threatening to go away, at another making a fresh assignation in his house:

Why do you hold out the hope of coming to see me, when you do not mean it? I know you too well, you are not brave enough to take such a step, and I do not really expect it of you, fearing you might risk too much. You want me to go away; it is done, my journey is arranged for tomorrow week. You desire it, that is enough. I know only too well everything is against me. How can I put up with such a life, living in Hanover without hearing from you? This is impossible. I would sooner go and dig the fields than bear this. If I could just die quietly somewhere I would be happy, for after all my suffering I do not expect to be happy ever again.

My companion [Prince Ernest] takes great care to keep us apart and if you want him to succeed, all you have to do is listen to what he says . . . I hope the love you have shown me will not let you be taken in by his lies. If you want to oblige me, please write and tell me who you talk to at court, it is not jealousy that makes me want to know, only curiosity. If you would be kind enough to answer me, the same messenger will be waiting to collect your letter, at the usual place. Comfort me, I beg of you, I suffer so much for the love of you. If by any chance you should be playing cards at the grand hall, my man will be waiting in the gallery leading to your apartments for fear of being seen.[7]

To indicate the intensity of his feelings, he put his personal seal at the end of the letter. It represented a heart burning over an altar, with a hand pouring oil on it, and the sun shining above. Underneath ran the motto: No impure flame burns in my heart.

His fever left him much weakened. Getting up too soon, he was thrown off his horse and had to take to his bed again. He could hardly walk. Aching and despondent, he was miserably wondering whether he would not be better advised to accept an offer from the King of Sweden to join his army and make a career for himself like his father and his grandfather, instead of frittering away his life on an unrewarding love affair fraught with so many difficulties. He had not yet learned that however earnestly the Princess might command him to go away, she would never mean to be obeyed to the letter. On this occasion she sent him a note that immediately resolved all his doubts. His plan of returning to his own country and making the name of Königsmarck even more distinguished melted into thin air. He answered by the same messenger:

While I was reflecting on my unhappy situation, your letter was brought to me, which I had little expected. I was so delighted to receive it I forgot to be ill and threw myself on it as if there was nothing wrong with me. You have done everything I wished to see you do, and it only remains for me to thank you for your kindness and assure you of my fidelity. . . .

If you do not believe me, I am prepared to abandon mother, family, friends, possessions and country, the better to convince you, and it only depends on you whether I should take the journey you know of.

My illness gives me a good excuse. I could pretend to be ill for quite a long time. If you agree with my plan, please let me know and I will act accordingly. This is the greatest proof I can give you at present, please accept it and make me happy; for the joy of seeing you far surpasses any ambition I might have for my future. I could not find better fortune, and the thought of possessing you is so precious to me that I do not think any more of any other ambition.

Your letter so purified my heart that no trace of jealousy is left in it. Your eagerness to hear about my condition convinces me that you love me. To satisfy your enquiry I will tell you that I am in great pain, but the pain of not seeing you is far worse than that of my fall. I could be much better in 4 days, but if you approve of my proposition, I shall keep to my room for 10 more. This will not stop me, as soon as I can walk again, from kissing you in the familiar places . . . .[8]

There was no more question of his leaving Hanover at this stage, and as soon as he recovered he resumed his duties. It was remarked however that he was spending much more time at the Palace than his duties warranted, and Sophie Dorothea took fright again. She absolutely forbade him to attend functions where she was present; or, if it was his duty to do so, to avoid coming near her, saving their meetings for more discreet surroundings. He saw the good sense of her command and tried to accept it, at the same time claiming his reward for good conduct:

You have laid down a law which is difficult to keep, but as this is what you want I must obey. I hope you will allow me to come and see you tonight. If you cannot arrange this, you come and see me tonight at my place. Let me know which it is going to be. If you decide to come to me, you will find nobody up in the house. The door will be open. Enter bravely and do not be afraid. I am dying of impatience to see you. Please send your reply quickly so that I know where I am. Goodbye dear heart.[9]

Apparently she did not pluck up enough courage to go to his house that night, for a few days later he was questioning the sincerity of her concern for him and wondering why she had not shown more opposition to his Swedish project:

> Anyone else would put you to the proof, to see whether your love will carry you so far to come to my place; but being me I love you too much to see you take this risk, and your offer to do so is quite enough. Still, in order not to lose the chance of seeing you (for I have so little time left to stay with you) I will come to you this evening, if you agree, and I am waiting to hear from you about the time of the meeting. If you think it is right for me to come to court, I shall do so, but if not, I won't.
>
> The joy of seeing you makes me forget all the unhappiness that my illness had caused me. On the whole I am quite happy, but I cannot forget how little opposition you showed concerning my departure, although you have a very good reason to dissuade me from it. I do not know what to make of it. I wish to God my departure would not prove unlucky for me.
>
> You accuse me of not loving you enough. How can you be so unjust? I will pass over this point without replying to it as I know that you must be fully convinced of my love for you, which is the purest that ever was and which will last as long as I live. I have often declared this to you in prose. Allow me now to do so in verse:

> As long as I draw breath,
> Your name I shall revere;
> To the day of my death,
> My love will persevere,
> Enduring to my dying day,
> Ending when I pass away.

> At 6 o'clock my man will be waiting outside the room of the good good friend.[10]

'The good good friend', Mlle Knesebeck, was indeed a staunch ally. She passed letters, kept a lookout for intruders while the lovers were snatching a private moment on their own, and tried to cover up all suspicious movements between the palace and the house down the road. Often Königsmarck addressed his letters to her instead of directly to the Princess; and sometimes Sophie Dorothea dictated her answers to her confidante, so that if they were intercepted, the handwriting would belie any accusation levelled against herself.

Königsmarck's illness had not left him altogether and he had a relapse. As soon as he was on his feet again, he presented himself at court; but Sophie Dorothea, feeling the need to keep up appearances, received him so coldly that the suspicious lover was prepared to believe the worst. Even after a tender note put things right, he could not help telling the Princess how much her pretended indifference had hurt him:

I must say that never did a letter arrive more in time, for I was about to accuse you of the blackest treachery; but your letter convinces me that you are incapable of such a thing. It is true I am not too happy with the cold airs you put on yesterday. That is why I spent such a miserable night. I was so wrought up I could not help crying. I was so agitated my fever returned and I was hot for three hours. Believe me, my divine beauty, that ever since I have known myself, I have never been in such a state. Do you know what I thought? 'God has sent me this illness to punish me, and as if this is not enough, He has also frozen my beloved's heart towards me. This is unbearable, I cannot bear it.' I threw myself down on my knees, my eyes full of tears, and begged God, if it were true you did not love me any more, to take my life away. I would have welcomed death with all my heart, for I really thought you had turned cold to me.

My pen is not skilled enough to tell you what depths of sorrow I was in, nor can I describe what immense relief your letter gave me. I kissed it a thousand times, and then a thousand more. I hated myself for having thought you capable of inconstancy. I throw myself at your feet and ask your forgiveness, and I promise that in future I shall not be so quick to imagine anything like that.

But I beg of you, never be fickle and do believe that I too am constant. To convince you all the better that I adore no one but you, I will sign this with my blood. You must know that as long as you love me you will always be worshipped by

Königsmarck
Signed in blood[11]

A serious affair

The summer of 1691 was well advanced when the Duke and Duchess of Celle invited the ducal family of Hanover to join them at their hunting lodge at Epsdorff, about eight miles from Hamburg. From his very early days at Celle, George William had established the pleasant routine of marking the seasons of the year by regular visits to his various hunting lodges. Eleonore usually accompanied him; and if, in her middle age, she did not take an active part in the sport, she was always ready to give the hunters a hearty supper after a hard day's chase. Epsdorff was more of a castle than a lodge, and quite fit to entertain a large party.

The invitation offered Ernest Augustus a much needed opportunity to hold a leisurely conference with his brother about their joint policy towards France and the Grand Alliance. The recurring French victories made the Duke of Hanover reconsider his position. That year he had sent no troops to the seasonal Flanders campaign against the French, and George Louis was at home. He too was invited to Epsdorff for the talks.

Pending a final decision, Ernest Augustus had been negotiating a separate pact with Sweden. In July he instructed Count Königsmarck, whom he considered *persona grata* with the King of Sweden, to go to Hamburg to meet the Swedish envoy in order to conclude the agreement with him.

It was a responsible diplomatic mission, which reflected the high esteem Königsmarck was held in by the Duke of Hanover. To an ambitious courtier such an assignment would have spelt advancement; to a lovesick young man it meant no more than a separation from his beloved.

The Epsdorff party was to leave Hanover first. When, on the eve of its departure, Königsmarck heard that the Princess had been suddenly taken ill and had to beft behind, he did not know what to make of it. He feared she was seriously ill, at the same time hoping she had only pretended to be so, in order to be allowed to stay behind with him. As usual, he wrote whatever came into his head, without a trace of self-consciousness:

Alas, I see I shall never be happy. No sooner had I recovered from my own illness, than my beloved is taken ill. My illness gave me great pain, but yours hurts me even more, so that I wish I were miles away. You might feel this is not a very kind thing to write, but I say this only because I cannot bear to see you in pain.

If fortunately your illness is not as bad as it seems, it would give me comfort; for I might think that you only pretended to be ill, for the love of me.[1]

It was not a feigned illness, but it did not last long. The lovers thought they were safe and made an assignation. To his horror, Königsmarck ran into George Louis, whom he had thought gone away. He managed to warn Sophie Dorothea just in time, and followed up his warning with a letter describing his frustration:

I see that the pleasure of kissing you, which I have been so much looking forward to, vanished entirely when that nuisance of a man turned up so unexpectedly. I admit I hated him on sight. Thunder from a clear sky could not have surprised me more. But there are bound to be unpleasant people who would disturb such a tender meeting as ours was going to be. All last night I lay awake, full of joy, thinking about our meeting; now our chance is gone and I am going to have another sleepless night, this time full of grief. I am quite certain that if you do not comfort me I shall bathe in tears. Comfort me, my divine beauty, and soothe a man who is dying for the love of you and who is so mad about you he is nearly out of his mind.

> For a wondrous fair
> I burn with a passion brave
> My reason doth declare
> I must love her till the grave.

This is my guiding principle and you shall see me carry it out to the letter. My greatest happiness would be to show you that only death could end my love for you. But for the love of God, remember the motto: *rien d'impure m'allume*. Adieu.[2]

Although Königsmarck was quite an accomplished young man by the standards of the day, he made no claims to originality. The verses with which he now and then embellished his letters—in French, German or Italian—were mostly based on some fashionable ballads going the round of the courts of Europe. This last one might well have been inspired by a gay drinking song, included in a collection published in Paris in 1670. It ran:

> For a wondrous fair
> I sigh day and night,
> But sometimes for the cup I care,
> To forget my plight.

It was a pleasant accomplishment to be able to adapt a well-known ballad to suit one own's feelings, and there might have been an added compliment implied to Sophie Dorothea, when he transformed a light-hearted anti-love song into a poem of eternal devotion.

When she was fully recovered, the Princess had to go to Epsdorff to join her father-in-law's party and her parents, whom she had not seen for some time. As Königsmarck had no reason to stay alone in

Hanover, he decided to rejoin his regiment stationed outside town, on his way to Hamburg. The arrangement seemed sensible to both of them and was reached after much discussion and protestations of love; but Königsmarck, hardly out of his beloved's presence, was already visualising her smiling at other men. From his house he wrote her a hurried note of farewell, with a warning:

6 o'clock
I cannot go away without thanking you for having smoothed away my worries. I would have been a broken man without our talk yesterday evening. I am going away as happy as any man can be who is leaving his beloved behind; but what comforts me is that I am well assured of your friendship and that my being apart from you will not cause me any harm by you. My soul is so much at ease that I am quite different from what I was. But I beg of you, no *tête-à-têtes*, not with anybody, particularly not with M.K. [M. de Kilmansegg perhaps, later husband of Sophie Charlotte Platen]. I shall find out everything, for I have good friends here whom you do not suspect in the least. Goodbye, beautiful goddess, think of me as much as I think of you. I kiss your knees a million times and am your eternal slave.[3]

In spite of his promises, he jumped to his usual conclusions when no immediate letter followed the Princess's departure:

Wednesday
I have been hoping to have a letter written in your fair hand, but I see you have forgotten me. Is it possible after all you have said to me? No. I cannot believe it and I want to find an excuse for you this time, but for Heaven's sake, do not make me languish much longer. Remember that a letter is my only consolation while you are away and that I cannot live without being reassured of your love. I will not go to Hamburg. Not an hour passes without my thinking of you and remembering your charms. I find comfort in doing so, it revives my heart which is so heavy with sadness. Why cannot I fly to you like my desire? I should this very minute be in your lovely arms, tasting the sweetness of your lips. . . .

I am shut up in my room, seeing nobody. I do not go out, I am far away with my thoughts, I think only of you. If one of my officers wishes to speak to me concerning the regiment, I fly into a rage for having to waste time instead of thinking of you. I hope after all this you will not ask me again if I still love you. It will kill me if you still doubt me.

But I must confess I have made another choice here. It is not a pretty girl, it is a bear which I keep in my room. I feed him and I intend, if you ever desert me, to bare my chest to him and let him tear my heart out. I teach him how to do this with sheep and calves and he is not bad at it. If ever I need his services, and God forbid that I should, I shall not suffer long. Goodbye, think of me.[4]

The visit to Epsdorff took an unexpected turn when Duchess Eleonore confronted her daughter with court gossip about her friendship with Königsmarck. Although most people still dismissed it as a harmless flirtation, the rumours were damaging to the Princess's reputation. The Duchess was greatly perturbed. While the menfolk were hunting or talking politics, she held long conversations with Sophie Dorothea, using all her maternal influence to dissuade her from following a course which was both imprudent and unworthy.

The Princess was torn between love and reason. She could neither give up nor go on brazenly. In her turmoil of mind she hit upon an idea which, painful as it might be, could once and for all force Königsmarck out of her life. She heroically suggested that he should find himself a wife and forget her. He was so crushed he never stopped to consider how much pain her gesture must have caused her, and wrote only of his own hurt feelings:

At last the miserable day has come which I had dreaded so much. I must marry, since this is what you wish. Very well then, I will follow your sentiments. You want it, that is enough for me. My death sentence has been written by the hand I adored. I must say I never thought to see such a deadly sentence passed by you. But why am I complaining? I should remember that I have loved you now for a year and I should know better than to trust one of your sex. Alas, I was weak and I believed all you said to me. Now I must have the strength to bear everything, but where shall I find it?

He was so carried away by his feelings that for the first time in his correspondence he dropped the polite form of address *vous* and started using the intimate *tu* instead:

Why do you inflict such misery on me? What have I done to you that you treat me like this? Your cruelty goes too far. If you had not wished to throw me into utter despair, you would never have treated me like this.

Recollecting himself, he continued in the second person plural again:

Why were you not given a less cruel heart and me a less tender one? We would have been better suited. I have never been but yours and I want to be yours all my life, but you do not encourage me to be constant; and you do not try in the least, by your behaviour, to strengthen my tender feelings, which in spite of their natural inclination tend to become weaker. If you acted differently, you would find in me such zeal and ardour that would convince you of my fidelity far better than anything I can write. You will please forgive me if I do not believe in the love you say you feel for me. Must your love be so languid? No, Madam, you keep your vivacity in your head, not in your heart. My trouble is that I am like the man who has a good case, but is so afraid of losing it, that he is willing to compromise.

You indicate that you want me to marry so that I can be saved from disaster, but you little think that it is marriage which will be my ruin. There are two ways to save me from disaster. The first, which is more agreeable to me, is not to make me marry, and if my ruin does follow, as well it might, not to abandon me. The second will be easier. It is to make me marry, but swear on your word of honour that you will always have for me the same feelings which you had proved to have. . . .

I will wait for your answer, which I hope will not be dictated, but written in your own hand, so that I know what to do. . . . But you do not love me any more, your head has triumphed over your heart; and it is not enough for you to try and stop loving me, you want to make me stop loving you. What a harsh command, how can I possibly obey you? No, Madam, in spite of your wish, I shall always worship you, and my love for you will be extinguished only with my life. I beg you to believe this of your most humble and loving servant.[5]

While in this turbulent state of mind, Königsmarck learnt that his mother had died in Sweden. He had always been a dutiful son, and her death could not have failed to move him. Besides, the old Countess used to look after his estates at home, which he tended to neglect. Her death was therefore a double loss to him.

He stayed in Hamburg only long enough to bring his mission to a successful conclusion. Then, declining yet another offer to join the Swedish service, he hurried to Epsdorff, ostensibly to report to the Duke, but in reality to plead with the Princess. The death of his mother, which he might have represented as the loss of the only woman who ever cared for him, must have helped to melt Sophie Dorothea's heart. She never really meant to give him up. She may not have suggested marriage, had she thought there was a real chance of it. She knew perfectly well that young Countess Rantzau, once Königsmarck's fiancée, was safely dead; and as for the projected match with Sophie Charlotte, Countess Platen's daughter, it had long been abandoned. The whole idea of his marrying seemed remote and impractical; and having made the noble gesture, Sophie Dorothea now sent a grateful note to the lover who had refused to accept her sacrifice. His answer reflected the tone of her letter and the nature of the meeting that preceded it:

Never in my life was I woken up more agreeably. Never was a man happier than me if it is true that you love me and you swear that your love will last for ever. . . . I am afraid my joy will show too much in my eyes and everybody will guess that it is only because of you. I will restrain myself as much as I can, but 'when the heart is full, the eyes betray it'. Your eyes too told me last night how you felt more than I dared hope. I am so happy I can hardly express myself. Tonight I hope to say to you what I cannot write.

Some officers are about to come in and stop me from going on. Adieu.[6]

The reconciliation was perfect. In a serene mood, Königsmarck found time to write to his aunt in Sweden and thank her for the letter of condolence she had written him a month earlier. Courteous clichés and pious declarations of devotion flowed easily from his pen, skilfully woven into a request for legal representation. Unlike his hurried love letters, this one was carefully thought out, calculated and insincere. It was also properly dated:

Epsdorff, 10 October, 1691

Madam,

Had I not known you to be entirely convinced of the deep grief that I felt at the untimely death of my late mother, I would have been justified in revealing it to you here in all its extent. But I know that having lost that which I held most precious in the world is enough to convince you of the truth of something that costs me dearly and which inflicts on me a pain I have never known before. My grief would have been all the more without your condolences over the sad event that had befallen me. Your letter was so kind and so helpful regarding everything that concerns me, that I am encouraged to hope, Madam, that in you I may find again that of which cruel fate had robbed me, someone to take an interest and give me help in all my future affairs at the court of Sweden. If to win this privilege I need only show you respect, obedience and submission, I hope I can attain this end quite easily, for I always act in such a way as might prove to you that I am, and always shall be, with perfect devotion and respect,

Yours etc.,

Shortly after the visit to Epsdorff, George Louis was taken ill with a severe attack of measles. Mindful of her mother's warning, Sophie Dorothea went out of her way to nurse her husband and give him all the attentions expected from a dutiful wife. It was a thankless task. George Louis was not grateful, while Königsmarck was madly jealous. Although George Louis never showed any passion for his wife, and while he was seriously ill could hardly have had any amorous designs on her, Königsmarck imagined her spending passionate nights in his bed. He wrote so fiercely and incoherently, that two independent transcripts of his original letter cannot make out his handwriting in the opening paragraph, which in translation remains therefore just as incoherent.

With what grief I hear that you have been in another man's arms cannot be expressed, but if he wants it that is enough for you, but you do it with reluctance and you take care to tell me that this is so. . . .
I must say I would never find it in me to make advances to someone I did not love and I would rather see all the Furies than an object I loath. . . . I adore you and love you to distraction yet I am not allowed to see you. Is there any torment like that in hell?[8]

He could not bear it when she was tending her husband's sickbed, and he could not bear it when she left the sickroom to join one of those gay sledge-parties from which he was banned. He sent her one note after another, trying to arouse her compassion, telling her he was looking so poorly everybody at court was alarmed about his condition. He was sick with jealousy. His love for Sophie Dorothea became the most devastating emotion he had ever felt, and he was a changed Königsmarck when he wrote to the Princess that he knew their love was no fashionable little flirtation, but a serious affair, *une affair serjose* (the spelling is characteristically his). But the more he persisted, the more she withdrew, until one day at court she unceremoniously told him to get out and leave her in peace. For a few days he took great care to keep out of her way, and the Princess, dismayed and anxious, must have sent him a sweet note of appeasement, for his next letters were full of joy and gratitude.

In November, as soon as George Louis was sufficiently recovered, Sophie Dorothea took herself to Wienhausen, another country residence where her parents were staying that month. After a short stay they all went together to Celle. Königsmarck could not bear the prolonged separation and did the same.

Duchess Eleonore was alarmed. She could not very well order the Count out of court; indeed she went out of her way to be civil to him and to keep his interest away from her daughter. But with Sophie Dorothea she was quite outspoken. She warned her again against evil gossip and counselled sending the young man away. At no time did the virtuous Eleonore believe that there was more than an innocent, if unwise, flirtation between her daughter and the Count.

Again Sophie Dorothea tried to put reason before love and told her lover to leave her alone. He threatened to volunteer for the Morea front, and cynically asked her to be kind enough, when he died in battle, to build a memorial for him, with an inscription saying that there lay a man who sought his death because he had not been allowed to gaze into the beautiful eyes of the woman he loved.

The threat had the usual effect. With the terrible rout of the Hanoverian troops two years earlier still fresh in her mind, Sophie Dorothea begged him not to do anything hasty. He did not need much begging:

> You know only too well that I live only for you and I would not go away unless it were because of you; but as you ask me to stay, I shall do so with joy. . . .
>
> So now you are prepared not to be afraid of your parents' rhetoric, and you do not wish to see me suffer. This is sweet of you, my divine princess, and I am so moved I can only think of how to behave to suit your wishes. . . .
>
> Though I did not have the pleasure of speaking to you yesterday, I am much happier today, and the only kiss I received, although in a hurry, relieved me so much that I slept peacefully. This is the first time since my arrival at Celle that I slept soundly. . . .
>
> Montalban enters, I must finish. I kiss your knees.[9]

Momentarily reassured, he was still obsessed by her recent show of coldness and the need to thaw it through a desperate gesture of going to the wars. He was haunted by the fear of losing her:

> Although I wrote to you only yesterday evening, I cannot help writing again to tell you that I have spent one of the worst nights I have ever known. I dreamt of you, but I saw you as unfaithful. This is what I dreamt.

Apparently I had asked you not to see a certain tall fellow, but in spite of your promises, you received him in order to say goodbye to him. I was told of it, and as I could not bear to see this infidelity, I pretended I had a letter to deliver to you from your mother. I entered your room rather suddenly and saw a most terrible sight. This big man was holding you in his arms, and what was worse, you were all alone in your room. You pretended to be annoyed with your Adonis and told him he was being impertinent. I wanted to leave, but you called me back. I was delighted, for it gave me a chance to whisper in your ear that you were the most ungrateful of women, and that I was never going to speak to you again. In fact I went to see M. de Podewils to ask him to post me to Hungary, which he did.

I do ask your forgiveness for this wicked dream, but I would consider it even more wicked if I did not tell you of it. Do not think I made it up, by God it is true. For the love of all that is dearest to you, please restore my peace of mind and put me out of my misery. I am afraid this dream might be an ill omen. It would be so unjust if a tender love like mine would bring infidelities on me, as indeed I hope it would not; for why should you wish to desert a man who loves you with all his heart and swears to be faithful to you? If such vows can attach you to me, I declare before God that I shall never be unfaithful to you and I shall love you as long as I live with the same passion I do now. . . .

I embrace you from my very heart and I kiss your picture a million times. Goodbye.[10]

He wrote this letter under the very noses of the entire court circle, possibly in the grand hall of the castle of Celle. There were Mme de Harling, Duchess Sophia's respected companion and one-time governess to her niece; Ermengarda Melusina Schulenburg, who took part in the game of cards; Prince Ernest, who seemed to dog Königsmarck's footsteps; Baron Hammerstein, and some others. Writing by candle-light in a far corner of the hall was not impolite, but it must have been noticed that the Count was writing more often and at greater length than most. There must have been some speculation as to the object of his writing, and Sophie Dorothea's fear that some of his letters might be intercepted was not unfounded.

GEORGE LOUIS, AFTERWARDS KING GEORGE I

The Morea threat filled her with love and remorse. Acting with unusual audacity, she went to see him one day at his own room in the castle. She was attended by her lady-in-waiting, and the interview must have been more tender than passionate, but it filled Königsmarck with happiness. For the first time in weeks he was able to shed all pretence and behave naturally and lovingly, without being watched by evil-minded courtiers. As soon as she left he sat down to describe the pleasure that her visit had given him:

I am pleased that for once you saw me as I am all the time; you could not have made me happier. Yes, Madam, this is how I always am, and even more so. .... It is my misfortune that most of the day you hardly see me, and when I do have the happiness of seeing you by day, I have to dissimulate so much that it must be impossible for you to guess what I really feel deep inside, unless my eyes tell you. .... You will perhaps make fun at my plan to go to the Morea. .... The fear of death does not discourage me from going to those terrible places, for it is to find death that I have chosen to go. But when I consider that I wished to die, I realise I have been stupid. I did not realise that death would mean being away from you. Death itself may not be unpleasant for me, but what makes it so cruel is the knowledge that it would permanently separate me from your beautiful eyes. This thought will always make death seem terrible to me, for as long as I live, I hope, but with death hope fades away. Let us both live and comfort one another. Nothing else matters to me in this world, as long as we love one another.[11]

During that brief visit they arranged for him to come and spend the night with her in her rooms. When she departed Königsmarck was beyond himself with excitement. His heart seemed to burst with anticipation. He had to share his happiness with somebody. In his moment of bliss, he turned to the woman he was going to see again in a few hours, wanting to share with her even the sweet agony of waiting:

The minutes seem like centuries, I cannot watch the daylight without hating it. Why can't the hours turn themselves into minutes? What would I not give to hear midnight strike? Make sure to have some rosemary water by, in case I faint with joy. What, tonight I shall embrace the loveliest woman in the world, I shall kiss her sweet lips, I shall gaze into the eyes that enslave me, I shall hear from your very lips that you are not indifferent to me, I shall embrace your knees, my tears will run down your cheeks, my arms will have the pleasure of holding the most beautiful body in the world. . . . Indeed, Madam, I shall die of joy. I feel it, nothing else is possible, be prepared for it; but provided I have the time to say that I die your slave I do not mind it.[12]

It must have been one of the happiest of their rare nights of love. Stealing back to his room just before daybreak, Königsmarck fell asleep. On getting up, he took great care not to go into any of the halls where Sophie Dorothea might be with her ladies, but waited patiently for nightfall, when he would rejoin her in her rooms. And as on the day before, alone and bursting with the need to share his excitement and his happiness, he turned again to the only person to whom he could talk about his love without committing an indiscretion. From his remote part of the castle he sent Sophie Dorothea a lover's thanks:

I slept like a king, and I hope you did the same. What joy, what pleasure, what enchantment have I not felt in your arms? God, what a night I have spent!! It makes me forget all my worries, I am the happiest man on earth. . . . How long the day will seem without you.[13]

Content and discontent

At the beginning of 1692 a new name made its appearance in Königs-marck's letters to the Princess. It was that of the Duchess of Saxe-Eisenach.

She arrived in Hanover with her husband and their entire court, as was the custom, to attend the carnival season in the 'German Venice'. The Duke's itinerary might have included some political talks with Duke Ernest Augustus and Duke George William. His visit was certainly important enough for the English envoy Colt to report it in his dispatches to London.

The Duchess however had eyes only for pleasure. She had a reputa-tion of being easy with her favours and no doubt expected the gay carnival to yield some fresh conquests. She must have met Königs-marck before, possibly during one of his visits to other German courts. From his references to her it would appear that she had known of his gallant disposition and was counting on it. She lost no time in renewing their acquaintance. When the courts of Hanover and Saxe-Eisenach moved to Celle for part of the carnival festivities, she went so far as to hint that, should Königsmarck wish to cultivate her friendship even further, he would meet with no rebuff.

Her overtures could not have been made in a more inopportune moment. Königsmarck was at the height of his passion for Sophie Dorothea, languishing for her by day, only living for the night, when he might join her in her rooms. Besides, he was only too well aware of his mistress's jealous nature. He therefore took care not to behave in any way that might lead to complications. But he could not help being flattered, and he would not have been himself had he not boasted to the Princess about his easy conquest and his newly-found virtue:

M. Gor has brought me a message from the Duchess of Eisenach, with her compliments, saying that although I had avoided speaking to her, she was going to show me that she thought of me more than I of her.

I swear to you that not only did this message give me no pleasure, but quite on the contrary, it annoyed me that she had it sent to me. I have not left my room all day, and I think I shall do the same tomorrow.

To please me, tell me how you are and when you will be back. I shall die of longing and grief if I do not see you soon. Goodbye, dear heart, think of your faithful lover and do not forget him in the midst of all this crowd of people. Once again, goodbye.

Thursday, at 12 after midnight. My pain in the chest continues, but I have had no fever.[1]

Quite possibly the gay Duchess of Saxe-Eisenach had not gauged the depth of Königsmarck's feeling for the Princess and genuinely believed she was not trespassing. Or if she had, she was not too squeamish to encourage the attentions of someone else's gallant. For Sophie Dorothea it was unbearable that a frivolous young woman should throw herself in the Count's way, apparently without encountering the least sign of disapproval. What she could not say in public, she did by letter, and her lover had to use all his powers of persuasion to convince her that he was not interested in anyone but her:

It is possible that after the declaration I made you, you are still not pleased with me? Are you not convinced of my love, and can you really believe I could be unfaithful to you? No, Madam, may I be damned if I ever love anybody but you, or let anyone but you possess my heart. You will see it by the manner I am going to treat the Princess Eisenach, and I hope you will be satisfied with me. Thank you for last night. Never in my life have I spent a better hour. If you would have the kindness to allow me to come to you tomorrow evening, it will give me back my life.[2]

Still she was not appeased. Clearly her rival was not in the least discouraged by the Count's airs, and he for his part must have enjoyed a flirtation in which he was playing the virtuous party. Sophie Dorothea, reluctantly adhering to her self-imposed rule of avoiding her lover in public, could do nothing to stop the young Duchess from pursuing him to her heart's content. The Duchess had the field to herself. Königsmarck had to double his protestations:

Surely, Madam, my manner towards the Duchess of Saxe-Eisenach must show you that, once you have taken possession of a heart, no other beauty can find a place in it, least of all that Princess. I hope you have no cause to complain of my behaviour to other ladies here. I was very attentive to your husband's mistress hoping to find out from her what the Countess [Platen] was up to, but she would not tell me anything. I stand well with His Highness the Prince [George Louis] and I show him more courtesy than usual.[3]

Sophie Dorothea decided to punish him a little and made it even more difficult for him to speak to her in the presence of others. He was reproachful:

I imagined that in possessing you I should be the happiest man on earth. I did not think I should have so few opportunities to speak to you, I will tell you frankly that this spoils my bliss, and I shall never be perfectly happy until I achieve that as well. . . .
Have you noticed how the Duchess of Eisenach besieged me? I hope that when I have answered her curtly once or twice, she will understand that I do not wish to have anything to do with her.

I love you because you are sweet. I do not love you for reasons of self-interest, ambition or vanity. . . . If in the next world we shall be able to keep the memory of this one, I am sure I shall never forget you. Indeed, my dearest, the sight of angels will never fill me with as much joy as the sight of you. . . .⁴

In the meantime life at Celle continued with as much splendour as Duchess Eleonore knew how to organise. One evening the entire company was invited to attend a comedy at the castle theatre. Everybody was there, the Duke and Duchess of Celle, their most important ministers and courtiers, the Duke and Duchess of Saxe-Eisenach, Count and Countess Platen, Mlle Schulenburg with George Louis and some of the young Princes of Hanover. Sophie Dorothea turned up in a gorgeous dress and delighted her mother by being attentive to her distinguished entourage and showing her appreciation of the play. She was gay and lively and seemed to be enjoying herself. Königsmarck felt left out. It is not known what he actually did to try to force her attention. He might have flirted outrageously, or he might have got disgracefully drunk during the supper and dance that followed. Whatever he did, it only won him a contemptuous look of disapproval. His pleading letter, written later the same night, indicated the enormity of his behaviour:

If you could only see how dispirited I am, you would forgive the fault I have committed. I admit I was piqued because you did not as much as look at me throughout the play, although I had seated myself right opposite you. I did not deserve this, and after the sacrifice I have made for you of the Duchess of Eisenach, I deserved at least a glance. You must have noticed that I hardly look at her, and when she speaks to me I answer her curtly so as not to encourage any further conversation. Her lady-in-waiting tells me that the Duchess finds me much changed, and a thousand things like that. But enough of this, it is not worth mentioning. Forgive me, my princess, I beg of you, and let me come and see you tomorrow. The dance made me so hot, I could not come and see you as I was, without changing my shirt. . . .
I wandered round your room for a good half-hour, hoping the

Confidante might come out. I even wanted to knock at your back door, but I did not dare. What a torment not to be in the arms of the one I love; and what a night I am going to have to spend! Good God, what did I think I was doing? And what demon possessed me? If you do not forgive me I shall be desperate, I shall take the first horse and go back to the regiment to weep over my sins. Goodnight and goodbye, sweet child, dare I still call you by this name? I do not deserve this privilege. I cannot bear this any longer, my anxiety torments me more than hell. Oh God, when shall I have your answer? For the love of God, let me have it soon for I cannot stand this any longer. I cannot keep still, I am so tense with worry. . . .[5]

Sophie Dorothea must have been placated; but what comforted her most of all was the fact that the visitors were about to leave. Colt reported to London that the courts of Hanover and Saxe-Eisenach were about to return to their respective residences, as the carnival festivities had come to an end. The Eisenach interlude was over.

The carnival season of 1692 was a happy one for the lovers, in spite of their petty jealousies and childish quarrels. There was much gaiety by day, and whether or not Königsmarck took part in it, by night he was able to make his way discreetly into Sophie Dorothea's suite of rooms. That comparatively worry-free period served to mature their relationship and give it depth. Königsmarck had already remarked that theirs was not a flirtation for the season, but a lasting attachment. He knew himself to be a changed man, and hardly needed the Duchess of Eisenach's lady-in-waiting to tell him so. He found himself constant without any conscious effort, and he was most anxious for Sophie Dorothea to understand that his life of flitting affairs was decidedly over. He penned another of his facile little poems, which the Princess never failed to find charming.

> Once I was a fickle swain
> Every moment in a whirl;
> From shepherd girl to shepherd girl
> I loved to change, and change again.

But since on Sylvie's charms I gaze
I'm bound to love her all the time.
This is for me the change sublime—
Never to change me all my days.[6]

Sylvie was only one of many tender names he had for her. She was his dear heart, his life, his little girl, his *aimable brune*; sometimes he called her *Léonisse*, or *Léonesse*, depending on which way the spelling muse would move him, or *Hermione* or *Iris*. And sometimes she was *le coeur gauche* or even *petite louche*, a nickname borrowed from a love-story of the time. The latter terms were partly endearments, partly code-names. The lovers had devised a very elaborate system of disguising names of people they were discussing in their letters, and although their code was too simple to be of any value if their letters had been intercepted, they clung to it with childish faith. Eleonore Knesebeck was naturally *la confidante*, *la gouvernante*, and more rarely, *Krumbuglen*. George William, Sophie Dorothea's father, was *le grondeur*; her mother, Duchess Eleonore, *le pédagogue*; and Duchess Sophia, *la Romaine*. George Louis, the husband, was *le reformeur*, and Duke Ernest Augustus, *Don Diego*. Aurora was nicknamed *l'avanturière* or *la maréchalle*, and Countess Platen *la baronne*, *la grosse*, *la perspective* or *dondon*. Prince Ernest was *l'innocent* and his brother Max either *le barbouilleur* or *Colin*. Königsmarck sometimes signed himself as *Tircis*, but more often as *le chevalier*, another character from the same love story that had yielded the *petite louche*.

Their inventiveness did not stop short at code names, but went on to cipher. Duke Ernest Augustus was 100, Duchess Sophia 200; the Duke of Celle was 101, and the Duchess of Celle 227. George Louis was 102, and Countess Platen 202. Places were also disguised and when Hanover was not Han, it was 300. The list was endless. Later they discovered the system of encircling each syllable by nonsense letters, thus making Colt into *jllicoltjlli*, Brockhausen into *illibrockjlli* and Hanover into *illihajilliverjlli*. The lovers and their confidante must have spent many pleasant hours adding to their list and improving it. They were too inexperienced in the art of plotting to know it could not have deceived a child.

The one blot on their happiness was Duchess Eleonore who did her best to keep them apart. Königsmarck was so sure of his standing with the Princess that he did not hesitate to criticise her mother to her, knowing full well that hers was the only voice of reason the daughter was still likely to listen to:

> What worries me most is that your mother has been at you again; for though she means well she is bound to watch you closely, and when she learns that you have been talking to me, she might tell the Duke of Celle. Try to avert that, or else we are lost. . . .
> It is cruel to see that the whole world may make love to you and that you can speak to anybody, without anyone finding fault with it, while I am the only one excluded. When I think that your mother actually pushes you into Baron Welling's arms, while at the same time she forces you to avoid me, I get so furious I feel like stabbing her, and I wish she went to the devil. If the earth were to open and swallow up both your mother and the Dowager [Princess of East Friesland], I should be absolutely delighted.[7]

The Dowager Princess, whom Sophie Dorothea had antagonised several years earlier when she refused to cede her a place of honour that was hers by courtesy if not by rank, apparently took it upon herself to criticise her behaviour to her mother; and although Eleonore was bound to stand up for her daughter, both middle-aged ladies were far too interfering for Königsmarck's liking. He classed them together:

> I have had a long conversation with the Duchess of Celle. I think she is the most hypocritical woman in the world. She says a thousand kind things to my face, and yet she tries to use her authority over you to malign me to you. . . . These ladies [Duchess Eleonore and the Princess of East Friesland] do their utmost to turn you away from me.[8]

It was during that happy time at Celle that the seeds of a new idea began to germinate in Sophie Dorothea's mind. Long before Königsmarck came into her life, when she resented being a neglected and unwanted wife, she would openly bewail her lot and wish she had been a French *marquise*—her mother's original rank—married for love, rather than a Princess of Hanover, disdained by her husband. She regretted not being able to lead the sort of life that might have been hers, had she been married in different circumstances.

Now, when for the first time in her life she experienced a reciprocated love, she began to form romantic plans for a distant future. She began to dream of running away with the man she loved, in order to live with him happily and respectably somewhere far away. At that stage however it was no more than a dream, and Königsmarck's reaction indicated that he too did not see in it, as yet, more than another assurance of her constancy:

> I know now it would be wrong of me to doubt you after the proposition you made me, saying that you want to leave all this splendid grandeur and retire with me to some corner of the world. After that I have nothing to worry about. I gladly accept your offer. Just say the word and I shall be ready for anything. If being persecuted by your parents might induce you to take such a step, I wish they would persecute you a hundred times more, so that you may act promptly. Why can't we run away tonight?[9]

That suggestion was to come up more frequently, as meetings became more difficult and exposure more imminent. But for the time being the lovers were still content with things as they were. When the court returned to Hanover, Sophie Dorothea obtained permission to extend her stay by a few days, ostensibly to enjoy the company of her parents. George Louis left with his mistress without calling on his wife to say goodbye. The news of his departure reached her through a note sent by Königsmarck, who also managed to stay behind, adding: 'All goes wonderfully well.'

By mid-March Sophie Dorothea returned to the Leine Palace to resume her duties as Princess of Hanover. While her husband was inspecting his troops in preparation for a new campaign, Königsmarck obtained leave to go to Hamburg and see to his estate there. Apparently he found a way to continue the pleasant routine established at Celle, for he delayed his departure from day to day. Eventually he tore himself away, and the Princess sat down to write immediately after their tender farewell. That letter was her first to be preserved.

Sophie Dorothea was a fluent writer. Her style was natural and her spelling impeccable. She expressed herself spontaneously, never using clichés and platitudes as her lover often did. Whatever restraint she put on herself in public, she showed none of it in her writing. She poured out her heart, baring herself with complete abandon, giving herself to her lover unreservedly and irrevocably. There was no trace of coquetry in her letters. For a woman who was constantly being accused by her lover of flirtatiousness, she was unusually direct, warm and unquestionably sincere:

I spent the rest of the night without sleeping, and the day talking about you and crying because you have gone away. Never did a day seem so long to me, and I do not know how I shall get used to not seeing you. The Confidante has just given me your letter. You may be sure I will do even more than I promised, and I shall not lose a single opportunity to prove my love and my sincere attachment. If I could shut myself up during your absence and not see anybody, I would gladly do so, for when I cannot see you everything irritates and annoys me. If anything might help me to bear your absence without dying of grief, it is only my hope to convince you, by my conduct, that nobody has ever loved as much as I love you, and that nothing equals my fidelity. It will stand any trial, and whatever happens to me, nothing will ever part me from the man I love. Yes, *mon cher enfant*, my love will only end with my life.

I was so different today and so depressed, that even my husband felt sorry for me and said he could see I was ill and that I ought to take care of myself. He is right, but my illness comes from loving, and I wish never to be cured of it.

I have not seen anyone worth mentioning. I went to see Duchess Sophia for a little while, but returned to my apartments as soon as possible, to give myself the pleasure of talking of you [with Mlle Knesebeck].

It is eight o'clock; I have to attend my court. God, how dull I shall seem! I shall retire as soon as supper is over, so that I can read your letters again. This is my only pleasure while you are away. Goodbye, adorable child, only death will part me from you; human powers will never succeed in doing this.[10]

Death nearly did part them that time. Königsmarck was hardly out of Hanover when his carriage broke down. Not wishing to turn back, he drove on relentlessly across the Elbe and barely escaped drowning, carriage, postillions, horses and all. But worse was to come, as he virtuously wrote after his safe arrival in Hamburg:

My servants had taken lodgings for us at our usual inn. Imagine my surprise when I learned that the Princess of East Friesland and the Duchess of Saxe-Eisenach were also staying there. I was wondering what to do, for they sent a message asking me to dine with them. But I remembered my promise to you, *petite louche*, and decided to move to some other quarters. I pretended I had some urgent business and left at once without seeing them, then put up at another inn.[11]

Hamburg was then a fortified town much patronised by the princes of northern Germany. It was a political centre where alliances were made and unmade, as well as a cultural one, where distinguished visitors could relax at the opera house, the first ever to be built in Germany. Countess Amelia Lewenhaupt, Königsmarck's married sister, was there with her husband, and the three had a great deal of family news to exchange. Not all of it was pleasant. Count Lewenhaupt had recently been granted a commission in the Hanoverian army, which was a promotion from his previous post at Celle. Some officer of his acquaintance said, while in his cups, that the Count had got the promotion because his sister-in-law Aurora Königsmarck slept with the right people. Both brother and brother-in-law were outraged and talked of vindicating the lady's honour by challenging the offender to a duel. The matter must have been settled amicably after all, for no further reference to it was made in Königsmarck's subsequent letters from Hamburg.

Something else was worrying him during his stay. Two of Sophie Dorothea's letters reached him with an unfamiliar seal. He suspected that they had been broken open and resealed by hostile hands, and was greatly perturbed about the Princess's safety. He immediately wrote to instruct her to stop writing to him until his return. Sophie Dorothea was badly frightened. When her lover returned to Hanover she scarcely spoke to him in public, and refused to continue their meetings in private. Their brief period of bliss was at an end.

Never doubt my fidelity

Three years of hostilities had not given France a definite advantage over the Grand Alliance, in spite of some spectacular victories. In the spring of 1692, hoping to beat his worst enemy at home, Louis XIV sent his fleet against England. But his luck had turned. Admiral Russel virtually annihilated it at La Hogue, opposite Torbay, thus proving that France was not invincible.

To vindicate their naval defeat, the French took the key fortress of Namur, which controlled the road to the Netherlands. The fall of Namur was a blow to the Grand Alliance, and William hurried out at the head of his army in order to liberate it. He took up positions at Lambeque, only six miles from Steinkirk, where the main body of the French army was encamped. There the two armies lay, almost within sight of one another, waiting for action. But the terrain was full of hedges and ditches, and neither side would attack. The delay suited William, who was hoping for reinforcement from Hanover. By the beginning of June Duke Ernest Augustus gave the word, and the Hanoverian troops were ordered to Flanders. Their commander-in-chief was again George Louis, who was this time accompanied by his brother Prince Christian.

Königsmarck should have been preparing his regiment and getting it ready for the march. But while other officers were busily drilling, inspecting and victualling, he was mooning around the Leine Palace, unable to goad himself to action as long as the Princess was avoiding him. It was small comfort to remember that it was he who had counselled caution:

Your reluctance to speak to me surprises me, though I still try to persuade myself you cannot very well do otherwise without arousing suspicion. Still, one should risk something when it is a question of saying goodbye for 6 months. This is what I think; that is why I stay here instead of going away. See how much I love you! I neglect my duty which calls me away for the rest of the year, although it is so urgent I ought to be leaving at once. But how can I leave without saying goodbye? I would rather die. . . .[1]

Sophie Dorothea sent word that he must be patient and on no account do anything foolhardy, like knocking at her back door or imposing on her while at court. It was not what he was hoping to hear:

Sunday,
Yes, Madam, I will suffer for your sake because you command me to, but when shall I have the happiness to be where I long to be, that is, in your arms? When shall I have this satisfaction? I lose all hope, for the way things are going I cannot flatter myself this will be very soon. I lose heart, and if I write without rime or reason, do not be annoyed with me; it is despair that drives me to it. If you do not believe me look at the hairs I pulled out of my head this morning. I cannot say that they turned grey overnight, but I swear they were not there 8 days ago. You must believe me when I say I am absolutely desperate. I stay on for the love of you, I risk honour, reputation, and ambition, for as I do not go to the front what will people say of me? And why should I risk all this, if I cannot see you again? I have reached the point where I must take hold of myself or else die. . . .
To stay on in Hanover like this is out of the question, for in three weeks' time you are going away to your father's. What should I

then do here with you gone? Please think it over and let me know your wish. I am ready to show you by my obedience that my love does not listen to reason. See what you have done to me; for your sake I sacrifice my ambition, the only thing I had preserved so far. See to what length my love goes! Judge for yourself what state I am in. Do not utterly ruin me, be more ambitious than I am; have ambition for a lover who has not got it anymore. . . .[2]

It was a dangerous situation; if he went on shirking his duty, the reason for his doing so would come out and Sophie Dorothea would be just as compromised as if she were caught giving him encouragement. In any case she could never resist him for long; her caution always deserted her at the slightest thought of his being hurt. She said goodbye to him in a manner that left no cause for complaint, and with a much lighter heart he left immediately for his camp, just outside town, from where the march to Flanders was about to start.

In camp, a grand military review was held, with Duke Ernest Augustus inspecting the Hanoverian force, accompanied by the English envoy Colt. The morale of the troops was high, for the news of the naval victory at La Hogue had only just reached them. After the review a general thanksgiving was held in Hanover. Sophie Dorothea was hoping Königsmarck might find a way to see her again:

Sunday, 12 June.
I have no news of you and I am desperate; I am very worried and fear a thousand things. But I cannot believe you are neglecting me; you have so convinced me of your love that I cannot have any suspicions on that count. But I love too deeply to be free from the anxiety that is inseparable from love. . . .
I was hoping to see you after the review. I could have done it with impunity, for my husband was staying in camp. That false hope kept me at my window for two whole nights. Every time I saw someone go by I thought it was you. It was no use Mlle Knesebeck sending me to bed, I would not listen to reason.
I must tell you what I have been doing with myself today. I retired early after dinner. There was some music in the evening, and I had a game of cards with Colt. . . . I must end now, it is three o'clock

and I must go to bed. Never doubt my fidelity, it is unshakeable. I want to live and die yours only.[3]

The thought of riding back to Hanover after the review for another private meeting with Sophie Dorothea had in fact occurred to Königsmarck, for he was naturally well informed of his Commander's movements and knew that he was going to remain in camp. The post horses were already saddled and waiting, when it suddenly dawned on Königsmarck that a certain tiresome little man who had been dogging his footsteps all day, was a spy in the employ of Countess Platen. There was no way of giving him the slip, and so Königsmarck had to overcome his eagerness and stay behind. He turned down an invitation to attend a victory party, and ordered his major to deputise for him. While his fellow officers were drinking themselves silly, he retired to his quarters and sought consolation in writing and dreaming. But he could not sleep. Only an hour or so earlier a brother officer, whom he considered a friend and well-wisher, had given him a discreet warning to pull himself together and not allow love to blind his eyes to duty and honour. Tossing and turning in his lonely bed, Königsmarck reflected that his affair with the Princess was no longer a secret. He trusted his friend not to say anything to anyone else, but he was so worried he wrote the Princess an exact account of the conversation. A more sensible man might have added a word of caution and counselled discretion, but Königsmarck was never a sensible man.

It was galling for Sophie Dorothea that instead of the lover she expected, her husband rode back the following day, to take her to a banquet given by Colt to celebrate the English victory over the French fleet. Colt spared no expense to make the banquet a further inducement for the Brunswick Dukes to keep their bargain with William, and in his dispatch described it as 'the greatest diversion that they ever saw in this place'. After the banquet, George Louis returned to camp, and from there started the march to Flanders, which was to keep him and his troops away for the next six months. With his consent, it had been arranged that during his long absence his wife would be allowed to live with her parents, either at their various hunting lodges or at Celle. Both Duchess Sophia and Ernest Augustus felt it was a sensible arrangement, and waived any objection they might have had in the past against her visiting them too frequently.

While she was preparing to join her parents at Brockhausen, two foreign envoys arrived at court with their parties and were given a grand welcome. The Princess was naturally expected to be gracious, and indeed did her best to be hospitable and please Duke Ernest Augustus. This social duty however seemed to her too tedious to be the subject of a letter, and she wrote only of her feelings:

Monday 20

Your letter was given to me as soon as I woke up. I found it charming, tender and just as I wished it. I ask you to go on feeling that way about me. If you ever change, I shall not want to live one single moment. Only you can make me find life agreeable, and since you left I have not had one moment's joy. When I think that each step you take removes you further away from me, I feel desperate. I thought a thousand times of following you. What would I not give to be able to do it and always be with you? If there is anything that may give me pleasure in my present state, it is to show you how indifferent I am to everybody and how sincere my love is. I avoid all men, I speak only to the ladies, and I am really enjoying it. Do not be grateful to me on that count, I could not do otherwise, and you are far too charming for me to be able to look at anyone else.

I have not left my room all day. On Sunday I am going to Brockhausen, so this evening I shall take my leave of Duchess Sophia.

If I were to tell you all I think of you and how much I love you, I should never finish. My love is beyond anything I could possibly express and I should be most happy if yours were like mine. I will not preach fidelity to you, but I need not remind you that I shall die if you are not faithful. I have said so a thousand times and all my peace of mind depends on it. You might well find a more attractive woman, but you will never find another who is so loving and to whom your wish is law. But why should you change? You are loved and worshipped and you have a sensible heart. Goodbye, *mon cher enfant*, know I shall love you to eternity.[4]

As the troops had not gone very far, communication was relatively easy, and news travelled fast. What the Princess omitted to mention in her letter, was reported verbally by the couriers. Königsmarck was appalled to learn that far from weeping at his absence, the Princess had actually attended a court entertainment in honour of the foreign envoys, and apparently conducted herself with her usual vivacity:

Venlo, June 21

So it is true you have forgotten me, and all for the pleasures of the theatre, the music, and worst of all, the company of the foreign visitors. I know all this from the Prince [George Louis] with whom I dined today. . . .

Since I last saw you I had been so careless with my appearance that I had neglected to have my beard trimmed. Attending the court quarters of the camp as I was, everybody stared. His Highness himself kindly asked what was wrong with me, for he had noticed my unkempt appearance. I pretended to have an attack of colic which gave me much pain.

God, he did not guess what state I was in. Until now I have had no fear that you might forget me, but since the arrival of the Piedmontese Count and the Austrian, I cannot doubt your inconstancy. Cruel, heartless woman! This is unbearable. But I must not complain. I know the names of my rivals, yes, I do, and that is enough. You are dealing with a man who loves you to distraction. You made me believe you loved me in the same way, it is incredible. But don't you think that I am going to leave it at that. Oh no, my heart is too proud to be deceived like that. I will revenge myself or I die. Yes, I will show the whole world how I take my revenge. . . .

So you kept to your room to weep over my letters, did you? Your room was the opera house, your tears were the result of too much laughing, and your pleasure, far from being the reading of my letters, was to listen to sweet compliments paid by other men. This is too much to bear, it does not bear thinking about, you will drive me to extremes. I shall try to have myself transferred to the service of the Elector of Bavaria, and then I shall seek out those who had robbed me of your ungrateful heart. . . .[5]

Not expecting this outburst of jealousy, Sophie Dorothea was staggered. But if Königsmarck was temperamental and immature, so was she. Far from showing understanding of a man who was so unsure of himself as to suspect a rival where none could be found, she in her turn upbraided him for his rash threat to offer his services to another prince. She too was unsure of herself, and while she protested her love and her innocence, the thought struck her that he might be planning to desert her for another woman:

Brockhausen, 30 June

Today I received two of your letters, but instead of finding them full of love, I saw nothing in them except reproaches which I do not deserve and never shall. I could not have been more surprised. I have not done anything since your departure with which you should not be perfectly satisfied, and as long as I live I shall never do anything which would not be agreeable to you.

These are my true feelings, and my only wish is to show you the depth of my love for you. Far from indulging the coquetry you so unjustly accuse me of, I shed bitter tears when I read those hard things you said. What grounds have I given you to form such a bad opinion of me? Is it because I loved you to idolatry? Or because for your sake I neglected all the friends I ever had? Or because for your sake I ignored my parents' warning and shut my eyes to the disaster that might follow? Nothing can describe my dejection. I cannot bear to think that you believe me capable of breaking my promises to you.

You talk of the pleasant people who might supplant you. They do not deserve the compliment you pay them, and I am ashamed to have to reassure you about them. I have spoken very little to the Piedmontese, and not at all to the Austrian. I have been telling you most accurately all I have been doing, and I am willing to take any oath you might choose to convince you of my innocence. Believe me and imprint it well on your mind that nothing will ever make me change. I love you beyond anything I can say, and even if you give me cause to repent, I shall never be able to stop loving you. My heart is too much yours for me to be able to withdraw it.

And yet you want to join the service of the Elector of Bavaria and leave me, and all this because of some delusion that has no grounds at all. Is that the way to love? Do you still love me or are you looking for an excuse to leave me? I have done nothing I would like kept from you. My words and my actions are irreproachable, and however severe you might be, you could not find fault with me. But I cannot forget that you want to leave me. It seems to me that this decision did not cost you much pain. I will have no peace until I know how I stand with you. If the most tender love and unshakeable fidelity could satisfy you, mine should.[6]

When writing this letter, the Princess had already been at Brockhausen for several days. She went out of her way to be sweet to her parents and tried to persuade them that for the pleasure of their company she would forgo all other. By day her father went hunting, and she spent most of her time with her mother, who again warned her against giving way to her emotions. In the evenings there would be a family supper, with a game of cards played with members of the ducal household, such as Judith de Beauregard, or General Chauvet. When it was time for her to retire, her father would escort her to her apartment with all due ceremony. Once alone in her room, she would take up her pen and start writing. Mostly she would write of her feelings rather than about the events of the day. The following was characteristic of her:

Brockhausen, June 22

My heart and thoughts are always with you and I have not had a moment's joy since you left; and when I think I shall be another four or five months without seeing you, I fall into a melancholy I can hardly conceal. A thousand thoughts depress me. I fear we might be separated, or someone might try to put obstacles in our way. I can see myself on the edge of a precipice. . . .

Goodnight, I am going to bed. What sad nights since you left! I cannot think of the joys we had without a pang of pain. Be faithful, *mon cher enfant*, all my happiness depends on it. I want to live only for you.[7]

There were regular couriers running backwards and forwards between Hanover and the army on the march. The Hanover mail, including letters collected from Celle and Brockhausen, was usually delivered to the court quarters of the camp, where a duty officer would sort it. One day, as soon as Königsmarck heard that the Hanover courier had arrived, he dispatched an officer to collect his mail. The officer returned with a heavy packet, but it contained only dull letters from Prince Ernest and Marshal Podewils. His disappointment led to a burst of anger:

25

The whole world writes except you. I have told you so so often I have nothing more to say. You danced at Colt's ball. I hope your letters to Antwerp will explain it, but there is no justification for your behaviour at Hanover, especially when the foreigners were there. Whatever the Duke expected you to do, you should have refused. This will be the last letter I shall ever write to you if I do not hear from you again.[8]

It was a cruel thing to say to Sophie Dorothea, who was trying so hard to allay her parents' suspicions and who had been caught impolitely daydreaming while a courtier was talking to her. She replied, as soon as she received the harsh letter, eight days later:

Brockhausen, 3 July

I am in agony and I cannot bear the pain your unjust suspicion causes me. You yourself instructed me to write to Wesel only once. This is what I did, and all my other letters were addressed to Antwerp. You should have received them and I do not know who is to blame for this negligence. You are making a grave mistake if you think I could possibly forget you. Time will prove my innocence and your injustice. I must say I am very hurt, for since your departure I have thought of nothing except how to show you my fidelity and how little everything else matters. . . .

I am annoyed at your being displeased with me for having attended Colt's ball. I could not get out of it, he was so insistent. It was not the foreigners who detained me in Hanover. They left days before I set out for Brockhausen. I have already told you I had hardly spoken to them and I have written to you exactly all I had been doing. If you do not believe me, there is no terrible oath I would not swear to prove my innocence. I am not capable of deceiving you. I love you passionately and no amount of unhappiness will ever turn me away from you. Still you think I deceive you and you do not want to write to me any more. You drive me to despair. How do I know that someone does not keep my letters back in order to estrange us? I have a thousand reasons to fear the worst and you depress me further by believing me unfaithful. You must never let it enter your head that I could ever fail in my love for you. I would sooner fail to myself, for you are a thousand times more precious to me. I want to live only for you, and if you change towards me, life will be unbearable.[9]

There were unusually heavy floods that year towards the end of June and the beginning of July. Roads were impassable and whole villages were under water. To Sophie Dorothea the distress of the peasants mattered little. The floods meant only one thing—couriers could neither depart nor arrive. She was imprisoned at Brockhausen with no news from the front. With a major battle looming ahead, and the danger of death threatening her lover, she was badly shaken to learn of the untimely demise of a young man from Duchess Eleonore's household, in the midst of his peaceful occupations at court:

Brockhausen, 25 June

Yesterday I learned of the death of Lescour's brother. I was shattered because I immediately thought of you. He was healthy, he was young, and yet he died. You cannot imagine what morbid thoughts I had. I fear for your life more than ever. If you really love me you must take good care of yourself for my sake. What will become of me without you? I could not stay a moment in this world, life would be unbearable. Since you left I languish, and the only thing that gives me strength is the hope of seeing you again. What would I do if I lost you? But I do not want to torment myself with such morbid thoughts. All my prayers are for your safety, I implore God night and day to keep you well.

If you knew how violent my love is you would pity me for being so far away from you. It grows every moment and your absence does not diminish it in the least. My love is constant, I have never loved so tenderly and so wholly.[10]

A few days later her fears for his safety became more real:

> Brockhausen, 27 June
>
> General Chauvet told me yesterday that as far as he could judge, there was going to be a battle soon. You know how much I love you, so you can imagine what state I am in when I think that the only person for whom I want to live is about to be exposed to a thousand dangers. If you love me stay alive. I shall die if you have the slightest wound. . . .
>
> I cannot see an end to my longing. The time I have to wait until we meet again seems like an eternity. But what joy when I do see you again! I will not be able to contain myself and everybody will know how much I love you. It does not matter, you deserve it. I could never love you too much. This is the way I feel, and I shall die with these feelings, unless you force me to change.[11]

When the floods subsided, the ducal family was at last able to leave Brockhausen, which was rather restricted for space, and return to the comfortable castle of Celle, the only place Sophie Dorothea ever called home. Eleonore had been unwell for some time, and there was talk of her going to Ems to take the waters. The Princess wrote to ask Königsmarck whether he would mind her going away with her mother, but while she waited in vain for his answer, she began to fear that the real cause for his silence was some terrible betrayal. She knew herself to be on the edge of a precipice, but could see no way back. She was wholly and irrevocably committed to her love. Much as she feared exposure, she feared losing Königsmarck even more.

> Celle, 11 July
>
> Many things confirm my suspicion that I have been betrayed. If Countess Platen takes a hand in it, you can well imagine what I may expect. But I have already told you, the only thing that makes me tremble is your temper. You will go and enlist somewhere else, and I shall never see you again. Maybe you already have, I am so

dejected I am sure it must forbode unhappiness. Still, if it costs you so little to give me up, you could not have really loved me. When the heart is truly affected one does not give up so easily, and one at least takes the trouble to consider things. But I cannot expect you to have the patience, I know your temper, you would break up with me altogether. Maybe later you will start thinking, but it will be too late and I shall bear the pain of loving you to idolatry, knowing that you never really loved me. The thought is so cruel it drives me mad. Goodbye, whatever happens I know I shall never be able to stop loving you, and you will be the bane of my life, just as you have been the happiness of it. But I love you, oh God how I love you.[12]

Königsmarck's replies arrived most irregularly. The Princess grieved to find them full of reproaches for things she had already explained in her previous letters, no doubt delayed or possibly even lost. She had to explain all over again:

Celle, 13 July

I am surprised you still write to me about the foreigners. I told you everything I have been doing every day and I do not recall any inconstancy on my part. Fortunately my memory is better than yours. You are the sort of person to malign me on no firmer evidence than a fly's leg, and I would have a hard time of it. But severe as you are, I defy you to find fault with my conduct. It is above reproach and my love is deep. My love and my fidelity are above anything I can express. I will not allow you to be in doubt about them, and the coquetry you accuse me of makes me despair. I renounced it forever when I gave myself to you, and my only thoughts are how to please you. This is my highest aspiration. . . . You must realise that I am incapable of deceiving you. I would not be fit to live if the thought ever entered my head. . . . For twelve days now I have learnt to what extremes my love can go, I think nobody has ever loved as passionately as I do.[13]

Two days later, she reported a narrow escape she had:

Celle, 15 July

I have just had an awful fright. My mother suddenly came into my room, although I had sent word I wanted to go to bed early. All I could do was to turn the sheet of paper over. I was terrified she might ask to see what I had been writing, I became quite white and started trembling. She asked if I was unwell and only stayed for a brief moment. My heart is still pounding, I have not quite recovered from the fright.

I envy the picture you have of me. It kisses you every day. You look at it tenderly while I will not have this pleasure for another four or five months, which will seem like centuries. . . . I miss you so much I shall never let you leave me again. I would rather expose myself to danger than live without seeing you. No man has ever been loved so truly and so tenderly. I would gladly renounce the world in order to retire to some corner where I would see no one but you. I have said so a thousand times and I will say so again and again. You may find a more attractive woman, but none as loving and as faithful as me. Your wish is law with me and my sole concern is to please you. . . .

The Piedmontese Count who worries you so much bores me to tears. I cannot help mentioning him although he is not worth it. I swear to you that I have had no conversation with him, nor had the slightest inclination to have any. You must be ashamed of yourself worrying about people who do not deserve to be looked at. You should know your worth better than that; you are so much above any other man that you must not fear anyone.

Keep your heart whole for me, I do not want to share it. I have given you all of mine and made you absolute master over it. Be as constant as I am faithful, and let us always love one another whatever happens.[14]

That night Sophie Dorothea nearly got caught again. The following morning she took up the story where she had left it:

Celle, 16 July

After I finished writing I went to bed. I read all your letters over and over again, I thought I was quite safe as I had said I was going to bed. Then mother surprised me a second time. All Mlle Knesebeck could do was to shove the letters under my blanket. I did not dare move, fearing that if I did the paper might rustle. At last mother left, to my great relief, for I was dying of fright. I do not like such surprises, but I cannot escape them.[15]

Still no letters came. The Princess's tone became reproachful:

> Celle, 20 July
>
> I do not know how to take your silence. It surprises me and I do not know what to make of it. Today I had a letter from my husband and I am depressed to think that he writes more regularly than you do. What has become of your ardour? Has the Brussels air cooled you off and has a new love blotted me out of memory? ... Please reassure me and tell me my fears are unfounded, I beg of you. I need it, I shall die if I do not find you as you should be, that is as loving and faithful as I am.[16]

And a few days later:

> Celle, 25 July
>
> I do not know any more what to think. The third post has arrived and still no letter. This is not the behaviour of the ardent lover you always seemed to be. Have you forgotten me altogether or are we betrayed? It must be either the one or the other. I am very worried and I have not a moment's peace, but I assure you that what I dread most is the possibility that you might have changed towards me. I do not think about other things and about what might happen to me. Is it possible that you have forgotten all your vows swearing eternal fidelity?[17]

All this time the Hanoverian troops had been marching on to meet up with the Grand Army of the Allies. Venlo, Wesel, Antwerp and Wavre were left behind, and in mid-July the united forces found themselves encamped within reach of Brussels. A rest was called and men and officers were allowed to go to town to take part in various seasonal entertainments. Everybody crowded into coaches and rushed to Brussels to attend parties and meet the local beauties; only Königsmarck stayed behind, preferring writing to carousing. By then he had received several of Sophie Dorothea's letters, and his jealousy melted away under the warmth of her love. For once in a happy mood, he gave her an amusing account of army life.

First he gave some reassuring news about himself. He had given up his vague notion of joining the service of the Elector of Bavaria, although the latter had been showing him much kindness. The Earl of Portland, King William's confidential adviser and one of his senior officers, assured him that the King held him in high esteem. Sophie Dorothea's portrait, which she had given him before his departure, was hidden in a safe place and was a source of comfort to him. And last but not least, he had decided to have his beautiful curls cut off. It was too difficult to keep himself well groomed while on the march.

Then followed some camp gossip. Prince Christian, a young brother of George Louis, was rumoured to be making plans to marry a widowed duchess. Prince Frederick Augustus of Saxony was being cheated at cards and had lost vast sums of money. And George Louis, Commander of the Hanoverian troops, had a meeting with William, the moving spirit behind the Grand Alliance. In a rare flash of humour Königsmarck added: 'The King's interview with our Prince was very dull, for both are men of few words.'

Shortly after their arrival, the commanders were invited to inspect the Grand Army. George Louis with his officers, Königsmarck amongst them, went in the party of the Elector of Bavaria. William walked around with his own party, and so did other princes. Königsmarck, who had fought and survived many wars, noticed a great many people of rank, but few men of distinction. On the whole he did not think much of the Grand Army, and his assessment was to prove tragically correct.

From the battlefield

Celle, 28 July [1692]

My husband writes that you are going to besiege Namur. God, what anxiety this news plunges me into ! I shall think of you exposed to danger all the time, and I shall not have a moment's peace as long as all I hold dear in this world is in peril. I pray for your safety a thousand times a day, and as I do it from the bottom of my heart, I know my prayers will be answered.[1]

That was how the Princess first heard of the battle of Steinkirk, which failed to liberate Namur from the hands of the French and ended in disaster for the Allies. The news of the battle took six days to reach Celle. By the time Sophie Dorothea was able to piece together the disheartening reports brought in by the couriers, it was all over.

The Grand Army had camped at Lambeque, virtually within glaring distance of the French troops at Steinkirk. When the long-awaited reinforcements arrived, William decided to strike. He launched the attack at daybreak, on the morning of 24 July. The French were caught off their guard, and in the semi-darkness of the early morning it looked as if the Allies were going to score an easy victory. But General

Luxembourg managed to ward off the attack, rally his forces and bring in reinforcements from the rear. By nightfall, after fighting all day since dawn, the Grand Army was forced to retreat to their base at Lambeque, leaving Luxembourg in possession of the field. Both sides had suffered heavy losses. The French counted some seven thousand killed and wounded; the Allies even more. William alone lost five regiments. The Grand Army was humiliated and defeated, and Louis XIV proved once again that his sun had not yet set.

At Lambeque all was recriminations and disunity, with each party blaming the other for the common defeat. Petty grievances assumed magnitude. Prince Frederick Augustus of Saxony, later Augustus the Strong, who had long suspected that his so-called allies had been swindling him out of huge sums of money at cards, seized the opportunity to avoid paying his debts, and threatened to leave with his troops. George Louis, whose Hanoverian regiments had been put on the reserve and did not take part in the fighting, was critical of William's strategy. Other princes were critical of George Louis's ability to command. Tempers ran high. It took all William's cunning and powers of persuasion to restore peaceful relations among his allies and put them on the march again.

On the eve of the battle Königsmarck wrote Sophie Dorothea a hurried note, which she received eleven days later.

From the camp at Halle, 23

Although I had intended to write to you tomorrow and reply at length to your letters of the 13th, 14th and 15th, which I received all at once, I have to forgo this pleasure, because the King [William] had decided that tomorrow we attack the French army, which is 2 hours away from us, at a place called Enghiem. At any other time this news would have delighted me, but I must admit that at the moment I find it distressing. You love me, the only person I ever found worthy of my love, and I was not wrong in believing you possess the best qualities in the world. But now I must risk my life and perhaps never see you again, my dear. I have risked my life a hundred times, through folly or high spirits, and I know myself well enough to say that I have never been afraid of death. But what now makes a coward of me, my divine one, is the fear of never seeing you again. Goodbye, beloved Dorothea, goodbye. How unhappy I am, and yet happy, though I cannot enjoy my happiness now.

But you must not think that your lover is a coward, no, my dear. Since to battle I must go, I will conduct myself as I should, and if I can, I hope to distinguish myself. There is one request I wish to make, dear heart. If I am unfortunate enough to lose an arm or a leg and be made a cripple for life, do not forget me, show some kindness to a poor fellow whose only joy was to love you. No, my dear, do not forget him, he is a man who truly loved you and will go on loving you as long as he lives, even if crippled. My eyes, which have been captivated by yours, may never see you again. I cannot think of it without shedding tears. What little chance I have of enjoying your love! How tormented I am!

The tower clock at Halle is striking 12. The men are bringing in cannon balls, powder and matches; it is the prelude to the scene we are to play tomorrow. I must go to my duty now. Goodbye, beloved child, how unhappy I am.[2]

Before he joined the fighting, Königsmarck called in one of his faithful officers, who was to stay on the reserve like the rest of the Hanoverian force, and confided to him a sealed parcel containing Sophie Dorothea's portrait and all the letters he had received from her since the beginning of the campaign, giving him instructions to burn it should he be killed. He held back only one letter, a very loving one, which he kept close to his heart, as a charm. After the battle he was convinced that it was the letter that had protected his life.

His taking part in the battle was entirely his own choice. As soon as he learned that William had ordered the Hanoverian troops to the reserve, he obtained George Louis's permission to volunteer for action with another regiment. He was too high-spirited to stand idly by while others were proving their valour. He attached himself to Prince Ferdinand William of Württemburg, commander of the Danish reinforcements, and never left his side throughout the battle. He fought valiantly, showing his usual dauntlessness, but unfortunately could be awarded no official recognition, for he had been fighting with a foreign regiment. His sole reward was the excitement of battle. He escaped without a scratch.

After the first news came through, there was a period of great tension and anxiety. Duke George William was informed that the Celle troops, unlike the Hanoverians, had been in the thick of the battle and had suffered heavy losses. While waiting for further details, the court was plunged into grief. Everyone had somebody at the front, and everyone fearfully awaited further information about the wounded and the dead. Sophie Dorothea was extremely agitated; but, like Königsmarck, she was self-centred even at the height of her anxiety. In the midst of her fears she wrote about her own suffering:

29 July

On getting up I learned there had been a terrible battle and that you had taken part in it. You can imagine my agony. Everybody noticed it and it was impossible to conceal. I am so worried and so agitated that I shall have no peace until I know you are out of danger. I am in a pitiful state. I think that every shot is aimed at you and that you alone run all the risks. God, what would become of me if something happened to you? I shall not be able to control my emotions and I shall go to you at once to look after you, and I shall never leave you again. I cannot tell you how I suffer. I know you have been in great danger and I still do not know how you are. I could die of it, I am so tense. You must swear to me never again to expose me to such dreadful anxiety. Never leave me again, and if you love me, stay the rest of your life with me and let us build up a happiness that nothing will ever trouble. I have not got the strength to write any more, I am beside myself and I do not know what I am saying. You have already made me shed so many tears since you left, I feel they will only dry with your safe return, for you are meant to stay until the end of the campaign. How I hate King William who is the cause of it all, he makes me suffer mortal pain by endangering the life of the man I love. Goodbye, and keep alive, I beg of you. My life is bound up with yours, I do not want to live a single moment without you.[3]

A few days later, although she had not yet heard from him directly, she learnt from the courier that the Hanoverian troops had not taken part in the battle, and that Königsmarck, who had, was safe. Her relief was mingled with reproaches.

1 August.

What joy to know you are out of danger. One must love as deeply as I do to feel as I do. I spent two days and two nights in mortal anguish, I do not think anybody has ever suffered so much. . . .

I want to rebuke you for having exposed yourself to danger so unnecessarily. Your foolhardiness drives me to despair. What have I done to you to be treated like this? Should you not take better care of yourself for my sake? I would be upset if you neglected to obey the call of honour; but I cannot forgive you for acting like a foolish young boy. Never again commit such a folly. What would become of me if I lost you? You do not stop to think that my life is bound up with yours and that I do not wish to live one minute longer than you.

I hope this battle will be the end of the campaign, for if we are going to go over to the attack again, I shall die of fear that something might happen to you.

Thank you for taking such precautions over my letters and my portrait, but they would have served no purpose, my grief would have given me away if something had happened to you. I would not have had the strength to conceal it. It would not have mattered in any case whether I was found out or not, for without you life would be unbearable, and imprisonment within four walls far pleasanter than going on living in society without you.

Thank God, I am rid of these sad thoughts. . . . Everybody remarked tonight on my cheerfulness. The fools thought it was because of my husband, though to tell you the truth, I have not thought of him even once, except in connection with you.[4]

About ten days after the battle, Sophie Dorothea received the hurried note Königsmarck had written just before the dawn attack at Steinkirk. She was overwhelmed.

4 August

Yesterday I received the letter you wrote on the eve of the battle, it pierced my heart and I am moved by what you wrote. You must know that whatever crippling injury you might have suffered, I would not love you any the less. Even if nothing were left of you except your head, I should still love you to distraction and I would willingly renounce society in order to live with you anywhere that pleased you. Still, I am very happy that you came out of the battle in one piece. All your parts are so beautiful and lovely that I would not want any of them lost. Take care of yourself, I beg of you. Never again commit the folly of exposing yourself to danger without need, or I shall be very angry with you.

Imagine how unhappy I am. I hardly recovered my peace of mind concerning your safety, when I heard that the troops are going to go on, and that another battle is expected soon, more terrible than the first. I cannot bear the anxiety. I would rather die a thousand deaths than lose you. . . . I have never loved you as much as I do now. Whatever I may do for you, I can never do enough, but at least I can promise you the tenderest love in the world, a conduct above reproach and a passion that will end only with my life.[5]

Although she rebuked Königsmarck for having risked his life when he could have honourably stayed behind, the Princess must have been proud of him when complimentary references to his action were made at court. It helped her to reconcile herself to her lot:

5 August

If you only knew how I miss you you would never have the heart to leave me again. But I must not have such thoughts, I must school myself to share your heart with your ambition. Mine is wholly yours, free of all other passions, and its only ambition is to please you. I love you a thousand times more than you love me. Goodbye, I shall love you to the end of time, I would become an example of the tenderest love and the most exacting fidelity that ever existed since the creation of the world.[6]

In spite of the bad news from the front, life at the courts of Celle and Hanover was not allowed to deviate from its pre-ordained course. The approach of autumn might well have heralded further hardship for the troops; but for court society it spelt going away to take the waters. At the end of August a cheerless convoy of escortless ladies, headed by Duchess Eleonore and her daughter, left for Wiesbaden for a six-weeks rest cure. The Duchess had taken a large convent-like mansion for herself and her household and was prepared to make the most of her stay. The company at Wiesbaden was not expected to be particularly entertaining, for all the men were still away at the front, but Sophie Dorothea did not mind. She had worked out that Wiesbaden was nearer the Flanders front than Celle, and with the temporary lull in the fighting she had formed a vague plan of a secret meeting with Königsmarck. He too was measuring the miles between them, and shortly before she set out on her journey he wrote to her in the same vein:

Our campaign is nearing its end, everybody is being informed about their winter quarters. I am secretly delighted with mine, because they are going to be at Dist or Louvain. Both are equally convenient, for they bring me twenty miles nearer Germany, and to a place where the postal service is reliable. I wish I could take the post home myself. If I could find a Pegasus I would pay him with half my blood, I would fly faster than Perseus to embrace my divine Andromeda.[7]

The journey from Celle to Wiesbaden took twelve days. There were only two or three gentlemen available to escort the ladies, and travelling was very tedious, as Sophie Dorothea reported from the first halt:

Einbeck, 12 August
Nothing happened which is worth writing about. All I do is drink, eat and sleep since the beginning of the journey. I think of you from morning till evening, it is my only occupation and the only one which gives me pleasure. I am delighted to think I am getting nearer you. If it were possible for us to meet, what joy for me! I dream about such a meeting, it gives me joy, although I know it is impossible.

I am told you are losing money at cards. I am sorry but one cannot be lucky in everything. I hope love will make up for your losses at cards.

I hope you will return to Hanover the same time as me. I am waiting for you with love and impatience, and I warn you again, you will not escape from me a second time. I would rather die than live without seeing you. . . . Goodbye, I am all yours and shall be so as long as I live, and as long as you want me.[8]

There was no news from Königsmarck during the journey, for it had not been possible to let him know in advance where the convoy would stop and where it would be safe for him to address his letters. Sophie Dorothea too wrote less than usual. For one thing it was impossible to write while travelling, and when the party stopped for the night there was no privacy. But there was another reason, more sinister than the first. Some of her letters had gone astray. Both she and Königsmarck ascertained the fact by checking dates and contents. When Mlle Knesebeck wisely suggested that writing *en route*, naming all their stopping stages, would be a giveaway in case of more letters being intercepted, the Princess cut down her writing to a minimum. She could not wait to get to Wiesbaden, where she would again write in the comparative safety of her room. As soon as they got to their destination she put pen to paper:

> 25 August
> I am in agony. I hear there has been another battle and I do not know what happened in the course of it. I shudder to think you might have exposed yourself unnecessarily and met with some accident. Take care of yourself, I beg of you, if you still have any feeling for me. What would become of me were I to learn that you had been wounded? For God's sake, take care of yourself. My life is bound up with yours. A thousand morbid thoughts come into my mind and I am so depressed. I can hardly write of anything else, I have plenty of leisure to nurse my grief and I am really glad to find myself in this solitude. . . . Goodbye, nothing will ever make me change towards you. I was born to love you. You are my only passion. I never had one before I knew you and I shall die loving you more than anybody has ever loved anybody.[9]

Knowing her lover's jealous disposition only too well, the Princess took care to give him a full account of her days at Wiesbaden. Mostly they were dull. Some amusement was offered when Duke George August of Nassau-Idstein, in whose domain Wiesbaden was, sent his envoy to pay his respects to Duchess Eleonore. The envoy stumbled so badly over his speech that Sophie Dorothea had to exercise all her self-control not to laugh right in his face. Not content with addressing the Duchess, he then turned to her daughter and pronounced another fumbling speech for her own special benefit. He must have seemed a figure of fun to the Princess, and his visit remained something to recall with merriment. Otherwise there was nothing much to keep her amused. She spent much of her time gazing at a portrait Königsmarck had managed to send her to Wiesbaden, until one day she nearly got caught when her mother, again, came unexpectedly into her room. On the whole the rest cure was not a success. The palace that the Duchess had taken was cold and draughty, and before long most of the ladies of the household were down with colds. Even Mlle Knesebeck was unwell. Sophie Dorothea took special care of herself, and ended up by putting on some weight. She wrote to Königsmarck that she hoped to escape illness for his sake. The time for his return to Hanover was getting nearer, and she would not want him to see her red-eyed and heavy with a cold.

Königsmarck too was concerned with his looks in view of the approaching reunion. He wrote to warn the Princess that the summer sun had tanned him so much he was as ugly as a Turk, and asked whether he should wear a wig on his return, or keep to his own hair. As the summer wore into autumn, his tone grew more cheerful, for the end of the campaign was in sight. With no imminent battle and so many princes and dukes about, life took on a more social pattern. His letters were full of stories about his comrades-at-arms and their doings. In one of them he described how Prince Frederick Augustus of Saxony, wishing to silence a jeweller from Brussels who demanded to be paid for his services, fed him some poisonous powder that nearly cost the poor man his sanity. Then, having borrowed a vast sum of money from Königsmarck, the Prince quietly departed, leaving behind many debts and a bad name.

In another letter Königsmarck repeated some gossip that had come his way from the hunting lodge of Luisburg, where Sophie Charlotte of Brandenburg was staying. The young Electress had seen fit to make fun of one of her courtiers, saying publicly that his legs were as thin as matchsticks under their padded stockings. The offended courtier burst into her chamber one morning, and without much ceremony stretched his legs on her dressing table by way of proving their natural muscularity. The Electress screamed, a page tried to evict the intruder, blows were exchanged and blood ran down faces and ruffles. There was quite a scandal, and it was only after a great deal of mediating that peace was restored.

Another letter told the Princess a saucy story that must have been the delight of the camp at that time. A Dutch officer had started an affair with the only daughter of a very respectable merchant and made a contract with her, signed with their blood, according to which he paid the girl five crowns every time she allowed him to enjoy her favours, while she paid him ten every time she made him come to see her. The frequency of their meetings was such that during the army stay at winter quarters the officer amassed no less than six thousand crowns.

As the girl had no money of her own, she helped herself to her father's. When the merchant discovered his loss, he lodged an official complaint with the young man's superior officers. They called a council of war and gave their verdict that the money had been honestly earned. They recommended however that the merchant should give his daughter two thousand crowns by way of dowry, and let her marry her lover. The officer agreed, for he wanted the money; the girl agreed, for she loved the young man; and the father agreed, for his daughter was pregnant.

Once Königsmarck described a camp party he had been to. The company was very select. It consisted of Prince George Louis, the Elector of Bavaria, three or four Hanoverian generals, and himself. Five *filles de joie*, two of whom were rather attractive, Königsmarck noted, had also been invited to keep the guests happy. But while the others took advantage of the opportunity, he alone restricted himself to food and wine. Women had ceased to be his pastime, and his chief amusement at camp was cards. Without realising it, he must have grown more mature. At another orgy which he attended, the Duke of Richmond amused his guests by challenging them to invent blasphemous swearwords, his own contribution being 'God's belly stuffed with apostles'. There was perhaps more than the usual debauchery, and Königsmarck, from the height of his twenty-seven years, wrote deprecatingly about 'the young of today' and told Sophie Dorothea how he had to reprimand them 'like a pedagogue'.

As for him, he would accept no reprimand when it came to his own failures, chiefly his senseless jealousy. When two officers' wives once made some remarks about faithless ladies, he immediately suspected that they were warning him about Sophie Dorothea's behaviour with another man. He hardly stopped to consider that the ladies were not supposed to know about his affair with the Princess, and that if they did, there was more danger in their knowledge of it than in their insinuating remarks about its alleged lack of stability. He reacted with his usual vehemence. He wrote to remind the Princess that he had friends everywhere who would observe her every move and report back on every flirtatious smile she might bestow on a potential rival. No explanation would appease him. He knew it was a weakness in him, but could not discipline himself to behave sensibly. Once, in a rare moment of truth, he wrote humbly to the Princess:

> Do not think, my angel, that my jealousy springs from the poor opinion I have of you; this would be criminal. My jealousy springs from the violence of my love, so I hope you will always forgive me when this madness comes over me.[10]

Ordinarily he could not think of her sweet smile, her sparkling eyes, her gracious ways and her general vivacity without being tormented by new misgivings. His suspicions reached a new peak when he heard that she was going to leave Wiesbaden earlier than anticipated in order to attend the Frankfurt Fair, traditionally an occasion for much jollity. It took all Sophie Dorothea's gentleness to assure him that she was attending the fair to please her mother rather than herself:

> 5 September
> You are right in supposing it is the journey that had stopped me from writing to you. I was distressed at not being able to write as often as I would have wished to. I am delighted to hear that the campaign will end soon, it cannot be soon enough for me. I am awaiting your return with an impatience that only equals my love.
>
> We are still on our own here, and those who tell you otherwise are misinformed. I am going to the Fair, and as the Princess [Christine Charlotte of East Friesland] has arranged to meet me there, my

mother told me to write to her so that we all arrive in Frankfurt at the same time. I beg of you not to let this news infuriate you. Nothing will happen to give you cause to grieve. I am very grateful to you for permitting me to take part in the festivities. You know very well you risk nothing by granting me this liberty, and you must believe I am incapable of abusing it. You have made me so indifferent to the rest of the world that you have nothing to worry about.[11]

In a moment of generosity Königsmarck had indeed written to say that a visit to the Fair would do her good, but he soon repented and wrote to Mlle Knesebeck that he did not really like the idea. He took heart again when he learnt that Prince Frederick Charles of Württemburg, one of the Allies, had been taken prisoner by the French and was not to be released for the duration of the hostilities. It meant that other princes, particularly the Prince of Hesse whom Königsmarck regarded as a potential rival, could not get leave to go to the Fair, and that consequently the Princess would have no scope for flirting. Sophie Dorothea must have felt quite offended at such little faith in her fidelity. For once she was angry. But even then she could not help writing with tenderness, and even with a touch of self-deprecating humour:

13 September

We are leaving tomorrow and will stay for only one day. I shall write again as soon as we arrive and give you a full account of all my doings. I am not going to say anything loving tonight, because you do not deserve it. But I fear that by tomorrow I shall not have the same strength of mind and I shall forget all my anger, for I am inordinately fond of you, and although I am not going to tell you so now, I feel I love you with a passion that can never be equalled.[12]

As good as her word, she wrote again the following day, within two hours of her arrival at Frankfurt, assuring him of her safe arrival and her love. His jealousy was forgiven.

Homewards

Towards the end of September 1692 Königsmarck startled Sophie Dorothea by hinting that some powers were at work to part them and make him go away from Hanover. The long separation had not lulled their enemies.

Indeed Countess Platen and her spies had been closely watching the progress of the lovers. The very existence of the affair was a constant reminder of her own failure, and its triumphant survival over distance and camp temptations an added insult. With the imminent return of the troops, she felt the time had come to strike. By then she was sufficiently furnished with incriminating evidence and it was only a question of playing her cards right. To her great annoyance, she found that even a powerful *maîtresse-en-titre* could not induce Duke Ernest Augustus to take a definite step. For one thing, if he were to condemn the Princess he would also be condemning, by implication, the behaviour of his own daughter, the Electress of Brandenburg, whose cuckolded husband was one of his most needed supporters in his quest for political aggrandisement. For another, even an old roué like Ernest Augustus must have realised how incongruous it was for his mistress to uphold the cause of virtue and seek to vindicate the honour of his son, who had long established himself with a resident mistress of his own. Countess Platen had to accept that for the time being Sophie Dorothea was out of her reach and that it would be wiser to direct her attack against Königsmarck. The problem was how to trap him, and the Princess with him, without appearing to do so.

It was no easy matter to find fault with his conduct during the campaign. On the contrary, his record was excellent. He had volunteered for action at a time when Prince George Louis and the Hanoverian troops stayed behind in safety. He had proved such a capable officer that he was put in command of three thousand men. He was popular with the German princes and with King William, and was on cordial terms with George Louis himself, who apparently had a high opinion of his military skill. There was no way of faulting him on professional grounds. It was clearly necessary to provoke him into some action that would throw him into disfavour with his master, or somehow make his continued service with the Hanoverian army so unpleasant, that he would resign of his own accord and seek employment somewhere else. Countess Platen set to work with her usual cunning and single-mindedness.

Königsmarck had always been known for his extravagance and ostentation. Before he went to the wars, when as an infantry officer he should have lived mostly at barracks and contented himself with a modest *pied-à-terre* in town, he instead took a large house and entertained most lavishly. At that time Countess Platen was only too eager to accept his invitations and attended some of his parties with many other distinguished guests from among the ducal entourage. Now his love of luxury gave her the weapon she was seeking. She spread the rumour that Count Königsmarck was about to take a larger and more fashionable house in Hanover, ostensibly to suit his sister Aurora, but in reality to enable him to arrange clandestine meetings with the Princess. When the rumour was well established, the Countess confronted Duke Ernest Augustus with the need to take some action to silence it and suggested a way of doing so.

Aurora Königsmarck was staying then in Hamburg with her sister Amelia Lewenhaupt, whose husband was serving with the Hanoverian army. Both sisters were friendly with Sophie Dorothea and had meant to join her at Wiesbaden, but she left for Frankfurt before they could arrive. They then decided on some other journey of pleasure and planned to go through Hanover. That was Countess Platen's opportunity.

Having repeatedly harangued Ernest Augustus about the need to stop the outrageous rumours concerning his daughter-in-law, she at last obtained his permission to take measures against Aurora whom she described, not without good cause, as an accomplice of the lovers. Through her insistence, the Duke took the unprecedented step of sending Marshal Podewils all the way to Hamburg to inform Aurora that as she had already spent a season in Hanover the previous year, there was no need for her to see it again, and that she would be better advised to re-plan her itinerary. The astounded Aurora retorted that she had indeed seen all there was to be seen in Hanover, and more, and certainly had no desire to set foot in it ever again. That was the sort of hot-headed reply that Countess Platen had anticipated. Aurora Königsmarck was pronounced *persona non grata* and her name as good as put on a political blacklist. Anyone who sided with her or sought to vindicate her name was to be considered as undesirable as she was. That clearly indicated her brother.

Königsmarck was slow to grasp the full significance of this development. In his simplicity he thought it was a genuine misunderstanding between his sister and the Duke. Only belatedly did he realise that the incident had been engineered by his arch-enemy with the express purpose of provoking him rather than Aurora. He had half a mind to ask Marshal Podewils to intercede for him with the Duke, but thought better of it, fearing that a genuine well-wisher like the Marshal would have only one piece of advice to offer him: resign his commission and take his services somewhere else. Instead he wrote to Sophie Dorothea, who by then had returned from Frankfurt to Hanover, and hinted that something was afoot. His letter arrived open. The anxious Princess wrote back asking him to be more explicit, and when she heard his version of the Aurora incident, set about making some nervous enquiries of her own. Having no reliable friends at court, she turned to her sister-in-law Sophie Charlotte, the Electress of Brandenburg, who had come with her husband to stay in Hanover.

Sophie Charlotte had never been fond of Sophie Dorothea, whom she could still remember as the undesirable bride from Celle. The

two young women had little in common, and the years had done nothing to bring them closer. But they were about the same age, and both
unsuitably married. This, and the fact that Sophie Charlotte was
known to have some fleeting affairs of her own, encouraged the
Princess to seek her help. Sophie Charlotte obliged with information
that caused Sophie Dorothea to write with mixed feelings:

I think I told you that the Electress of Brandenburg told me they
are going to send you away, but on a pretext that has no connection
with me. We have this information from Countess Platen herself.
I cannot describe the state I have been in for the last four of five
days.[1]

Königsmarck did not share Sophie Dorothea's newly-found trust in
her sister-in-law. He suspected she was either laying a trap of her
own for the Princess, or else been given misleading information by
Countess Platen, in order to lull him into a false sense of security. He
knew the Countess too well to take anything she said at face value,
and was genuinely worried for the Princess's safety. As was usual with
him at moments of great agitation, he sought to silence his fears with
a flow of over-dramatised statements:

10 October,
6 hours from Charleroi

... The order that our troops are to besiege Charleroi could not
have come at a better time as far as I am concerned. I shall seek my
death there and relief from all my troubles. Think only of yourself
and take every possible care so that their suspicions may not get
you into trouble. I beg of you to do this. I will bear all disgrace
with joy if I could see you out of danger. I will gladly be the
unhappiest of men, I will give up the only woman I ever loved, I
will leave the Hanoverian service, I will be deprived at one blow of
my beloved, my calling and my consolation. The King of Sweden
wants to take my property away from me, and even at cards I
am persecuted by bad luck. I have borne ruin and disgrace without
taking action, happy to be able to love you with a lasting love, but
now I must live without you. I cannot do it. If I must leave you I

must leave life too. Charleroi will help me, there I will seek death to end my sorrow. . . .

If I am not fated to die yet, I will never leave you, not even if I were poisoned, murdered, beaten black and blue or burned alive. I talk like a man who has lost his reason. I do not see how I can win you by suffering all these insults. I am bringing trouble on your head. I must give you up, but if I must die, I will die avenging myself on those who are forcing me to leave you.

My greatest grudge is against Countess Platen, and on her I will avenge myself for she is the source of all my misfortunes. I will seek out her son, pick a quarrel with him and despatch him to the next world. After that I will tell everybody how she persecuted me, tell them also all the foolish things I once did with her, and then, if the Duke still shuts his eyes, the first time I meet her off her dung-hill I will insult her publicly, so that as long as she lives she will never dare show her face in public again. But how small such a revenge is in comparison with the harm she has done me! For she robs me of the only joy I have in the world. I lived only for you, I wore your chains with joy; you were my joy, my divine beloved, my all. Imagine what misery this jade of a woman brings upon me. If I were the Lord of creation I would sacrifice her, fling her to the bears, let the lions suck her devil's blood, let the tigers tear out her cowardly heart. I would spend day and night seeking new torments to punish her for her black infamy in separating a man who loves to distraction, from the object of his love. . . .[2]

The Princess knew her lover too well to take his threats for anything more than an expression of anguish. She countered by passing on an advice offered by her new confidante the Electress of Brandenburg. Königsmarck should make up to the Countess, whose persecution was basically a result of her thwarted advances, and renew his old association with her. His position at court would then be reassured, and he could carry on his intrigue with the Princess under La Platen's very nose.

It was not pleasant advice, but it was realistic. It was a measure of Sophie Dorothea's fear of exposure that she recommended to her lover a course of action, the mere thought of which must have stabbed like a dagger. But Königsmarck was revolted and upbraided the Electress for her callousness. The only thing that the Princess might learn from her with advantage, he wrote angrily, was her supreme indifference to what people said about her. She let them talk until they got tired of the subject and transferred their attention to something else.

Sophie Dorothea would not hear anything against her new friend. She accepted her invitation to go and stay with her at Brandenburg for a few days, and Königsmarck, although still suspicious of Sophie Charlotte's loyalty, conceded that as the Elector was influential with Duke Ernest Augustus, perhaps it was wise of Sophie Dorothea to keep on the right side of his wife.

It was late autumn 1692. The Flanders campaign was over for that year, and officers were getting their leave passes to return home. Königsmarck was not amongst them. In a letter addressed to Mlle Krumbuglen, which was another code name for Mlle Knesebeck, he expressed his exasperation:

17 October, Louvain

I have arrived here at last, but have not yet got my leave. I do not know what it means, for all the other officers who have applied have got theirs by now. I am determined, in case I do not get it, to ask for my discharge. I may as well do so, since they are looking for a pretext to get rid of me. Whatever I lose here, I might find again if I enter the service of the King of England. But all the kings in the world will not console me for the loss of my goddess. What am I to do? If I enter his service I shall hardly ever see you. How shall I survive? No, I cannot do it. I might do better to attach myself to the King of Sweden, for at least I should be nearer and could find a way of seeing you more often.[3]

The officers who had not gone home were detailed to march the troops to their various winter quarters. Königsmarck marched his to the garrison of Dist, which he thought the most desolate place he had ever been to. He was billeted 'with the nuns', which he did not much like, and he had hurt his foot. Although he had been instructed to send his personal equipment on to Hanover, there was still no news of his application for leave. He was exasperated to see George Louis leave for home, since this would reduce the chance of a secret meeting with Sophie Dorothea. He wrote sadly that worry was aging him. When his servant combed his hair he found ten, no, twelve grey hairs in his head.

For want of anything better to do, he went to a drinking party, where he made everybody raise their glasses to a mysterious lady called *Léonisse*. That was one of his favourite code names for the Princess. *Léonisse* was the heroine of *The Prince of Tarente*, written by the Duke of Bourbon, and she was, as Königsmarck once explained to Sophie Dorothea, 'an incomparable woman'.

> 6 November, Dist
>
> . . . I made up a song in German about my love, and when I sang it at a party it was much admired. I told them the lady's name was *Léonisse*, and they all drank a toast to that name as well as to the song. That cheered me up a little and I drank with them until we got tipsy. To make the wine sweeter I removed an old red ribbon from my watch, rather soiled it was, and dipped it in the drink. You know where the ribbon came from. That was the only day in three weeks which gave me any joy.[4]

Soon he had far better cause for joy.

In one of her letters Sophie Dorothea had hinted there might be a chance of a secret meeting. Towards the end of October she felt circumstances were propitious. Although her husband was back from the front, he was away at Celle for talks with Duke George William. The Princess decided to be bold. She sent word to her lover to forget about his leave pass and come to her with all possible speed. She was alone in Hanover, and it was safe.

Königsmarck did not have to be asked twice. He sent back an ecstatic reply, following hard behind:

> 2 November, Dist
>
> Since you command me to lose no time in coming to you, I am starting at once, without waiting for my leave permit, whatever

happens. It is not very wise, as it will give them the pretext they want. But as you wish to see me, I fly, I rush to the spot where you are. Why can't I be there tonight? You smooth away my fears when you say that if we behave prudently we should be able to evade our enemies. Let me know your plans, and I shall tell you what I think of them. My life and my happiness depend on them. . . .

My own life, what can I do to show my gratitude? I am so happy, my angel, my divine one, my delight, my only comfort! Your virtues surpass all, your charms are above all your sex, your beauty greater than a goddess. I cannot live any longer without you. I am dying to be near you, but there are still so many days between us. Goodbye, my soul, my idol. Goodbye.[5]

He rode day and night, writing only brief notes from the various stage posts on the way:

6

This is to warn you that I shall arrive tomorrow evening. Do you understand me? Should this reach you tomorrow, Monday, before dinner time at 10 o'clock, let me have a word from you so I know what to do. Should you receive this note after 10 o'clock, I will wait for the usual signal.

A few hours later he added a postscript:

I hoped to be able to find post horses here, but could not get any. I shall therefore arrive not on Monday, but on Tuesday, the 8th. Do not be alarmed at the broken seal. I opened it myself to add these words.[6]

After a week's journey, hindered by unforseen obstacles and delayed by slow post horses, Königsmarck at last entered Hanover on Tuesday, 8 November, disguised, unkempt and bursting with excitement. Once in Hanover he felt on safer ground. He could rely on his secretary, George Conrad Hildebrandt, who was as loyal to him as Mlle Knesebeck was to the Princess. From his hiding-place he wrote a brief message:

Tuesday, 8

Although the non-stop travelling has tired me out, I cannot wait the whole night before throwing myself at your feet. Do not refuse to see me right away, or I shall die. You will see me in a mean disguise, but I hope you will not mind. I can come to you secretly, no one has noticed my arrival, I can stay in hiding as long as you wish. I only wait for a word from the Confidante. I will come when I see the usual signal. The answer can be sent to my secretary. He will know where to find me, and he will pass it on to me without fail. Goodbye, I am dying for the hour.[7]

At long last the lovers met, after five months of separation. In one another's arms they forgot their jealousies and their fears. For a few days they were oblivious to the world. Then Königsmarck left his hiding-place, went to his house, put on his uniform and reported to Marshal Podewils to hear what punishment was awaiting him for having gone away without leave.

Henry Podewils was one of the most highly-respected personalities in the court of Hanover. Born in Pomerania, he took part in the Thirty Years War, then went to France, making it his country of adoption and fighting valiantly for Louis XIV. But he was a Huguenot. Not waiting to be dismissed for his religion, he resigned and went to Protestant Hanover, where Duke Ernest Augustus welcomed him with open arms. Already in his mid-sixties when he arrived there, he was successively appointed General, Field-Marshal, President of the Council of War, and Governor of the Leine Palace. He died in 1696, full of years and honour.

Although a strict disciplinarian, the Marshal had a kind heart. He had taken a liking to Königsmarck, and treated him like a son. Once or twice he warned him in general terms against getting involved in amorous pursuits that might endanger his life, let alone his career, and did his best to bring him to his senses. He was also fond of Sophie Dorothea, whose mother, the great benefactress of Huguenots in exile, he liked and respected. He had known the Princess since her childhood, and was one of the few people who were asked to attend her wedding ceremony at Celle. Both she and Königsmarck, although they did not follow his advice, felt that in him they had a real friend. In their correspondence they called him Le Bonhomme.

The old Marshal knew only too well what had induced the young Colonel to rush away from Dist without waiting for his leave permit. He could not find it in his heart to recommend the expected punishment, which entailed sending the offender in disgrace to Hamburg, and decided instead to make as little as possible of what should have been regarded as a gross breach of discipline. He left the matter in the balance for a few days, and by the time it came up it had lost its sting. The court of Hanover was feverishly waiting for news about Duke Ernest Augustus's promotion to the status of Elector, and the political activity concerning the last stages of the long-awaited event took precedence over everything else. Königsmarck was allowed to stay on in Hanover as if he was on legitimate leave. There was a marked coolness towards him on the part of Prince George Louis, back from Celle, and Duke Ernest Augustus, but no action was taken against him.

The lovers had another brief spell of happiness. The Princess managed to avoid accompanying her husband and her father-in-law on their long-projected journey to Berlin to see the Emperor, and enjoyed her lover's company without fear. By day they exchanged tender messages, by night they met in her apartments or in his. Königsmarck had nothing to find fault with:

Last night made me the happiest and most contented man in the world. Your embraces showed me your tenderness, and I could never doubt your love.[8]

And a few days later:

On rising from my dear bed, which I found softer than ever, I was given your letter. In it I found, as I knew I should, the most constant love in the world.[9]

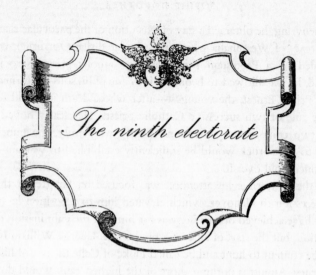

The ninth electorate

Duke Ernest Augustus's amazing advancement from a state of complete dependence to the powerful dukedom of Hanover was only partly due to blind fortune; to no small extent it was due to his own driving force and his ability to manipulate circumstances to his own advantage. Shrewd by nature, he was always on the alert. The more he progressed, the more ambitious he became.

His first chance came when his elder brother offered him a handsome regular allowance as consolation-prize for marrying Sophia; his second, when the see of Osnabrück fell vacant. His third and greatest opportunity came when he succeeded to the duchy of Hanover through the premature death of an heirless drunken brother. Soon afterwards he was able to conclude his long-drawn-out negotiations to secure Celle for his offspring. Turning the tables on his eldest brother, he became the Emperor's highly-thought-of ally, while George William was content to follow his lead.

It was characteristic of Ernest Augustus that no prize was too small for him. Although after his succession to Hanover the bishopric of Osnabrück could not have been of paramount importance to him, he was still loth to abandon his hold over it. After some clever manoeuvring, he obtained a stay of execution of the particular clause in the Treaty of Westphalia which had stipulated that Osnabrück would be ruled by a Protestant prince and a Catholic priest in rotation. Instead, he was allowed to bequeath it to one of his sons—it turned out to be Prince Ernest, the youngest—after whose death it would revert to the rule of two successive Catholic priests. He clearly hoped that after two consecutive generations in his own family, the Luneburg claim to Osnabrück would be sufficiently established to warrant their continued hold over it.

At the same time his attention was focused on far greater things. His accession to Hanover, which elevated him to a position he could never have achieved otherwise, was for him not the culmination of his ambition, but the start of an even grander one. George William might well be content to hunt and be called Duke of Celle the rest of his life; for Ernest Augustus nothing short of the highest rank would do. His heart was set on making Hanover the ninth Electorate of the empire.

The idea had not been entirely his. It had already been entertained by John Frederick, his brother and predecessor, who instructed Leibnitz to expound it in a carefully-prepared statement as early as 1677. When Ernest Augustus succeeded to Hanover, he embraced his brother's plan without reservation. Indeed, he had better grounds to support his application to the Emperor, for the unification with Celle, which after his son's marriage to Sophie Dorothea was only a matter of time, made Hanover of a size comparable with some of the other eight electorates.

Keeping his duchy as one indivisible unit was an obvious precondition, for only if it were as large and important as Saxony or Brandenburg would the Emperor seriously consider an application to raise its status. Putting the future grandeur of Hanover before the immediate material welfare of his younger sons, Ernest Augustus decided to break away from the traditional German custom of subdividing an inheritance among all surviving heirs, and announced his resolve to establish in his family the principle of primogeniture. Although still considered alien, this principle was by no means unknown in German courts; it had already been established in the Wolfenbüttel branch of the house of Brunswick. But among the Luneburg princes it caused much consternation and bitterness. With the exception of George Louis, who was to benefit from it, all the younger sons protested strongly against the plan to deprive them of what they had always regarded as their fair share. Most vociferous amongst them was Prince Frederick Augustus, the Duke's second son.

Born in 1661, only a year younger than the official heir, he raised heaven and earth to have his father's decision revoked. He appealed to his mother for support, which she gave wholeheartedly, but which was of little use, for Ernest Augustus had never let her take part in state affairs. Frederick then took his troubles to his relative Duke Anthony Ulric of Wolfenbüttel and asked him to intervene on his behalf. Although himself a beneficiary of the principle of primogeniture in his own house, Anthony Ulric was well aware that its establishment in Hanover was only a means to pave the way towards the status of electorate. As he had no intention of allowing a Duke of Hanover to exalt himself above the head of a Wolfenbüttel he willingly embraced Frederick's cause. He wrote to Duchess Sophia pleading her son's case, and she passed his message on to her husband, who was then making the most of his last visit to Venice.

On receiving his wife's communication, Ernest Augustus was beside himself with rage and immediately threatened sanctions. Anthony Ulric retreated and asked George William of Celle to intercede on his behalf with his brother. In the end the rift between the elder Dukes was patched up, but Frederick Augustus was not allowed to escape lightly. His father instructed him to leave Hanover at once and join the Imperial army fighting against the Turks. So great was his anger with his son, that he did not equip him with troops, as was the custom, and as indeed he had done for George Louis, but sent him off to seek his fortune like the son of any poor nobleman. The Prince's disgrace was the talk of the court, but Duchess Sophia, whose heart ached for her banished son, could do nothing for him. In December 1685 she wrote to a Wolfenbüttel relative:

Poor Gustchen is altogether cast out, and his father will no longer give him any maintenance. I try to laugh it off by day, and cry all night, for one child is as dear to me as another. I love them all, but I grieve most for those who are out of luck. One must accept God's will, but this is not easy, because I am such a fool where my children are concerned.[1]

Gustchen fought valiantly against the Turks, hoping to win the Emperor's gratitude and institute a suit in Vienna to recover his hereditary rights. He little suspected that his father had been pulling strings in the same quarter to further his own ends. In 1690, before he had a chance to proceed, Frederick Augustus took part in the Transylvania campaign and was killed.

It was now the turn of the third brother to take up arms against his father. Prince Maximilian, a survivor of twins, was born in 1666, the same year as Sophie Dorothea. As a child he had shown great piety, keeping a prayer book under his pillow to have it handy first thing in the morning. As a young man he showed more interest in the ladies, and even Sophie Dorothea, his brother's wife, did not escape his importunacy. He was charming and frivolous, and a great spendthrift. More than once he had to appeal to his mother to help him out of debt, which she did discreetly out of her own allowance.

Having watched his brother's unsuccessful attempt to approach their father openly, Prince Max decided to have recourse to secret diplomacy. First of all he secured the approval, if not the active participation, of two of his younger brothers, Prince Charles and Prince Christian. Then he got in touch with Duke Anthony Ulric, who must have forgotten his discomfiture of five years ago and was prepared to have another go at the Duke of Hanover. Baron Bernstorff, the Duke of Celle's chief minister, was also approached and included in the secret league. Finally Max communicated with Count Dankelmann, minister to the Elector of Brandenburg, who seemed to favour the young Prince's case. At his father's own court Maximilian enlisted the help of Count Möltke, the Duke's Master of the Hunt, and his brother. With all these powerful ministers behind him, he hatched a plot, the exact nature of which never came to light, though its prime aim undoubtedly was to dissuade Ernest Augustus from perpetrating his un-German notion of primogeniture. Unfortunately, Max reckoned without his sister Sophie Charlotte, the wife of the Elector of Brandenburg.

Somehow she got wind of the plot and communicated her suspicions to her father, who immediately acted on her information. According to one version he contrived to catch Count Möltke in the midst of a Borgia-like attempt to poison him. Apparently the Count offered him some snuff which the Duke accepted, but which, instead of sniffing, he gave to his favourite spaniel who as a result died before their very eyes. The Count was ordered to withdraw and wait at the bottom of the grand staircase, from where he was escorted to prison.

The story sounds too far-fetched to be credited, but in the general confusion that surrounded the plot, it might well have been accepted in certain quarters. The fact remains that one fine morning of December 1691, Hanover was shocked to learn that Prince Max and some other highly-placed court officials had been put under arrest. Sir William Dutton Colt, then newly appointed by William III as envoy to the courts of Celle and Hanover, reported the event in his despatch to London:

The gates have been shut for two days at Hanover, accompanied with a great consternation. Yesterday first the two Möltkes were brought to Court under a guard, where they are kept close, and all their papers taken. One is the Grand Master of the Hunt and hath been employed in the business with the Duke of Saxe-Gotha, and the other was Lieutenant-Colonel, and had waited upon the Prince Max; and there is also secured a secretary to the Duke of Wolfenbüttel, who formerly served Prince Augustus, the Duke's second son, who was killed in Transylvania. And next day Prince Max was secured under guard in his chamber, none of his servants being suffered to come near him but the Duchess, who is under great affliction, and the Duke say'd publicly that there were designs against his person and Government, and many storeys are dispersed about.[2]

There was a lengthy trial, during which Prince Max learned to his horror that he had been betrayed by Baron Bernstorff, his so-called Celle ally, who had been nothing better than an *agent provocateur*. Duke Anthony Ulric managed again to wriggle out, without permanent damage to himself, while Count Dankelmann, the Brandenburg ally, was beyond reach, for Ernest Augustus was too wise to antagonise the Elector by incriminating his chief minister. The brunt of the affair had to be carried by Maximilian and Möltke.

Max was first unrepentant, claiming that he meant no harm to his father, and only wanted to force him to relinquish his unjust plan of disinheriting his young. For a long time he was kept under house arrest; his guards were doubled and even his mother was not allowed to go near him. Indeed, she herself had to give evidence before the Council, when it was established that her part in the plot had amounted to no more than a mother's natural concern for the future of her sons.

In the end the Prince recanted and undertook to honour the principle of primogeniture for as long as he lived, but the interrogation of Count Möltke continued. Attempts were made to force him to reveal the names of more accomplices. It was rumoured that Countess Platen tried to make capital of the situation in order to serve her vendetta against Sophie Dorothea. She was supposed to have offered Count Möltke his release if he agreed to implicate the Princess in the plot and to have vowed his death when he gallantly refused. In actual fact the Countess, for all her influence, was not in a position to grant life or death to a state prisoner. Count Möltke, for all his gallantry, would not have refused his freedom, if he had the slightest chance of buying it by incriminating someone else. And lastly, Sophie Dorothea could have hardly been implicated in a plot which went directly against her own interests. As wife to George Louis, whether estranged or not, she was bound to approve of primogeniture, which in the end would benefit her own son. The rumour must have been one of many that went round the court, for want of accurate information.

Whatever the facts of the plot, Ernest Augustus was clearly determined to teach his rebellious sons a lesson they would not easily forget. If he could not very well execute Prince Maximilian, Count Möltke was a convenient scapegoat. In July 1692, seven months after his arrest and just as the Hanoverian troops in Flanders were getting ready for the battle of Steinkirk, the Master of the Hunt was conducted to the riding place behind the Royal Mews, and was publicly beheaded.

Prince Max, who had been held under arrest in the castle of Hamelin, was allowed to go unpunished, but he too had to pay the price. He was sent to the wars, and like his brother Frederick Augustus before him, was made to join the Imperial army. But he was more fortunate than his brother. His escapade was put aside, and before long he was again a familiar figure at court. In years to come, he was to plot again against the law of primogeniture, but nothing came of it. He lived to make a distinguished career for himself, and like his fellow-conspirator Anthony Ulric, ended by becoming a Catholic. He died at the age of sixty.

With his sons properly subdued, the road was open for Ernest Augustus to follow his cherished dream of elevating Hanover to the status of Electorate. For years he had been buying the Emperor's goodwill by supplying him with troops, throwing them into the imperial campaigns against the Turks, and later against Louis XIV. Their performance did him credit, for they were well-trained, disciplined, and apparently adequately-paid, which must have accounted to some extent for their valour. The Flanders campaigns of the Grand Alliance gave Ernest Augustus further scope to prove his worth as an ally.

But his application to be rewarded with an Elector's bonnet did not have a smooth passage. The existing Electors did not much relish the idea of having to share their authority over imperial policies with yet another partner. There were eight of them since the Treaty of Westphalia: the two Protestant ones of Saxony and Brandenburg; the three Catholic ones of Bohemia, Bavaria and the Palatinate; and the three spiritual ones of Metz, Treves and Cologne. The spiritual and Catholic Electors advanced the argument that the creation of another Protestant electorate would upset the balance of religious power. The Protestant ones were worried about elevating the junior branch of the Luneburg Brunswicks over that of the Wolfenbüttel Brunswicks. Count Platen, assisted by the learned Otto Grote, President of the Council, had to make several trips to Vienna to present his master's case, and William of Orange, recently made King of England, also took a hand. The last stages of the negotiations were very tense, and Ernest Augustus waited anxiously in Hanover to hear the latest developments. His strongest ally was his son-in-law, the Elector of Brandenburg, and it was he who eventually helped to tip the scales in his favour. Vienna conceded that Greater Hanover, including Celle, had achieved sufficient political and military importance to justify its elevation to the desired status. In March 1692, while in Hanover proceedings were being held against Prince Max and Count Möltke, the Hanoverian representative in Vienna was notified in writing that the Emperor had decided to confer an electoral bonnet on Duke Ernest Augustus and his heirs. The Duke then hurried to Vienna for the investiture, which took place in December of the same year. As soon as the ceremony was over, he despatched a courier to Hanover to instruct the court of his triumphant return.

The whole city turned out to meet the new Elector. Together with Duchess Sophia, who had met him earlier at Brandenburg, he made a state entry into the town. Church bells rang, and cannons were fired. A thousand new pieces of gold were distributed to the Palace servants.

The real ceremony took place a few days later. The court assembled in the banqueting hall of the Leine Palace, drawn up in a semi-circle, with the Duke and Duchess in the centre. At a given signal, Count Platen stepped forward to read aloud the imperial edict, while Otto Grote presented Ernest Augustus with the electoral bonnet and a diamond coronet, each laid on a cushion. The Duke placed the bonnet on his head with his own hands, and pronounced the magic formula: 'By the grace of God we assume this earthly dignity.' He next handed the diamond coronet to the Duchess, and waited for her ladies to fasten it securely to her powdered head-dress. Turning to the court, he cried: 'Long live His Majesty the Emperor,' and the whole Palace resounded with loud cries of 'Hoch! Hoch!!' It was a great day for the house of Hanover. Past plots and animosities were laid aside, and the whole electoral family presented a united happy front. Even George Louis, from then on styled the Electoral Prince, and Sophie Dorothea, from then on styled the Electoral Princess, buried the hatchet and together acknowledged the congratulations offered to every member of the electoral family.

Perhaps alone among all the jubilant Luneburgs, Duchess Sophia, now the Electress, paused to consider the price which had been paid to achieve that single honour. Of her six sons, one was under a cloud and two were dead, all as an indirect result of their father's ambition. Young Charles, her favourite, although only very slightly involved with his brother Max's plot, had joined the Imperial army and had been killed in the Turkish campaign in Albania at the beginning of 1690. She had hardly recovered from the severe shock of his death, when news reached her that Frederick Augustus, her 'Gustchen', who had been made to join the Imperial army like a poor gentleman as a punishment for his rebellion against primogeniture, was also dead, killed during another campaign against the Turks. In one year she had lost two of her sons, while the other four were on active service and in constant danger of their lives. For all her courage, the Electress's coronet weighed heavily on the mother's head.

As for Königsmarck, he hated every minute of it. His recent breach of discipline had not been forgotten, and although he was allowed to attend the official ceremony, he was hardly taken any notice of. He was practically an outcast. As he watched the Princess proudly standing by her husband, triumphantly acknowledging the homage due to her new rank, his heart was consumed with new jealousy. He was jealous of his mistress's husband. He forgot how constant she had been; how she had been giving him rendezvous night after night in spite of the danger involved; how she had pretended to be ill in order to avoid accompanying George Louis on his recent political journey to Berlin; how she had to submit to a daily massage by the court physician in order to be cured of her pretended illness; and how she nearly fell really ill from the course of treatment that had been prescribed for her. All reason forsook him. He could only think that Sophie Dorothea was dazzled by her husband's new rank and was eager to win back his favour. A few days before the actual ceremony, when the news had just reached Hanover, Königsmarck penned one of his coarsest jealous outbursts:

Electoral Princess! Now we can call you that, for apparently the Electoral Prince invested you last night with this honourable title. Has his love-making more charm now that he has achieved higher rank? I cannot sleep for rage when I think that an Electoral Prince has robbed me of my charming mistress. This morning I would have offered you my contragulations on your new rank, but I doubted whether your husband had done his duty by you. If I am to judge by his keenness to see you, the investiture will not start before 10 o'clock in the morning. . . . I hope it will take place immediately after your getting up, so that the Electoral pleasures stay fresh in your mind. I dare not remind you of the pleasures we two had together. They will seem to you so meagre by comparison, that you will forget them altogether. I use the word meagre after the song that goes: Alas my prince, how meagre your love-making is.[3]

The festivities turned out to be premature. Although the Emperor had issued the decree promoting him to the rank of Elector, other dukes refused to recognise Ernest Augustus as such. An opposition was formed, consisting of Duke Anthony Ulric, the Duke of Mecklenburg, the King of Denmark in his capacity of Duke of Holstein, and the Elector of Saxony. At one point they were ready to take up arms against Hanover, and only an imperial intervention stopped what might have developed into a war within the empire. Even then Ernest Augustus could not persuade the Electoral College to admit him, and when he died in 1698, his claim was still in abeyance.

On his death the indefatigable Anthony Ulric renewed his opposition and actually marched on Hanover, only to be easily rebuffed by the superior military strength of the new Elector, George Louis. In 1703 Anthony Ulric conceded defeat and acknowledged the precedence of the Hanoverian Elector at the Diet. Still it was not the end of the road. The outbreak of the War of the Spanish Succession caused further delays, and it was only in 1708, sixteen years after the investiture, that the Hanoverian envoy was allowed to take up his seat in the Electoral College in Ratisbon. Electress Sophia, by then an old lady of seventy-eight who had lost four of her seven children, was at that time nearing the realisation of her own cherished ambition, the English Succession.

A beggarly lover

By the beginning of 1693 Count Königsmarck's financial position had deteriorated alarmingly. In less than five years he had managed to squander a vast proportion of his inheritance, while his expenses continued to mount. Once one of the richest bachelors roaming the courts of Germany, he was now beset by debts he had no hope of repaying.

His revenues came from two sources. One was his estates in Sweden which, apart from his native castle of Agathenburg, included several rich domains like Wormsio and Campenhof. The other source was outside Sweden and included properties in Hamburg and Holstein. Although the joint revenue from all his estates was considerable, the young man was bogged down by family obligations before he could even start to call his money his own. He was obliged, possibly through special clauses in his brother's and uncle's wills, to give regular allowances to some female relatives including his widowed aunt and his sister Aurora. He was also responsible for his sister Amelia's dowry, and years after her marriage he was still behind with his payments. The correspondence between brother, sisters, brother-in-law and aunt always revolved round money matters, and on one occasion Count

Lewenhaupt nearly brought a lawsuit against his brother-in-law for non-payment of his wife's dowry.

The management of his estates would have been difficult for Königsmarck even if he had been a thrifty young man with a taste for a quiet life; being the extravagent person that he was, he found the task well beyond him. He entrusted his affairs to his superintendent who, in his name, mortgaged property, borrowed money, bribed influential personages and represented his master in the various court cases that were brought against him by creditors. Worst amongst them was the King of Sweden who, particularly after the death of Königsmarck's mother, the respected Countess Marie, threatened to confiscate his estates, on the ground that they used to be crown property. In vain did the loyal superintendent send one desperate appeal after another for Königsmarck to return to Sweden to take the battle into his own hands. The Count would not leave Hanover.

But the real source of the trouble was Königsmarck's extravagance which, even in an ostentatious court like Hanover, was unsurpassed. His stables contained fifty-two horses and mules, and he had a household staff of twenty-nine. How disproportionate this vast number of servants was to his station in life can be gauged from the fact that Count Platen, the all-powerful chief minister, kept thirty-eight servants, while the average minister had only fifteen, or twenty at the most. An inventory of Königsmarck's house, made in 1693, showed it to be furnished most lavishly. That year his debts were so heavy and his creditors so pressing that he went to Hamburg to try to raise money on his property there; but the moneylender he approached, a Portuguese Jew, refused to lend him anything.

Königsmarck was also a keen gambler, who played for the sheer excitement of the game rather than for gain. When he won he went on playing until he lost; and when he lost he shrugged his shoulders and reported it to the Princess with his usual *insouciance*. At camp, the more he abstained from the usual orgies, the more time he spent at the card-table. Like so many people who think nothing of money, he was also generous. He allowed his boon companions to borrow large sums off him, without ever claiming them back. One person who borrowed freely and rewarded him with nothing better than promises was Frederick Augustus of Saxony, later Augustus the Strong, who should have been indebted to Königsmarck not only for his generosity, but also for the introduction to his sister Aurora, who in due course became his mistress and mother to one of his three hundred and fifty-four children.

The pay of a colonel in the Hanoverian army was not high. A promotion to the rank of general, which Königsmarck was entitled to expect after the Flanders campaign, would have nearly doubled it. But no such promotion was offered; in fact it was deliberately withheld. While younger officers were receiving advancement and awards, Königsmarck was passed over time and again. It was of course a deliberate policy to make him dissatisfied with his position and goad him to part company with Hanover and whatever held him there. He refused to take the hint, held on fast to his Hanoverian commission, and turned down all outside offers.

He must have been considered a capable officer, for the offers continued to come in. He could still join King William's army; or the Elector or Bavaria's; or even Denmark's. And from Sweden, in the midst of his bitter legal quarrel with the King—*ce roi barbare* as he called him—a tempting offer came, promising him a general's rank with a very high pay. This last commission might have straightened out his finances once and for all, but he had little hesitation in turning it down. Equally he turned down offers of marriage that might have been advantageous to him. When Count Bielke, the Swedish envoy to Hanover, offered him the hand of his daughter in marriage, Königsmarck refused so categorically, that the Count nearly took offence.

The only reason for his dogged refusal of promotion away from Hanover was his disinclination to put distance between him and the woman who had become the focal point of his existence. He was going towards his ruin with his eyes open, but nothing mattered as long as he could be sure of Sophie Dorothea's love:

. . . I love and I am loved, is there a happiness like mine? Indeed not. I can now call myself the happiest of mortals, even the happiest of Gods. Oh lovely *Léonisse*, the kindness you show me makes my love for you complete. It makes me despise the favours of fortune, and all the whims of ill-fortune will not change my love. For you I will give up all my interests, family, career, relations, sisters—wife and children if I had any—and follow my love anywhere in the world.[1]

For once he was not exaggerating. When, in a moment of bitterness, he complained to Mlle Knesebeck that for love of the Princess he had sacrificed his career and his honour, he was telling her the stark facts of his life.

He was however too intent on the present to be long worried about the distant future. He lived from day to day, hinging the whole of his daily routine on the expectation of a rendezvous. Soon after his return from Flanders he and the Princess worked out a complicated system of signs, based on the cooperation of the Confidante and a man servant, which was meant to facilitate communication. But every now and then the system broke down, as it would seem from what he wrote one day:

Tuesday

Yesterday morning the Confidante had a letter from me, but she brought back no answer, which rather shocked me last night when I found no message in my hat. You will remember asking me what I was looking for and my answering that I was making sure my gloves were safe in my hat, for some had been stolen. You said: 'You are quite right, a pair of fringed gloves had been stolen from Count Horn or Count Oxenstierna.' I was annoyed with the Confidante for she gave me the signal without my finding any note in the hat. I was hoping it was because she had not had a chance to put it in, but I was most surprised, when I left the card-table, not to find anything in it although the Confidante gave me the sign for the second time. I wanted to speak to her, but little Prince Ernest followed so close behind her, and Stubenvol was so close to me, that I could not do it. God have mercy on us, I do not know how we shall get out of this business without his help.[2]

When a rendezvous had been arranged, Königsmarck would announce his presence from a distance by whistling a bar or two from *les Folies d'Espagne*, a popular tune which must have been performed by the court musicians at the Leine Palace theatre. One bitterly cold night he waited in the street from midnight until two in the morning before he accepted that his signal would not be answered. He was frozen and angry, although reason told him the Princess was right not to take unnecessary risks.

Having taken such elaborate precautions over their meetings, he had a rude awakening when Marshal Podewils summoned him one day and gently warned him to watch his step. The Marshal would say nothing more beyond hinting that it had something to do with 'some of the ladies of the court'. Young Prince Ernest was far less delicate. He took Königsmarck aside and told him quite plainly that his 'conversations' with the Princess might bring disaster on his head. Suddenly Königsmarck realised that half the court was aware of what was going on, and that his affair was on every tongue. He nearly fainted with fright, and so did Sophie Dorothea when he told her. But they were both too far gone to cut the knot that bound them. Life without one another was unthinkable. Königsmarck noticed with astonishment he was behaving in a way that a couple of years ago would have seemed laughable to a man of his experience. Now he was sometimes content just to see his love from a distance, or to wait for hours under her windows to catch a glimpse of her, or even of her lady-in-waiting. He was behaving like a romantic youngster, he ruefully wrote early in 1693:

See what I have been reduced to! I consider it the greatest happiness in the world just to be able to see you a thousand feet off; indeed it would be a great comfort to me if I could have this pleasure. Writing to you is another precious pleasure and I would not give it up for a kingdom. My only fear is that my accursed fate will rob me of it, and that would be the end of me. I beg of you, take every care so that we should not be deprived of it. You know from your own feelings, I hope, that one could not go on living without it.[3]

That no storm broke over their heads was due in the end not to their greater precautions, but to Königsmarck's having made his peace with Countess Platen, on her own terms. He grovelled to her, flattered her, courted her and proved to her unmistakably that she was still as desirable a woman as she wished herself to be. He hated her for forcing him to debase himself and unhappily told Sophie Dorothea that, to save their love, he had to betray it. The Countess triumphed over her rival, but her triumph must have been nearly as bitter as her former rejection, for Königsmarck, having paid the price, made no attempt to be gallant or even ordinarily courteous. When summoned to the Countess's house for one of her notorious supper-parties, he would come late, hardly eat, hardly talk, and whistle tunes most of the evening. Once when the Countess arranged a foursome for dinner and got up to be taken in, Königsmarck hurriedly offered his arm to the other lady. He later told Sophie Dorothea that he could see the blood rush to La Platen's cheeks under her heavy makeup. There could not have been much intimacy between him and the Countess; but the main thing for her was that she could flaunt him again as her gallant, and humiliate the Princess.

Although Sophie Dorothea was the first to advocate this ignoble course, she was also the first to resent it. She could not very well reproach her lover for placating an enemy, but she could not help picking up a quarrel with her. They had a fierce row, and the Countess, holding Königsmarck in her grip, demanded an apology. Sophie Dorothea had to swallow her pride and do as she was asked. After that there was a sort of uneasy truce that lasted for several months.

It might have been partly due to Countess Platen's influence that Königsmarck was allowed to stay on in Hanover when other officers, including the Electoral Prince George Louis, left for Flanders to prepare for the spring campaign of 1693. The ostensible reason was the chance of a new assignment, where his services would be more useful than on the Flanders front. He was held in reserve in case of a military encounter with the King of Sweden, much nearer home.

Three years earlier the Duke of Celle had inherited the duchy of Saxe-Lauenburg, near the Holstein border, and had at once begun to strengthen the fortifications of Ratzeburg, its main city. At first none of the neighbouring sovereigns thought it necessary to interfere, but in 1693 things changed. Both Sweden and Denmark had had enough of the Grand Alliance and were contemplating an alignment with France. Their main quarrel was with the two Brunswick Dukes who had been William's most active supporters amongst the German princes. They therefore demanded the immediate demolition of the reinforced fortifications of Ratzeburg, claiming that they constituted a military risk to the Danish-held Holstein. The Emperor was inclined to give way, as he hoped to buy the goodwill of the Swedes and the Danes and save the Alliance, but the Elector of Hanover, backing his brother, would not hear of pulling down the fortifications. Together the two brothers mustered troops against a possible attack on Ratzeburg. Königsmarck volunteered to go to the new battleground, should hostilities break out. As his infantry regiment had remained in Flanders, he was transferred to the cavalry and made a colonel of dragoons.

Sophie Dorothea was dismayed at the thought of her lover going to the wars again; but Königsmarck was pleased, for he could stay near the Princess for a little longer, without being accused of shirking his duties. He took his new appointment seriously, spent much time and energy equipping his dragoons, and drilled them every day. His exertions were not rewarded. His useful services were tolerated rather than sought. He was clearly out of favour.

About the middle of March he was ordered to go on a recruiting tour. He set out with Marshal Podewils, but they could not go far, for the river Leine had overflowed. The old Marshal was in no hurry to accomplish the mission, and so they put up at Einbeck and waited for the water to subside. Königsmarck complained bitterly:

Monday, Einbeck

It is terribly uncomfortable here. Every night we have to put up at some other miserable inn. Ever since we left Hanover I slept on nothing better than straw ... but though I was poorly bedded I had the impertinence to want you next to me all the time, not stopping to think how uncomfortable you would be. If my wishes could come true you would indeed have to be pitied, for you would often find yourself on a hard bed and a rough seat.[4]

It was certainly no pleasure trip. Königsmarck worked hard, getting up at five in the morning and dropping off, exhausted, at nine in the evening. Marshal Podewils was a hard taskmaster and would not allow any slackening in the performance of duty.

Shortly after his return Königsmarck had to go away again, this time to Hamburg to try to raise money and meet his two sisters. He had some outstanding debts in Flanders, and it was rumoured that one of the reasons for his unwillingness to return to the Flanders campaign was his fear of being pounced on by creditors. He was not altogether displeased with the rumour, for it gave the lie to the other one, that he stayed back to be nearer the Princess. Anyhow, his twelve-day visit to Hamburg was not very successful, and he returned empty-handed, just in time to see Sophie Dorothea whisked away by the Elector and the Electress to their castle at Luisburg. Clearly Sophie Dorothea was under constant supervision, and there was a tacit conspiracy between in-laws and parents to keep her away from temptation without bringing anything into the open.

The Princess was desperately trying to convince her suspicious in-laws that she was above reproach, and to her great delight an ideal opportunity to do so presented itself immediately on her arrival at Luisburg.

Several years earlier, when she was still a young bride, her brother-in-law Prince Max had made some improper advances to her. Although he seemed to have been long cured of his weakness for her, the Princess continued to harp on his misbehaviour and made a constant show of her offended virtue. Königsmarck was of course madly jealous of Max, although there was not the slightest indication that he had any reason to be.

On her arrival at Luisburg, Sophie Dorothea found that she was expected to share her suite of rooms with Prince Max, who had also been invited to the castle. Without allowing her ladies to unpack, she immediately sent for the chief steward and demanded to have Prince Max evicted. The steward tried to point out that the Prince was being lodged not with her, but only next door to her, but the Princess would not be swayed. She burst like a fury on the Elector and Electress who were already at supper, surrounded by the usual company, and demanded in very shrill tones to be protected against the importunacy of an amorous brother-in-law. She pointed out that the room adjoining hers should be reserved for her husband, even if he were absent, and that it was most indelicate to throw her into another man's company. Still wearing her travelling cloak, she threatened to leave there and then and go to her parents.

The scene was so effective that Ernest Augustus had to give in and assured the Princess that, even if the Electoral suite was three times as large as it was, and no other room left in the castle, she should still not be made to share it with anybody. Prince Max was moved elsewhere, and virtue was vindicated. Sophie Dorothea was pleased. She had proved to her in-laws what a dutiful wife she was, and at the same time relieved her lover of his jealous fears. Not content with her triumph at Luisburg, she wrote to tell her husband how virtuous she had been and how conscious of her wifely duties. Her show of virtue might have been more convincing if she could have refrained from bringing Königsmarck's name into her letter. Her husband's reply was sarcastic:

You have acted like a veritable Lucretia towards Prince Max, and I am beginning to realise that my honour is very safe in your hands. I was surprised to learn that Königsmarck was going to join the Rhine campaign; it will not be good for him, for he has not paid his debts there, and to judge by what is being said about it, I think he might get into serious trouble if he goes there.[5]

The Princess was piqued to learn that her show of virtue had misfired. Later she learnt that even the Elector had not been duped, and that he had told the Electress he was fed up with his daughter-in-law's tantrums, and was not to be bothered ever again with such trifles. She was even more piqued to learn that while she was being so faithful to her lover in the face of such temptation as Prince Max might have put her way, Königsmarck was apparently enjoying her absence. It came to her ears that barely two hours after her departure to Luisburg, he rushed over to La Platen and had supper with her. She did not mind his going over to her house, Sophie Dorothea wrote, but she could not bear the thought that he did so before the dust raised by her departing carriage had a chance to settle. The business of the supper-party was the subject of several of her letters, and bitter reproaches were exchanged. Königsmarck pleaded that he went to the Countess's to allay suspicion, that he behaved boorishly to her, and that he spent the best part of the evening strolling about with a male companion. In the end he swore never to set foot in the Countess's house, whatever the consequences. That brought the Princess back to her senses. She wrote with alarm:

Tuesday

Do not commit the folly of dropping La Platen altogether. You know my feelings on the subject, it is absolutely essential that you should humour her, and I beg of you, in the name of my love, to continue your visits to her as usual. It is not your visiting her that I object to, it is only the fact that you did so the very day of my departure. It hurt me. It was so thoughtless and I was terribly downcast.

And although she was not able to keep her promise, she added bravely:

But let us not talk of it any more. I love you, and it is not in my power to be angry with you for any length of time. You were forgiven long before you wrote to explain. I am a fool to tell you so, but do not abuse my weakness for you.[6]

After a few days at Luisburg the Electress Sophia, always conscious of her duties, took her daughter-in-law to nearby Brockhausen, to pay her respects to the Duke and Duchess of Celle. George Louis, who had to be consulted on his wife's every move, had given his approval in a letter to his father; but to his wife he wrote sarcastically, as she quoted to Königsmarck:

Sunday, Luisburg

I have just received a letter from the Prince in which he gives me his permission to go to Brockhausen. But he does not want me to stay too long, because he does not like the news I gave him of how the Electress had given you a length of ribbon for your personal standard, and of how the other ladies of the court did the same. Here are his very words: 'There must be a dearth of news for you to write and tell me about the graciousness of *madame ma mère*. I have no doubt you followed her example.' There is something in the tone of his reply that I do not like.[7]

The courtesy visit to Brockhausen lasted only a day or two; not only because George Louis did not want his wife to stay there too long, but also because the Electress Sophia did not want to be Duchess

Eleonore's guest a moment longer than duty required. On her return to Luisburg, having acquainted herself with the lie of the land, the Princess wrote to Königsmarck one of her most daring letters, which would have compromised her there and then had it been intercepted like some of the others:

Friday

After languishing for three days and worrying for a thousand reasons, I had today the joy of receiving two of your letters. I shall start with what is dearest to my heart, which is my desire to see you.

As I have already told you it is quite easy, for Knesebeck sleeps in the small room next to mine. You can come in by the back door and you can stay twenty-four hours if you so wish, without the slightest risk. As for me, every evening I take a walk with Knesebeck under the trees near the house. I shall be waiting for you from ten o'clock to midnight. You know the usual signal, make your presence known by giving it. The gate of the palisade is always open. Do not forget it is you who should give the signal, I shall be waiting under the trees. I keep imagining the joy of our meeting. I have longed for it every single moment of the day ever since I left you, and this is why I have been putting off my departure for Celle. My mother and father have been urging me to join them as soon as possible. When I see you I will tell you about my state of affairs, it is too long to do so in writing. I can only think of the happiness of seeing you again. I think I shall die of it. . . .

I am cross with you for not visiting Countess Platen any more. It is very important that you should. I beg of you to go on seeing her as usual. You have so well reassured me against my jealous fears, that I begin to be calm and believe that you will always be mine. You too must believe that I love you more than ever and that I shall be yours as long as I live.[8]

This time Königsmarck took the precaution of obtaining his leave. It was not difficult, for the department issuing officers with their leave passes was under Marshal Podewils. He arrived the following day, had a wash and shave, and scribbled a last note in a bold hand about some confusion concerning the dates of some previous letters. Then, realising he had reached the end of the sheet, he added the essential message in faint writing between the lines:

Saturday

Tomorrow night at 10 o'clock I will be at the rendezvous. You will know me by the usual signal, I shall whistle *les Folies d'Espagne*. If I understand right, the spot is between the house and the stables, where the Prince's horses used to be kept. I shall be there at 11 o'clock.[9]

Whether he arrived at ten or eleven, he stayed with the Princess most of the night, and possibly all the following day and part of the next night. When he left, letting himself out through the gate of the palisade, he noticed two men strolling about six feet away from him. He hurried past them without turning his head for fear of being recognised. He never found out who they were.

For the Princess it was one of her happiest days. It inspired her to write a little poem, something of a feat for her, as she herself remarked with a touch of her French *esprit*:

Thursday, 22 June

Yesterday I made up a song, proof that love can work miracles. I cannot help writing it down for you. It goes to the tune of *Dans Mes Malheurs*.

My Thyrsis gone my life is boring,
He alone is my joy and my treasure,
He is my magic and my calling,
On him alone I set my pleasure.[10]

An accomplished poet by his own standards, Königsmarck complimented the Princess on her achievement and encouraged her to write some more. To her credit she modestly replied she was well aware that her poem had little merit beyond reflecting the true state of her feelings.

By nature and upbringing Sophie Dorothea was more suited to be a wife than a mistress. She hated the need to lie and deceive, and longed for a miracle that would set her free. During the early stages of her affair she had on several occasions asked for permission to leave Hanover and stay with her parents, not so much in order to facilitate her meetings with her lover, but to be away from a husband she disliked. Her request was granted only for the duration of the 1692 Flanders campaign, when George Louis was away and protocol did not require his wife's presence at court. During her stay at Celle that year her father spoke to her about the need to make her peace with her husband. At that time Duke George William thought that his daughter was simply being vindictive over the Prince's continued liaison with Mlle Schulenburg, and he therefore advised her to stop being capricious and accept her lot as a dutiful wife.

Having failed to secure a measure of freedom by a permanent residence with her parents, Sophie Dorothea began to dream of having an establishment of her own. It was not such an extraordinary request on the part of an Electoral Princess, whose rank entitled her to some extra privileges. Indeed, had she been known to be ostentatious and greedy, wanting an independent establishment simply to overshadow the magnificence of Monplaisir, she might have found more sympathy for her request. But coming at a time when it was obvious that it could mean nothing but setting the seal on her estrangement from her husband and allowing her to live her own life independently of court supervision, it fell on deaf ears.

She went about her business quite ingenuously, complaining to her mother that she was always kept short of money, having none of her own, and had to depend on her father-in-law's generosity for the slightest thing. She asked her mother whether she could not have part of her inheritance during her lifetime, and although she was told this was not possible, for reasons she did not yet fully understand, she felt that some provision could be made for her. She told Königsmarck:

23 June

My mother has started something that would be quite useful if she is successful. She wants the subjects of Celle to present me with 30,000 crowns. She discussed it with Bernstorff, who promised to spare no efforts on my behalf. He said a thousand friendly things to me, offered his services and assured me I must have no hesitation in asking for his help. He wants to see me settled in my own establishment, I think you want that too. It is certain that if I could persuade Bernstorff to take up my case, my father will do all he is asked. We must try every possible means. This business means so much to me I must not neglect the slightest chance. All my happiness depends on it.[11]

The Princess never suspected that it was Bernstorff, chief minister to Duke George William, who had himself negotiated the treacherous marriage contract that had deprived her of all her rights to her possessions. While pretending to be sympathetic to her case, he led her on to betray her true intentions, storing the knowledge against a day when it might pay him to pass it on to Count Platen, his opposite number in Hanover, whose wishes he was said to study more loyally, and more lucratively, than his master's.

He put the Princess off with vague promises and complicated legal excuses, until she demanded to see her marriage contract for herself. It was only then, eleven years after her wedding day, that she realised for the first time the full extent of her dependence. Of all the rich properties that her father had bought her as a child, of all the deeds of inheritance he had bestowed on her, nothing was left. All had been signed away to her husband or to his eldest son, in case he pre-deceased his wife. She did not have a penny of her own. She reported to Königsmarck with great agitation:

Wednesday

Yesterday I read over my marriage contract, it could hardly be more disadvantageous to me. The Prince is the absolute master of everything, and I do not own a thing. Even my allowance is so vaguely worded that they can easily cheat me out of it. I was very much surprised at this, for I have not expected anything like it. I was so hurt that tears rushed to my eyes. My mother was upset and spoke to me most kindly and tenderly, nobody could have been kinder. She even went as far as to offer to sell her jewels so as to give me a regular allowance wherever I want it. At last we decided it would be best to speak to my father so that he puts the matter right. My mother did so this morning and his answer was favourable and I hope I shall get what I want. My mother asked me to speak to Bulow and ask him too to push the thing, to show him the marriage contract and point out how unjust it is; so that without anyone being able to guess my plans, I have the finest pretext ever known. My mother acts most honestly on my behalf, and I am annoyed with you for calling her crazy. I have never loved her as much as I did yesterday and today.[12]

The Duke of Celle might well have felt embarrassed at having sold his daughter so short, but he was in no position to take up her case. The fortifications at Ratzeburg and the need to recruit and maintain an army against the Danes emptied his treasury; and he could not possibly ask his brother, the Elector of Hanover, to revoke an agreement signed by his own hand simply to gratify what was after all no more than a woman's whim. By then he must have heard some rumours about his daughter's *penchant* for the Swedish count, and he no doubt felt that the less rope a wife was given, the better for her family. His own relations with his wife had undergone a change within the past few years. Although faithful to her to the end, he no longer allowed her to influence him as much as she did during the first ten or fifteen years of their marriage. In the matter of political orientation he shook off her influence altogether and declared himself openly against her beloved France. In domestic matters he was also bent on having his own way. Sophie Dorothea overheard a frightful row between her parents concerning her half-brother Buccow, the Duke's natural son by a Venetian lady of pleasure. The Duke intended to grant his son's latest impudent demand for promotion, while the Duchess objected. The quarrel lasted a long time, and harsh words were exchanged. True enough, a few hours later the Duke and Duchess made it up and were more affectionate to one another than ever, but the daughter could not forget how unjust her father had been, and how immovable. She began to realise she had little to hope from him.

It was stocktaking time for her. Her affair was in its third year, fraught with ever-growing difficulties and far from rewarding. She could barely count on twenty meetings a year, she once sadly calculated. Her mother was constantly warning her; the Electress was suspiciously solicitous; the court was rife with gossip; Countess Platen could break the truce and produce incriminating evidence; and even George Louis, who as the husband should have been traditionally the last one to find out, had been making unusually sarcastic remarks in his letters. The storm could break any day. In her fear and unhappiness Sophie Dorothea began to look into her conscience. A firm believer in matrimonial fidelity, she had been swayed by passion to ignore her conviction. Now, in her hour of misery, she was overwhelmed with remorse. Her love was a sin and retribution was at hand. Königsmarck had to use all his sophistry to persuade her that God could not possibly frown on a love as true as theirs. For the first time since he started writing, he firmly declared that if they could ever live openly together, he would never commit adultery again:

> Thursday morning
> You regard your love for me as a sin and you fear God will punish you for it. Good Heavens, what a thought! Do not let such thoughts enter your head, for I fear this kind of thought will turn you away from me. You know what gives our love strength. What we wish for ourselves is in accordance with divine law and it is up to Him who is above to take us out of the sort of life we are living. I swear to Him that after that I shall never again sin against the 6th commandment and I shall lead a devout and blameless life. You too must make a vow to God, perhaps He will grant our prayers. I wait for this blessed moment with the greatest impatience.[13]

There was, however, no immediately foreseeable chance of an open union. A great deal depended on financial independence, and while Sophie Dorothea was unable to gain hers, Königsmarck was rapidly losing his. He was sufficiently man of the world to realise that love could not long survive in poverty. It was with this in mind that he once wrote:

> If I want property, or desire to win glory or own great fortune, it is only for the love of you, so that you may love me even more. For a beggarly lover, without considerable wealth, cannot hope to be long held in esteem by a lady of your rank.[14]

Without being mercenary, he urged Sophie Dorothea to continue nagging her parents about her allowance, and not take no for an answer. His approach was sensible, but he would not be himself if he did not dramatise the situation. He balefully wrote that he could foresee a time when she would be forced to live permanently under her husband's wing, while her abandoned lover would have to beg for bread in some remote corner of the earth. Sophie Dorothea took him to task for entertaining such unworthy thoughts:

> Wednesday
>
> The more I read your letter the more I am moved. You say you will be forced to go to some corner of the earth where someone will throw you some bread so that you would not starve to death. Do you count me for nothing? Do you think I could ever abandon you whatever happens? If you were ever reduced to that state, nothing would stop me from following you and I would want to die with you. But for God's sake, let us not abandon ourselves to such morbid thoughts, perhaps we shall be happier than we think. Let us love one another all our lives and find comfort in one another for all the unhappiness brought on us.[15]

These noble sentiments could hardly be expected to be shared by Königsmarck's creditors. He mortgaged his estates, and when the hostilities with Denmark were over, sold his Holstein property. The sum he realised was not sufficient to meet all his obligations, so he borrowed some more from the Hanover *Hofjüde*. It never occurred to him to cut down his expenses. In the midst of his difficulties he gave a lavish banquet in his new house, which to the Princess he later described as a dull and sober affair. His standards of entertainment can be deduced from the fact that at this sober meal one guest ate six partridges all by himself and drained a whole barrel of cherry wine.

Colonel of Dragoons

Königsmarck's marching orders against the Danes came when he least expected them.

For several months Sweden and Denmark had been making threats, hoping to frighten the Brunswick Dukes into submission and get them to dismantle the fortifications of Ratzeburg peaceably. They therefore encouraged lengthy negotiations while maintaining a high level of military preparedness. Contrary to expectations, and in spite of the mediation of an Imperial envoy, the talks came to a halt. Hostilities became inevitable. At the last moment the Swedes left it to the Danes to take action over something that was happening on their very doorstep, and so, in the summer of 1693, Denmark sent troops to attack Ratzeburg. The Danes had the numerical superiority and it was feared that, if not successfully rebuffed, they might follow up their advantage by marching on neighbouring Celle, possibly even on Hanover. The ducal Council of War instructed the Hanoverian troops to take up positions on the left bank of the Elbe and be ready for a confrontation.

Königsmarck had spent the night between Sunday and Monday, at the end of July, in Sophie Dorothea's chamber. Her husband was safely away in Flanders, but she was highly nervous, imagining spies behind every curtain. Long before her lover was ready to leave, she pushed him out and made him go. They parted on a rather cool note, the Princess hurt at his lack of sympathy for her fears, Königsmarck vaguely suspicious that she was trying to get rid of him for some other reason. When he arrived at his home, in the small hours of the morning, he found the lights full on, servants rushing about, and his horse already saddled. His marching orders had arrived while he was out, and he had to make up for lost time. There was no chance to write a note and find a safe way to have it delivered. In sheer vexation and despair he hurled himself on his horse and rode him non-stop to Celle, the first assembly point on the route towards the Elbe. From his quarters there he wrote a note explaining his sudden departure and entrusted it to a peasant to take to Hanover. It never arrived.

The Princess was at a loss what to make of his absence. It was a whole day before she learnt that the dragoons had been ordered to the front, and a whole week before she had any direct news from him. Because they had parted on a note of discord, she ascribed the lack of letters to a lover's cooling-off. Her agony was indescribable. When no message arrived for several days, she wrote one of the most tormented, most reproachful and most touching letters in the whole of her correspondence. It was also the last one to be preserved:

5 August

As you well know how much I love you and how sensitive I am to anything that does not indicate the same feeling on your part, you can easily imagine what state I am in. It is frightful, and I do not know any more what to think of you. This is the sixth day since you left and I have not heard a single word from you. How can you neglect me and humiliate me like this? How have I deserved such a treatment? Is it for loving you to idolatry, for having sacrificed everything for you? But what is the use of telling you all this? When a man falls out of love, nothing can revive his good will, he gets so fed up that he does not want to hear about that love ever again.

My uncertainty is a thousand times worse than death. Nothing can equal the torments of this cruel uncertainty. I imagine a thousand reasons to doubt the love of the only person whose love I want, and what makes things worse is that whatever reason I have to complain about you, I cannot help loving you so tenderly and so truly, that I feel I shall never be able to stop loving you.

How painful, oh God, and how humiliating to love without being loved. Still, it is my destiny, I was born to love you and love you I shall as long as I live. If it is true that you changed towards me, and I have a thousand reasons to fear so, I wish you no other punishment except that of never finding, wherever you might be, another love and fidelity like mine. I wish that in spite of the pleasures of new conquests, you should never stop regretting the love and tenderness I had for you. Nowhere in the world will you ever find anyone as loving and as sincere.

I love you more than ever, with a tenderness that no one but me can feel for you. But I keep repeating the same thing over and over again and you must be tired of hearing it. Do not be displeased, I beg of you, and do not rob me of the only consolation I still have, that of complaining to you of your own harshness. I am so over-wrought I can hardly think of anything else, though I should be worrying about the letter you were to write from Celle. Although everything had been done to trace one, I had not had a single word from you. Everything conspires against me. You do not perhaps love me any more, and I myself am on the brink of utter disaster. This is too much strain all at once, and I am bound to break down under it.

I must finish now, tomorrow I shall go to Communion. Goodbye. I forgive you all you have made me suffer.[1]

Königsmarck stopped at Celle for a few days, where he was asked up to the castle to dine with the Duke and Duchess. In between discussing the war situation, they tactfully asked whether the Princess was still in Hanover or whether she had gone with the Electress to her summer residence at Herrenhausen. He replied truthfully that the last occasion when he saw them both together was about a week earlier, when he had the honour of playing cards with them. Later he might have said a great deal more, for according to his own admission he got so drunk he could hardly remember anything of what was said or done. Fortunately the drinking part of the evening was not shared by Their Highnesses, and whatever he said in his cups fell on the ears of equally drunk fellow-officers.

From Celle he rode on at the head of his regiment to Luneburg, and eventually reached the front line at Artlenburg, on the left bank of the Elbe. There the troops lay in wait for the Danes, who had encamped opposite them on the right bank of the river. The Commander-in-Chief was Marshal Podewils, and the officers included such familiar personages as Prince Max and Sophie Dorothea's half-brother Buccow. Buccow was in charge of the left flank of the cavalry, while Königsmarck commanded the right one. He spent days on end on horseback, inspecting his positions and patrolling the area. There was a shortage of officers, and he had to undertake extra duties. At midnight he went on guard duty for three hours; at three he went to bed until seven in the morning; and at seven he had to report to Marshal Podewils who detailed his duties for the rest of the day until the next guard duty at midnight. There was hardly any time for writing. He exerted himself as much as he could, for he realised that was his last chance to win promotion. In fact he impressed the Duke of Celle, who arrived later on to inspect the preparations, but the Elector of Hanover remained unmollified.

In the meantime the court of Celle, the more vulnerable of the two, was watching the Danish situation with great anxiety. There was talk of having to evacuate the womenfolk to a place of safety, and Berlin or Amsterdam were mentioned as possible places of refuge. The Princess, who had joined her parents at Celle, felt the situation was providential. There was her chance to run away, for in the confusion of the evacuation no one would notice her absence until she was safely away somewhere with her lover. Again it was the practical Königsmarck who pointed out, not that desertion in the face of the enemy was punishable by eternal disgrace, but that the plan could not stand up to realities:

20

If I was sure you really wanted to run away with me when the Danes cross the river, I would gladly let them do so. But my angel, when it comes down to realities and material things, I do not think you will be as quick to accept as you are to suggest, for we must have something to live on. This is the great obstacle.[2]

Neither Denmark nor Hanover wanted to strike the first blow, and while the two armies stuck to their positions on either side of the Elbe, negotiations started again, during which a cease-fire was observed. After a period of fretful waiting, a Danish general took the law into his own hands. Either on his own initiative, or more likely, on a hint from his King, he ignored the cease-fire agreement and attacked, while the Hanoverian troops still believed they had another whole day of truce before them. The Ratzeburg fortifications were demolished before the rescue force had even heard of the treachery. Immediately the *casus belli* was removed, the King of Denmark sent a message of regret at the unfortunate misunderstanding and offered to make peace. Having lost the very thing for which they were prepared to fight, the Dukes decided to accept their discomfiture with as much grace as possible. Negotiations started all over again but the troops were instructed to be on the alert till they were safely concluded. Königsmarck was forced to stay on at Artlenburg until the end of the year. There was no more danger to his life, but equally no more chance of promotion. His military career in the Hanoverian army had come to an end.

The camp area on the river was probably marshy, for an epidemic spread among the troops, carrying off many victims. Königsmarck complained about the 'infected air' and daily counted his losses: three hundred infantrymen and dragoons, three captains, five lieutenants, four ensigns, several valets and servants. Marshal Podewils was taken ill and had to be transported to Luneburg for proper medical treatment. Other dangerous cases were transported to Celle. Königsmarck seriously thought of applying for three days leave, to avoid contact with the infected, but instead had to take over from his sick Marshal.

His worry for his own health gave way to violent fear when he heard that Sophie Dorothea had been attacked by the same fever and was very ill. He wanted to desert and rush to her bedside, but held himself back. Instead he dashed off note after note full of worry, urging the Princess to rest, to conserve her strength, and to avoid eating fresh fruit. When, after several bouts of fever, Sophie Dorothea rallied sufficiently to write that she had lost weight and her looks, and therefore possibly his love, he sent a passionate denial. For a man so permeated with the clichés of his day, this was a most fervent burst of sincerity. The Princess could have had no doubts left:

I am sorry to hear you have grown so thin but (with your permission) I find your question ridiculous and absurd. If I loved nothing in you except your beauty I would forgive it, but you must be convinced this is not the only thing which I adore; it is your merit and your sweet temper. I must admit I am charmed to see how beautiful you are, but I protest that even if you were as ugly as Mme Kopstein I should not love you one bit less. Tired of you? Can one ask such a thing of a lover who loves you so dearly? No, no, *Léonisse*, you are not convinced of my sincere love. What must I do to convince you of it? I shall have no rest until I know you are absolutely convinced. Do you believe that a love like mine could be founded on anything as transient as beauty? Although you have much of it, and more than anyone of your sex, I can tell you it is not your beauty which has put me into the state I am. It is true that your beauty set me on fire, and that without it I should not perhaps have been as happy as I am, but what has made me as I am towards you is your mind, your sincerity, your ways, and finally your soul, so noble, so perfect, which produce in you a sweetness beyond compare, generosity without equal, a kindness beyond description. It is these virtues that have placed me in my present state of sweet slavery, in which I mean to remain to the end of my days.[3]

The year 1693 was drawing to a close. It had not been a good one for the house of Luneburg. The demolition of Ratzeburg and the enforced peace with the Danes on their own terms was a bad blow to the joint prestige of Hanover and Celle. The Flanders campaign had fared no better. The French had recaptured Ghent, taken Charleroi, and won several other battles. The ducal exchequers were empty, while troops had to be maintained. A united front in the face of adversity had long been a family rule, and the two courts now came nearer to unity than at any other time in the past.

The Electress Sophia and the Duchess of Celle, in spite of past animosity, saw eye to eye concerning their children's marriage. Appearances had to be kept up, scandal avoided and an open break stopped at all costs. With the return of George Louis from the Flanders campaign there must have been a family council during which he was advised to resume the semblance of normal conjugal life with the Princess. As this in no way debarred him from continuing his regular arrangement with Mlle Schulenburg, he did not make any objections. But Sophie Dorothea, still recovering at Celle from her illness, was revolted. She protested, begged, threatened and shed tears. It served no purpose. Both parents and in-laws were adamant. Some time in October she informed her lover, still away by the Elbe, that she was back in Hanover under the conjugal roof. Königsmarck was appalled:

At two o'clock I received the fatal news that your husband is in your arms. Oh, what utter despair his arrival throws me into! I am beside myself and only death can deliver me from the torment his presence makes me suffer. Oh how I hate him! I loathe him! I never wish to set eyes on him again! But alas, he was born to be my Lucifer and I fear he will always be that. If it is true you love me do all you can, plead, nag, act so as to bring about the success of your mother's plan, or else I shall be the most pitiable man in the world. If you really love me, your sole concern should be the success of your enterprise. Do not spare words, do not spare your tears. If you love me as much as I adore you you will succeed in the end.

Let me find comfort in your eyes. Let your eyes, when looking at me, be tender so that I can see by your expression that the fatal return of your husband exasperates you; and above all let me see that the caresses of the newcomer are like death to you. Oh, I cannot bear this deadly thought, I am dying with desperation. He will give you a baby I am sure, and this will be the death of me. Alas, your shepherd is much to be pitied, but my shepherdess too is unhappy. I feel for you and I pity you, you will have some bad moments. . . .[4]

That she certainly did. She could hardly hide her revulsion for her husband, and tried to avoid him by shutting herself away from society. She must have been so deliberately disdainful, that even Königsmarck felt she was overdoing it and counselled her to 'show the Prince some warmth'. He was still hoping that the Duchess of Celle might be able to settle some money on her daughter, which would enable them to run away and start life afresh together.

Towards the end of the year the last of the troops were recalled from the Elbe, and Königsmarck was able to return to Hanover. No hero's welcome awaited him. The Princess was under constant supervision, the Elector was cold, Countess Platen was suspicious. His friends kept advising him to resign his commission and offer his services somewhere else, and there were some indications that if he were not going to do so of his own accord, he would be dismissed. He realised that dismissal was a comparatively light punishment for his affair with the Electoral Princess; death would have been a more likely one. The thought had been with him for a long time and gave him a terrible nightmare:

Last night I had a dream which I hope will never come true. My head was cut off because I was caught with you. I suffered more than a soul in purgatory. My greatest anxiety was to know what had become of you. My judges were your husband and Marshal Podewils. I would not want another night like this for anything in the world. I woke up all in a sweat and my valet said I had been sobbing in my sleep: 'Where is she? Where is she?' I was not afraid to die, my greatest fear was not to be able to know what became of you. It is in cases like that that one realises how much one loves.[5]

Königsmarck's affairs were at their lowest ebb. Sophie Dorothea was closely watched and more unattainable than ever. His presence in Hanover was clearly undesirable, and he was deep in debt. He could see no way out.

1 July 1694

In the spring of 1694 the Elector of Saxony died of smallpox, caught from his mistress. He was succeeded by his twenty-four-year-old brother Frederick Augustus, later Augustus the Strong and King of Poland.

Königsmarck had met him during the 1692 Flanders campaign, when the Prince, five years his junior, was in command of the Saxonian army. The two became good friends, in spite of Augustus's habit of borrowing without repaying. In one of his letters to Sophie Dorothea Königsmarck described the young spendthrift as an honest man at heart, and someone who could make a good Elector. That remark was no more than an assessment of personality, for at that time, two years before the event, nobody could have foreseen that the reigning Elector of Saxony would be suddenly carried off by smallpox.

In the years to come, Augustus proved to be a ruler on the grand scale. During his long reign Dresden became one of the most beautiful capitals of Europe. From a city of brick he turned it into a city of marble. He built galleries and museums and filled them with beautiful collections of pictures, porcelain, glass, precious stones, armoury and metalwork. At the same time he was extravagant in his habits, unscrupulous, lustful and despotic. Of his lust his countless mistresses and his three hundred and fifty-four children bore evidence. As for his extravagance, it manifested itself in whatever he did, whether in card-playing, the buying of jewels, or entertaining. Once, in the midst of a campaign, he invited no less than forty-seven kings and princes to feast with him. He had a huge cake baked in their honour, three feet high, twelve feet wide and twenty feet long, and displayed it all round the camp. It was sliced open with a silver axe, wielded by a cook dressed up as a carpenter. The feast lasted thirty days.

Augustus's unexpected accession opened a door of escape to Königsmarck. Rembering the thirty thousand crowns he had lent the young Elector during the Flanders campaign, he calculated that if he were repaid, he could settle all his debts and perhaps realise his romantic dream of running away with Sophie Dorothea to start afresh in some other part of Europe. The Princess for her part felt sure that if she ever did run away with him, the court of Hanover would be only too willing to sever connections with her and grant her the divorce she had set her heart on.

It must have therefore been with her consent that Königsmarck set off for Dresden to claim his debt. The Elector received his old friend and boon companion with open arms and invited him to attend his coronation ceremony. Of the repayment of outstanding debts no mention was made; but instead, the lucrative post of a general was offered, with further chances of promotion. Weighing up the ruins of his military career at Hanover with the new prospects before him, Königsmarck accepted. It may be assumed that he took this decision after a great deal of corresponding with Sophie Dorothea, and that she agreed to his joining the Saxonian service as a preliminary to their joint departure from Hanover.

His deferential petition to be repaid, and the offer of a generalship in lieu, must have taken several weeks to be negotiated. In the meantime he became a familiar figure at court, where he joined with other guests in Augustus's favourite war-game of pelting one another with raw eggs. He was often invited to the Elector's table and took part in his drunken orgies. Königsmarck had never been a man to hold his liquor well, and in Dresden, under the influence of drink, he committed the most serious indiscretion of his life. He disclosed to a large audience of distinguished drunks some of the most scandalous bedroom secrets of the court of Hanover.

His sister Aurora claimed in her memoirs that the guests round the electoral table were playing a sort of truth game, when every one in his turn had to tell some true anecdotes of his past love life. Not to be outshone by the others, Königsmarck talked freely about his relationship with Countess Platen; how she had wooed him and conquered him to suit her ambition; how she kept several young lovers under the very nose of the elderly Elector; how she painted her face like a mask to hide its horrible flaws; how, to keep her hold over him, she offered to marry him to her daughter, fathered by the Elector; how Prince George Louis kept an ugly mistress and was cruel to his beautiful wife; and how he, Königsmarck, was in the Princess's confidence and knew at first hand how cruelly she was persecuted by the whole court.

Königsmarck's scandalous revelations were reported back to Hanover with all possible speed; unfortunately not by one of Countess Platen's spies, who would have reported only to her, but by a discredited courtier who hoped to make capital of the situation and sent detailed reports of what had been said to all parties concerned, including the Elector Ernest Augustus. Countess Platen was not only mortally offended, but seriously worried for her own safety. It was essential to convince the Elector that while Königsmarck was speaking the truth about Sophie Dorothea's hatred for the court, he was not to be believed when he insinuated anything against the virtue of the electoral *maîtresse-en-titre*. Immediately she received the Dresden report she rushed to the Elector and gave him her own version of it so artfully and so convincingly, that by the time he read his own copy he easily discounted anything it alleged against the Countess and was only incensed against the Colonel who, while still in his service, had the impudence to denigrate the court of Hanover. In this mood Ernest Augustus was persuaded without difficulty to punish Königsmarck on his return. All he intended was perhaps a summary dismissal from the army and a repetition of the instruction once given to Aurora, never again to set foot in Hanover. Countess Platen however was not the woman to be satisfied with anything less than a full-scale revenge.

The time was ripe. Sophie Dorothea had become more obstreperous

than ever, refusing to share the conjugal roof with her husband, pleading constantly for a separate establishment and formally asking to live
permanently with her parents at Celle. What precipitated this last
open request is not quite certain. According to some versions she had
suddenly learnt, for the first time in her married life, that her husband
had a daughter by Mlle Schulenburg. She was so offended at his
flagrant infidelity that she went to remonstrate with him; and George
Louis, as prone to wife strangulation as ever, seized her so violently by
the throat, that her ladies-in-waiting had difficulty in rescuing her alive.
After that she drove straight out to Celle to seek the protection of her
father.

A more likely explanation of her hurried visit to Celle is that the
Princess, knowing herself to be under constant surveillance and being at
the end of her tether, decided to shorten the waiting period for her
lover's return from Dresden by going to Celle. A quarrel with her
husband, one of many since they resumed co-habitation, was the excuse
rather than the cause of her departure. It was facilitated by the fact
that George Louis himself was about to go on a prolonged visit to
Berlin, to stay with his sister the Electress of Brandenburg. He too
had more than enough of his wife, and before he left he was reported to
have said: 'There has been enough quarrelling; on my return I shall
write to your father and demand a separation.' This was just what
Sophie Dorothea was hoping for.

Unfortunately the Duke of Celle was not in a benevolent mood. He
had had enough of his daughter's tantrums and had already agreed with
the Hanover in-laws that a wife's place was with her husband's family.
After allowing her a short rest at his summer residence of Brockhausen,
he sent her back to Hanover.

Hanover was virtually deserted then, with George Louis in Berlin
and the rest of the court at the nearby summer residence of Herrenhausen. Etiquette demanded that the Princess, when passing by
Herrenhausen, which was on her way, should stop to pay her respects
to the Electress Sophia. She did nothing of the sort. In flagrant violation
of protocol, so dear to the old lady, she drove right past the residence
straight into Hanover. The court was scandalised. The Princess had
again proved to be a defiant wife and a disrespectful daughter-in-law.
Court gossips were quick to attribute her rebelliousness to the evil

influence of the absent Königsmarck. Countess Platen knew that if she played her cards right, she could ruin both with one blow.

Königsmarck in the meantime concluded his business in Dresden and proposed to wind up his affairs in Hanover and obtain his release. The date for his taking up his new post as a general in the Saxonian army had not been specified, but his duties were made clear. He was to proceed to the Rhine and take command of a regiment of cuirassiers. In the second half of June he returned to Hanover, where he met the Princess, back from her abortive visit to her parents. They might have discussed a plan of elopement, but the instructions he gave to his secretary suggested that his intention was to leave for Dresden on 5 July, to take up his new appointment.

On Sunday, 1 July, Königsmarck left his house at ten o'clock at night and went to see Sophie Dorothea at her apartment at the Leine Palace. He was never seen again.

The sudden disappearance of Königsmarck mystified all Europe. The lack of concrete evidence as to what happened to him gave rise to all sorts of rumours and conjectures. Within a year of his disappearance a romantic novel was published which purported to tell the true life story of a well-known cavalry colonel and his sad end. Other fictitious accounts sprang up like mushrooms; and in 1732 the *Histoire Secrette*, published by Baron Poelnitz, set the seal on a version that remained in favour for more than two hundred years. It had all the ingredients of popular melodrama and has been too long sanctioned by tradition not to be mentioned.

According to this version, Königsmarck returned to Hanover some time in June, unaware that his indiscretions at the court of Dresden had earned him the disfavour of the Elector Ernest Augustus. In fact he was rather surprised at the cool reception he received when he presented himself at court. However, he did not worry much about the attitude of a Duke whose service he was about to leave. He communicated with the Princess by messenger and made provisional arrangements for their elopement. They rejected France, which was their first choice, and decided to run away to Wolfenbüttel, where Duke Anthony Ulric was bound to receive with open arms another rebellious member of the hated Electoral family of Hanover.

Accordingly Königsmarck instructed his secretary Hildebrand to dismantle his household and pack all valuables in readiness for the flight. On the morning of 1 July, which was a Sunday, he received a note written in a strange hand, asking him to call on the Princess at her private apartment at ten o'clock at night. Shortly before the appointed time he left his house, disguised in some light, shabby, clothes, and proceeded to the Leine Palace. On giving the signal under the Princess's window he was immediately let in, although Sophie Dorothea said she had never dictated that note and that it must be a forgery. Still she allowed him to stay, for she had not seen him for more than three months. Later they discussed their flight, and Königsmarck informed her that he had a carriage waiting outside, ready to drive them to Wolfen-büttel and to happiness. But the Princess, who until then had wished for nothing better, was suddenly seized with pangs of maternal love. Aurora Königsmarck, in her memoirs, was able to quote the very words Sophie Dorothea used to postpone her departure:

My children! My children have never offended me; not should I bear the Reproaches of my Conscience if I set out without leaving such an Impression of their unhappy Mother's affection upon their Minds, as Time itself shall not be able to eface.[1]

In vain did Königsmarck go down on his knees and begged her to come away there and then. She insisted on waiting for the morning, when she would be able to kiss her children goodbye, and instructed him to return with the carriage the following night at the same time. He then left to return to his house.

All this time Countess Platen and her henchmen had been lying in wait for him. Through her spies she had heard of the intended flight, and no sooner did she ascertain that Königsmarck had entered the Princess's apartment, than she ran to the Elector's chamber to notify him of the outrage. The Electress Sophia was away at her summer residence; George Louis was in Berlin; and nobody dared stop the *maîtresse-en-titre* from entering Ernest Augustus's private chamber at such a late hour of the night. The Countess reported that Königsmarck had just been seen entering the Electoral Princess's bedchamber and said that with the help of four halberdiers she could catch the culprits *in flagranti delicto* and bring them to justice. Having received the Elector's sanction, she hid the halberdiers in a large chimney recess, plying them with wine, while she herself hid behind a curtain. She had taken the precaution of locking all the doors leading out of the Princess's gallery except the one near the chimney.

Königsmarck knew he was trapped as soon as he found his usual exit locked, but he decided to sell his life dearly. When the four armed men pounced on him he fought valiantly until his short sword broke in his hand. Even then he wounded three of them badly. Eventually they overpowered him and stabbed him to death. Lying on the floor with blood pouring from his mouth, he still managed to whisper that the Princess was innocent. Countess Platen, who had come out of her hiding-place to watch the battle, kicked his mouth shut with her boot. A few minutes later he was dead. He was only twenty-nine.

The Countess, who had not been authorised to kill Königsmarck but only to bring him to justice, was put out at his death. Leaving the halberdiers in charge, she rushed back as fast as she could to the Elector's chamber and informed him of the misadventure. By then Ernest Augustus was too deeply involved to turn away from her, so he gave her *carte blanche* to obliterate all traces of the accident. The halberdiers were instructed to throw the corpse into the palace latrines, cover it with quicklime, and brick the wall up. All this was done speedily and silently, and by dawn all the parties to the murder were safely in their beds.

Sophie Dorothea spent the rest of the night after Königsmarck's departure packing her jewels and getting ready for the flight. She heard some muffled sounds in the remote gallery, but took no notice of them. She did not suspect anything had gone wrong until the following morning, when her children failed to pay their morning call. Instead, a grim-looking official instructed her not to leave her quarters until further orders. She waited all day and all night, but Königsmarck did not come. It was only on the third day that Mlle Knesebeck came to her with the dreadful news that the Count was dead. The Princess replied with fortitude that his lot was happier than hers, who was doomed to suffer the iniquities of the world for the rest of her life.

Such is the traditional account of the events of 1 July. We are on

surer ground when we come to what happened after that fateful night.
Apparently Königsmarck's failure to return to his house was not
immediately noticed by his servants. They were used to his nocturnal
outings and probably had standing orders not to disturb him in the
mornings. It must have been well past midday on Monday when they
discovered that his bed had not been slept in. When the rest of the
day passed without word from his master, his secretary Hildebrand
began to worry for his safety. On Tuesday morning he went to see
Marshal Podewils and reported the Count's disappearance. The
Marshal did not suspect foul play and assured the secretary that his
master was sure to return within a day or two alive and well. Not
content with the reply, and being more familiar with Königsmarck's
dangerous love-life than the Marshal, Hildebrand sent a message to the
Elector Augustus in Dresden alerting him of the Count's disappearance.

He was still wondering what to do when on the morning of 4 July
court officials burst into the house with a search warrant, broke open
Königsmarck's desk, confiscated all his letters and papers, then sealed
the rooms and their contents with the official seal. Hildebrand was
sure now that his master's disappearance was not due to an ordinary
street brawl, but to some move by the authorities. On 6 July he broke
the news to Aurora Königsmarck, who was staying in Hamburg with
her sister Amelia Lewenhaupt. In his letter he told them that he had not
seen his master since ten o'clock on Sunday night, that he feared foul
play, but hoped the Count was still alive. He advised the sisters to wait
for further news before taking action and in the meantime asked for
some money to meet the large daily expenses of feeding fifty-two
horses and mules, twenty-nine servants and an unspecified number of
artisans. . . .

The sisters waited for a few days as advised, then wrote appealing
letters to influential dukes and princes of their acquaintance, including
the Elector of Hanover. When no satisfactory answer was given,
Aurora travelled to Hanover to conduct her inquiries in person. She
was peremptorily reminded that the place was out of bounds to her, so
she adjourned to Celle, only to be put off by Bernstorff, who had his
instructions from the Platens. Eventually she left for Dresden to beg the
Elector of Saxony to intervene on behalf of her brother, who was not
only his old friend, but also a general in his army.

At thirty-two Aurora Königsmarck was considered one of the most seductive women in the courts of Germany. She combined beauty with culture, social graces with a lively mind. She spoke and wrote French, German and English, wrote poetry, painted landscapes, sang, and even composed an opera which was put on in Hamburg. She also had all her brother's high spirits and unbridled love of pleasure. She was well aware of her natural endowments, and did not spurn to show them to their best advantage. She would come to court balls dressed as a goddess, with one of her generous breasts perfectly bare.

Whether dressed as a goddess, or more demurely as a sister in anguish, Aurora had no difficulty in persuading Augustus to take up her case. He had already heard from Hildebrand, and sent an envoy to Hanover to start an enquiry. It was thought that Königsmarck was still alive, possibly incarcerated in one of the Leine Palace dungeons. Accordingly the envoy was instructed to demand his restitution, on the ground that he was a major-general in the Saxonian army, under orders to proceed to active service on the Rhine. A carefully-worded reply informed the envoy that at the time Count Königsmarck was last seen, on the night of 1 July, he was still a colonel in the Hanoverian army, and therefore the Elector of Hanover could not be expected to hand him over, even if he knew where he was. The implication was that the fickle Count had disappeared of his own volition, and that the Hanover administration would not allow outside intervention.

In the meantime strange rumours trickled out of Hanover and Dresden and reached other courts. Count Königsmarck was well-known and well-connected all over Europe, and his mysterious disappearance gave rise to a wave of curiosity. Questions were asked in France, Denmark, Sweden, Poland and in several German courts unfriendly to Hanover. Ernest Augustus's failure to provide a satisfactory answer gave rise to ugly speculations. King William in particular desired to hear the hard facts of the case. On 24 July George Stepney, the English envoy to Dresden, sent a despatch to James Cresset, the new English envoy to Hanover, reporting on what he knew, and asking for any clarification available:

I have great curiosite to know what piece of mischief has been brewing at Hannover. If you dare not trust it at length, I must beg

you to satisfy me in Cypher, as likewise with the particulars of your
Princess's ruine. Amours are fatall in these parts; wee have had a
scene of them here and may hereafter have more the like nature. But
at present the Tragedy is removed to your Courts, and I fear Daggers
and poyson will be as familiar among you as they are in Italy. Your
Princes have been often there and may have learned the humour of
the country of despatching people without Noise. A servant or two
of Count Königsmarck run frequently betwixt this place and
Hannover (as I have heard Count Berlo's dog did betwixt the Camp
and Brussels after the Battle of Fleuros), seeking out their master,
but have no tidings. Our Elector sent one of his Adjutants, Mr.
Bannier (a swede likewise) to Hannover, I believe with a design to
stopp the blow if it was not yet given. But I suppose the Corps by
this time is in the common shore, and our Elector by the accident has
cleared the debt of 30 thousand R he had lost to him two years ago at
play.

I have been told his sister raves like Cassandra and will know what is
become of her brother; but at Hannover they answer like Cain,
that they are not her brother's keeper and that the Body should be
found (which I believe as little as that of Moses), yet the circumstances
of the Murder will be left as much in the dark as the manner of
despatching Sir Edmonbury Godfrey has been. He [Königsmarck]
was not recommended to me by Mr. Stratford. I knew him in England,
at Hamburg, in Flanders and at Hannover for a dissolute debauchee
whom I would always have avoided. By chance I ate with him here
at Count Frizews and our new privy counsellor Haxthausen, and by
chance likewise they did suppe with me, whereas they were invited
to Mr. Bomeburgh's who too late remembered it was a fish-night
and so shifted off his own company on me. This is all I have had to do
with the spark, and if he has been so black as we think he is, his
Fate (be what it will) is not to be pitied.[2]

Believing that Königsmarck was still alive and in prison, Augustus
gave his envoy fresh instructions to insist on a satisfactory answer.
Other courts began to take an unhealthy interest in the case, as far as
Hanover was concerned. Denmark, which had never recognised the
ninth electorate, was not loth to make the disappearance of the Swede

an excuse to take the proud Elector down a peg or two. Anthony Ulric of Wolfenbüttel, who could not forgive the elevation of the junior Luneburg branch over his own, was only too ready to join in a concerted action against Ernest Augustus. From a purely domestic affair, the Königsmarck case developed into an issue with wide political repercussions.

As usual, Ernest Augustus enlisted the support of his son-in-law, the Elector of Brandenburg, and together they put the case to the Emperor. With the widening rift between allies, it was no longer a question of the fate of one man, but of the future of the Grand Alliance. Strong pressure was brought to bear on Saxony to stop interfering. Imperial disfavour was threatened. In view of such powerful opposition Augustus's zeal cooled. The more time passed, the more Königsmarck's disappearance seemed an unworthy cause for a rupture between two friendly electorates. Ernest Augustus's envoy produced a formula of retreat that was acceptable to both Saxony and Hanover. He conveyed to Augustus that the Elector of Hanover much cherished his friendship and would do anything in his power to please him, but unfortunately he had no knowledge of what had become of 'the person for whom application was made', and that in all likelihood he was 'rather dead than living'. In his despatch from Dresden on 21 August, the English envoy Stepney described the last scene of the drama before curtain fall:

> The Elector of Saxony seemed very moderate after this answer, as if he doubted not the truth of what had been offered, and replyed only that he hoped as an instance of friendship that the Elector of Hannover would give him notice as soon as he should learn any tidings of Count Coningsmark, and I believe here that the affair will end without causing any breach betwixt the two Electors. The Count's sister is gone hence, but I know not which course she steers.[3]

And so the search ended. Aurora went away, presumably accepting the consensus of opinion that her brother was dead; either slain on the night of his disappearance, or killed later while in prison. Whatever her feelings, her part in the case was played out. She left for Brunswick, where Duke Anthony Ulric made her welcome, and where her brother's costly furniture and effects were delivered to her, having been released by the Hanover authorities.

But Aurora's visit to Dresden had not been altogether unsuccessful, for she made an impression on Augustus the Strong, eight years her junior. When she returned there the following year, he courted her so ardently, that the thirty-three-year-old Countess lived up to the code name of *l'avanturière*, once given to her by her brother and Sophie Dorothea, and accepted the position of resident mistress. The liaison was celebrated with as much pomp as if it were a wedding. On a fine May morning in 1695 the whole court set out from Dresden to the nearby summer residence of Mauriceburg, with Aurora and her sister Amelia leading the cavalcade in a magnificent coach. Half-way to their destination they were met by a deputation of scantily-dressed goddesses and satyrs, led by Augustus dressed as Pan. The festivities at the summer residence did credit to the Elector's renowned extravagance, and lasted fifteen days. Nine months later Aurora gave birth to a baby boy, who grew up to be one of his father's best known sons, Count Maurice Saxe. The liaison lasted two years, a long time by Augustus's record, and then petered out in the face of fresher attractions. Aurora bought her entry into the Abbey of Quedlinburg, where she lived as its deaconess —some say devoutly and some say as adventurously as ever—until she died at the age of sixty-four, still a very attractive woman.

For the next two hundred and fifty years the fate of Königsmarck continued to intrigue Europe and serve as an inexhaustible source of conjecture to writers in many languages. Walpole believed the mystery was solved and the case closed when a skeleton was found by builders at the Leine Palace during the reign of George II. In his reminiscences he stated that 'the body of Königsmarck was discovered under the floor of the Electoral Princess's dressing-room, the Count having probably been strangled the instant he left her, and his body secreted'.

But the later discovery of two more skeletons casts a doubt over the identity of the first one; while their presence in the disused cellars of the Leine Palace, along with many other old human bones, may be explained by the proximity of a monastery cemetery. In recent years Dr Georg Schnath has made a new appraisal of the Königsmarck case, based on his researches in the archives of many European capitals. From his findings a new version emerges.

On the night of 1 July 1694, the twenty-nine-year-old Königsmarck left his house at ten o'clock, dressed in light summer clothes, which he used to put on as a semi-disguise instead of his conspicuous dragoon uniform. He was observed to enter the Leine Palace, but not to leave it. Once inside, whether before he saw the Princess or immediately after, he was set upon by four people and mortally wounded. His assailants were not halberdiers or guardsmen summoned at random, but four well-known courtiers, who must have been picked out some time in advance, either for their venality, or on the contrary, for their established respectability.

Two were notorious ne'er-do-wells whom Königsmarck had mentioned several times in his correspondence. One was the Italian Count Montalban, who had once stirred up an ugly scene at the Electress of Brandenburg's boudoir by placing his thin legs on her dressing-table. The other was Stubenvol, who had once consumed six partridges and a barrel of cherry wine at a supper given by Königsmarck. Both men had a personal grudge against him and never neglected an opportunity to do him a bad turn. They both held high positions at court. Montalban was the Osnabrück estate manager, while Stubenvol was a gentleman-in-waiting, and the husband of Ernest Augustus's natural daughter Laura, born to him by one of his Italian mistresses. Königsmarck distrusted both Montalban and Stubenvol, and described them as a couple of mischief-makers, cheats and seducers.

He had no such bad opinion of the other two who took part in the plot. In fact he had exchanged cordial letters with them and considered them friendly. One was Klencke, who later was entrusted with several diplomatic missions and won much honour. The other was Eltz, who rose to be a Privy Counsellor.

That Countess Platen was the originator of some dark plot there can be little doubt. She must have drawn Montalban and Stubenvol into her scheme by promising them the Elector's favour if they helped arrest Königsmarck and prove his guilt. The other two may have been led to believe that their presence at the nocturnal assignment was required primarily as unbiased observers who might later be called upon to give evidence.

It was not unusual for the Countess to give instructions in the name of the Elector; if she did not do it in her capacity of a mistress she did so in her capacity of the chief minister's wife. The four courtiers had no reason to doubt the legitimacy of her step, and when called for action late one night, had no hesitation in following her to the Princess's gallery. The instructions she gave must have been ambiguous; perhaps she gambled on Königsmarck's instinctively drawing first at the sight of four armed men. There was a scuffle, during which three courtiers might have fought more in self defence than with design to kill, while Montalban dealt the mortal blow. Later he alone was held responsible for the murder; he became the sudden recipient of vast sums of money from governmental sources, which were paid out to him in such a way that they could be reclaimed the moment he opened his mouth. It was a reward as well as hush-money. It must have been a relief to all concerned when he died some seven or eight months later.

Once the plotters had a corpse on their hands, it was a question of disposing of it as quickly and as quietly as possible. It was midsummer, with the nights at their shortest. There was no time for ceremony. The four courtiers put the dead man's body in a sack, weighted it with stones, and gently dropped it into the Leine river running by the side of the Palace, where it disappeared without a trace.

Divorce

On the night of Sunday, 1 July 1694, Sophie Dorothea went to bed as usual. No sounds from the far gallery disturbed her sleep.

It was only when the best part of Monday had gone by without a word from Königsmarck, that she began to suspect something was wrong. It was not usual for him, when in Hanover, to leave her long without a letter or a message. He must have told her that he was leaving for Dresden on the Thursday, and she could not therefore have consoled herself with the thought that he had been suddenly called away, as he was the year before at the time of the march to the Elbe. A total silence could have only meant a cooling-off, or an accident. Whichever the Princess chose to believe, she must have been in a terrible state of suspense.

Not knowing where to turn, she confided her anxiety to Councillor Albert Philip Busche—not to be confused with General John Busche, Countess Platen's brother-in-law—whom she must have considered friendly. Two or three days later, with Mlle Knesebeck returning from her thousand errands with the same reply that Königsmarck was untraceable, Sophie Dorothea threw caution to the winds and sent the Councillor a letter of appeal:

Sir,

I weighed again what I had told you. I tremble with fear that if C[ount] K[önigsmarck] is in the hands of the lady you know, it might be prejudicial to his life. Have you kindness to inquire into this matter, and let us wait a few more days in order to have all possible information about the poor C[ount]'s fate. I rely entirely on your discretion, for in my present state of mind I am completely out of my senses.[1]

It was naïve of her to imagine that anybody at court would try to find Königsmarck for her; but she clutched at any straw. She must have heard through Mlle Knesebeck that Königsmarck's house had been searched and his papers confiscated. It was probably then that the two women agreed to deny any suggestion of a love affair between the Princess and the Count. They kept that agreement to the end, in spite of harsh interrogations and threats. Shortly afterwards Mlle Knesebeck was arrested, while her mistress was brutally told that Königsmarck was dead.

The Princess's position was invidious, for the letters seized in Königsmarck's desk were compromising in the extreme. They revealed her love; they discussed a possible elopement to Wolfenbüttel; they expressed hate for the court of Hanover in general and for some high-placed persons in particular; they contained expressions of loathing for George Louis; and last but not least, they included derisory remarks about the Duke of Celle, whom his daughter described as harsh, weak-willed, and besotted by age. The letters were shown to the Elector of Hanover, who passed them on to his brother. Neither doubted their authenticity. Leibnitz later wrote that they proved the Princess's guilt beyond doubt.

The exact nature of her guilt was never quite specified; in fact it was deliberately left vague. As soon as Königsmarck's disappearance began to draw attention, it became clear that any linking of his name with the Princess's would cast a suspicion of foul play on the court of Hanover. In Dresden rumours were rife that the Count had been killed to vindicate a husband's honour. If the Princess were to be accused of a love affair, it would be very difficult to convince Europe that her lover had not been murdered by her in-laws.

There was another complication. In England and France Jacobites were referring to eleven-year-old Prince George Augustus as 'Young Königsmarck', although he was born years before the Count ever came to Hanover. It was essential to refute any possible allegation of irregularity in the Hanoverian line of succession. Far from accusing Sophie Dorothea of adultery, it was necessary to proclaim her virtue. If Königsmarck's removal had been intended as a first shot at the Princess, it had badly misfired.

There the case could have rested. Sophie Dorothea could have been allowed to retire to Celle and live with her parents; or she could have been given the separate establishment she had been asking for, and lived quietly away from Hanover. Now that her lover was dead and honour was no more in danger, appearances could have been saved. With goodwill the whole thing could have been smoothed over and relegated to the past, like so many other family scandals.

But there was no shred of goodwill towards Sophie Dorothea. The sins of twelve years were laid at her doorstep. Her wilfulness, her disrespect for protocol, her intolerance of the unofficial court hierarchy, all served to win her enemies. They included the most influential people at court: Countess Platen who wanted revenge for personal reasons; Count Platen, the Elector's chief minister, who considered her as a pawn in a game, to be discarded when its usefulness was over; and George Louis, the husband, who loathed her for herself and would never forgive her for making a cuckold of him. They all wanted to get rid of her.

Getting rid of a Princess could only mean divorce. There had been several precedents in the courts of Germany, and the principle was never challenged. The question was on what grounds to demand it. Count Platen was entrusted with the problem, and together with Baron Bernstorff, his opposite number at Celle, he worked out an ingenious solution. It was known that the Princess had often asked for separation; it only remained to prove that when unable to get it, she was guilty of desertion. That she would welcome a divorce was beside the point. She had to be proved the guilty party, to enable her husband to retain his good name, and her property.

Accordingly George Louis, who was still 'acting Comedyies and making merry with his sister the Electrice' of Brandenburg at her court in Berlin, was made to write a courteous letter to his wife, asking her to resume co-habitation with him on his return to Hanover. His request must have seemed the height of sarcasm to Sophie Dorothea, and so she played right into Count Platen's hands and haughtily refused it. Moreover, as soon as she was convinced that her lover was dead and that no useful purpose could be served by her staying on in Hanover, she demanded to leave the place and go to her parents at Celle.

Her demand was welcomed by Platen as proof of wilful desertion. He transmitted it to the Elector, whom the Princess was not allowed to see, and the Elector communicated it to his brother at Celle, indicating that it was not his wish that the Electoral Princess should be received by her father as if he condoned her behaviour. Duke George William was sufficiently incensed against his daughter to fall in willingly with his brother's wishes. For years he had been content to follow Ernest Augustus's advice in all matters concerning the welfare of their duchies, and he might have genuinely believed that the future unity of Hanover and Celle, as important to him as it was to his brother, depended on the peaceful dissolution of an unsatisfactory marriage. He left the matter entirely in the hands of his chief minister Bernstorff, who found the ideal answer. The Princess would be allowed to leave Hanover; but instead of going to her parents at Celle, she would move to the castle of Ahlden, in the territory of Celle.

Sophie Dorothea could not have been altogether surprised when her father refused to let her come and live with him. Ahlden seemed a good compromise, and she therefore accepted it without hesitation. She was greatly disappointed when she learnt that the date of her departure had to be delayed by a day or two. But her eagerness to leave did not stop her from packing all her belongings and instructing her household to pack theirs. If Platen had counted on the Princess's impetuosity, her careful preparations took him by surprise, as he ruefully wrote to Bernstorff on 15 July:

> The Princess's departure cannot be taken for desertion, because she has indicated her wish to take with her all her household and her belongings.[2]

At long last the day of departure arrived. On the morning of 17 July a sad convoy left the Leine Palace, headed by the Electoral Princess and escorted by dragoons who looked more like gaolers than a guard of honour. Twelve years earlier a much grander convoy had driven in the opposite direction, conducting a young bride to a court which awaited her with pre-conceived hostility. Her departure from Hanover was the predictable outcome of long years of intrigue and personal vindictiveness. Sophie Dorothea left without regret, never to return.

Removing the Princess to Ahlden, a small village twenty miles from Celle, that nobody in Europe had heard of before, gave rise to further speculations about Hanover's part in Königsmarck's disappearance. Towards the end of July identical notes were sent to the Celle and Hanover envoys in Vienna, Ratisbon, Stockholm, Berlin, The Hague and London, instructing them what to say in case awkward questions were asked. The notes denied any connection between the 'still inexplicable disappearance' of Count Königsmarck and 'the coldness that had been observed to exist for some time' between the Electoral Prince and the Princess. They further implied that the person who inspired the coldness in the Princess was Mlle Knesebeck, her lady-in-waiting, who had such an evil influence on her mistress that she had to be dismissed from service and arrested. As for Ahlden, the notes concluded, it was a comfortable castle, situated near Celle, and the Princess went there of her own free will.

Whether the Princess had gone to Ahlden of her own free will, or whether she had been escorted there under duress, her departure could no longer be represented as desertion. In one of his reports, Vice-Chancellor Hugo of Hanover had to admit that although it was known that Sophie Dorothea desired separation, her desire was strengthened, if not caused, by her husband's attitude, for before leaving for Berlin he threatened in front of witnesses to write to his father-in-law and ask for a dissolution. There was ample proof of mutual dislike, but none of the Princess's guilt.

Count Platen then fell back on his original idea, once rejected for political reasons, of accusing the Princess of adultery. Mlle Knesebeck was subjected to a rigorous interrogation about her mistress's behaviour, but firmly denied all allegation of misconduct. Platen later wrote to

Bernstorff that her replies were so much like the Princess's that they must have been concocted together. When he realised he was not going to get any incriminating evidence out of the obstinate lady-in-waiting, he sent her to prison without trial. Legal minds were momentarily at a loss.

Fortunately for the prosecution, Platen was quick to grasp that his best ally was Sophie Dorothea herself. She was so intent on obtaining her release, that she was willing to supply whatever evidence was required. And indeed, when it was tactfully intimated to her that the course of justice would be facilitated if she freely admitted to wilful desertion, she readily agreed to cooperate and promised to sign anything that would speed up the process. No evidence was needed, for the Princess saw eye to eye with the prosecution. After that, a divorce was a foregone conclusion. All that remained to be done was to give the procedure the sanction of legality.

Anticipating the verdict, the Elector of Hanover and the Duke of Celle got together to work out the shape of Sophie Dorothea's future life. They agreed that her inheritance would continue to be the property of Prince George Louis and his son even after the divorce. The Elector authorised his brother to provide for his husbandless daughter, and the Duke of Celle undertook to allow her eight thousand thalers a year, from the Celle treasury, to be increased by four thousand on his death, and by another six thousand on the Princess's fortieth birthday. It was also arranged that Ahlden would become her permanent residence.

This agreement was worked out and signed towards the end of August. At the same time a consistorial court was formed, consisting of four lay judges and four clerical ones, chosen in equal numbers from Celle and from Hanover, as if they were opposing sides in the case. Councillor Albert Philip Busche, whose help Sophie Dorothea had sought in finding Königsmarck, was nominated president. Councillor Rudolph Thies was appointed to represent the Princess.

Legal preparations began in all earnestness. Conferences were called, letters were exchanged, and lengthy documents were submitted in learned German, interspersed with French and Latin. Bernstorff had several meetings with the judges and tried to show them where their duty lay. In mid-September he reported to Hanover that all was going well, but the main point was not to let anybody realise that the verdict had been determined in advance.

In order to make it easy for Councillor Thies to confer with his client, Sophie Dorothea was forced to leave her refuge at Ahlden and return to Hanover territory, if not to Hanover itself. She was lodged at a magistrate's house in Lauenau, where Thies was able to call on her and report developments. He genuinely tried to dissuade her from pleading guilty to a charge of desertion, which he knew was unwise. The Princess did not listen to him. She wanted her freedom, and that was all that mattered to her.

When the court convened in Hanover for its first hearing, on 20 September, it soon appeared that Bernstorff had not prepared the ground well enough. The four clerical judges were not satisfied with the evidence presented to them, and demanded that the Princess should be given a fair hearing. They gave her the choice of appearing in person, or, if she preferred, of putting down her case in writing. Bernstorff was alarmed, fearing his carefully planned case would come to pieces. He need not have been. Nothing could have been more odious to the Princess than to return to Hanover and appear before a court. She gladly put her signature to a statement that her lawyer had prepared for her instead:

Since our illustrious husband George Louis, Electoral Prince of Hanover, has delivered a complaint against us to the consistorial court formed in Hanover by our father and father-in-law, requesting the dissolution of marriage between our husband and us; and since our father has sent to us Marshal Bülow, to hear from us what we had to reply to the plea of wilful desertion, we hereby command Councillor Rudolph Thies to convey our answer.

We declare that we have well and freely considered the contents of our husband's complaint, and that our intention is clear. We abide by our often declared resolution never to resume co-habitation with our husband, and we desire nothing so much as the dissolution of marriage requested by him.

We hereby authorise and command our lawyer Councillor Thies to present our declaration in answer to the letter of 20 September 1694, sent to us by the above mentioned court.

In witness thereof we have signed this with our hand and have caused our seal to be affixed to it.

Sophie Dorothea

Lauenau, 26 September, 1694[3]

The document was taken to Hanover and submitted to the Elector's Vice-Chancellor for examination. The wording was found faulty, and the Princess was asked to sign an amended one. Still the four ecclesiastics were not satisfied, and insisted on a verbal declaration. It was no use her signing a third document. A delegation came to Lauenau to talk to her and try and persuade her to return to her duty. Sophie Dorothea was firm and repeated her resolution never to co-habit with her husband. This time the clerical judges were convinced. The court sessions could be resumed.

All this time Duchess Eleonore had not been allowed to see her daughter, or else she might have succeeded in warning her that the suggested divorce was not going to be the release she had been hoping for, but a public condemnation by court. The Duke of Celle seemed to be content to let the law take its course. Whenever he showed signs of weakening, there was Ernest Augustus at his side, to remind him of his duty. The Elector spent much of his time with his brother, and even went to stay with him at his hunting-lodge at Göhrde. It was said that to safeguard the future, he extracted a promise from him never again to see his daughter. As for the Duchess, the Elector hoped to placate her by suddenly increasing her annual allowance, in the form of an act signed by him and his son.

But Eleonore was not to be placated. As soon as Ernest Augustus left for Hanover, and George William freed from his influence, she started a new campaign. There was not much she could do by then, but at least she could oppose the court recommendation to forbid Sophie Dorothea to re-marry after the granting of the divorce. Once the Elector was out of the way, the whole court of Celle was behind the Duchess. Councillor Thies made an outspoken speech at court, demanding for the Princess the right to re-marry.

Immediately there was panic. Vice-Chancellor Hugo of Hanover wrote letter upon letter to Bernstorff, ordering him to convince the court of Celle that the future of the united duchies was in jeopardy should the Princess be allowed to produce further legal issue. The whole delicate structure of the Celle inheritance would be questioned. Political expediency had to come before personal emotions.

In the face of such reasoned and persistent opposition, the Celle resistance broke down. The court went into its final session, and on 28 December, some four months after it was first convened, gave its verdict. It was exactly along the lines visualised by Count Platen and Baron Bernstorff:

In the matrimonial suit brought by the illustrious Prince George Louis, Duke of Brunswick and Luneburg, against his consort the illustrious Princess Sophie Dorothea, Duchess of Brunswick and Luneburg and Electoral Princess, we, the President and Judges of the matrimonial court of the Electorate and Duchy of Brunswick-Luneburg, declare and pronounce judgement, after all attempts to settle the matter amicably have failed.

In accordance with the documents and verbal declarations submitted by the Princess, and after detailed examination of circumstances, we agree that her continued refusal to resume co-habitation and grant conjugal rights has been established, and is consequently to be regarded as wilful desertion. After careful consideration we pronounce the ties of matrimony null and void.

Since in similar cases it has been permitted to the innocent party to re-marry, which the guilty party is forbidden, the same will apply in this case, in favour of his Highness the Electoral Prince.

Published in the Consistorial Court of Hanover, 28 December, 1964.   (signed)

Albert Philip Busche

Francis Eichfeld
Anthony George Heldberg
Gustav Molan
Paul Puchler

Gerard Molan
Maurice Spilcker
David Rupert Erythropal
Henry Christopher Hattorf[4]

The verdict was communicated to the Princess of Lauenau, where she obliged Platen by signing yet another document, assuring the court that she had no intention of lodging an appeal. She still believed that divorce meant freedom, while the ban on re-marriage must have seemed pathetically irrelevant to a woman who had just lost the only man she ever loved. Her final declaration was taken to Hanover on the last day of the year. Immediately notes were sent to the Celle and Hanover envoys in foreign courts, advising them that the Princess was no more a member of the Electoral house of Hanover. Her name was struck out from the church prayers and deleted from official documents. Her pictures were taken down from the walls of the Leine Palace. Courtiers were discreetly warned not to mention her. To all intents and purposes Sophie Dorothea ceased to exist.

The divorce was pronounced just as the carnival season of 1694–5 was about to begin. James Cresset was shocked to see Hanover so jubilant. In one of his January dispatches he wrote:

> The Carnaval here is very provoking, but they cannot live without it, they are a sort of people that can rejoice even in their own disgraces. . . . I think them as little in their senses as at Dresden. The Duke of Zell has been at Hanover halfe of the time and the other with his Dutchesse at Zell. The divorce was finished but the day before their frolicks began here. The sentence was pronounc'd upon malicious desertion . . . those who don't like the proceeding say there is a nullity in the manner of it, that those persons were no competent judges, and that the Princesse may appeal to the Emperour whenever she pleases. She is still confin'd.[5]

In Versailles, the Duchess of Orléans, as contemptuous as ever of Eleonore d'Olbreuse, was delighted to hear of the downfall of her daughter. She made short shrift of both of them, when writing to her aunt the Electress Sophia:

Versailles, 13 February, 1695
How could the Duchess of Celle ever imagine that her daughter would not be unhappy, when she had brought her up to have such

ideas in her head? Where in the world can one find such men who love nobody but their wives, and who have no mistresses and boys as well? If wives were to lead the same sort of life as their husbands, one could never tell with certainty who the true heir was in the family. Does not this Duchess know that a wife's honour consists in having nothing to do with anybody except her husband, and that there is no disgrace for men to have mistresses, but only to be deceived by their wives? That wives bring a thousand misfortunes on their heads if they fling themselves into similar enterprises? Her daughter's unhappiness will teach her these truths only too well.[6]

When asked by Louis XIV for the latest news from Hanover, the Duchess of Orléans informed him that the real victim of the case was Countess Platen, who had befriended Königsmarck only as a possible son-in-law. When his disappearance was laid at her door, she took it so much to heart that she fell seriously ill and had to keep to her bed. The Countess was much less of an *intriguante* than Sophie Dorothea, concluded the Duchess of Orléans. In later years she pushed her malice even further by hinting that young Prince George Augustus—later George II—was not fit to ascend the throne of England, because of the doubt about his paternity.

The only person to proclaim Sophie Dorothea's innocence was Eleonore Knesebeck, who was therefore summarily dealt with by the Hanover authorities. She was arrested twelve days after Königsmarck's disappearance, interrogated by Platen, and sent to prison at Springe without trial. Six months later, shortly after the divorce had been pronounced, she was moved to the ancient fortress of Scharzfels, on the edge of the Harz mountains, where she was to stay hidden from the rest of the world. Her family knew nothing of her whereabouts, and it was only after long months of searching that her married sister, Mme de Maitch, succeeded in finding out what had happened to her. Living in Brunswick as she did, she got in touch with Duke Anthony Ulric, the champion of all Hanover enemies, and together they worked out a daring plan of escape. A friend, disguised as a builder, succeeded in being admitted to the fortress in order to mend the tiles on the roof. From his perch he threw a rope down to Mlle Knesebeck's room, hauled her up through the hole he had made, then lowered her down some eighty feet into the castle ditch, with himself following. Together they made their escape good to Brunswick. Mlle Knesebeck had been incarcerated for well over three years.

The commandant of the fortress swore that his prisoner had been closely guarded, and that she must have been spirited away by magic. The very hole in the roof was proof that it had been the work of Satan, for no human could have made it. The authorities examined Mlle Knesebeck's room and found the walls, the door and even the bed-stead closely inscribed with her reflections, scraps of verse and texts from the scriptures. For pen she had used charcoal taken from the chafing-dish. Her writings were duly copied out and presented to the members of the Hanover Privy Council, who must have flinched at the reading:

> The government must have committed a great wrong, or else they would not want to silence me. If they can answer to the whole world for what they have done to the Princess, why do they not let me speak up too? If the sentence is just, how should I dare to speak against the Elector, poor and obscure girl that I am? And if his judgement is right, how could I speak a lie? What does the govern-ment mean by stopping my mouth? What are they afraid I might say? It is clear they committed a great injustice, so they suffocate and oppress me with power, iniquity and violence, so that their injustice does not come into the open.[7]

Eleonore Knesebeck, only a few years older than Sophie Dorothea, must have been a very determined woman indeed. Three months after her escape she went to Vienna to seek justice at the Emperor's court, disregarding the danger of being arrested on the way by Hanoverian agents. On her return to Brunswick her sister made her promise never to leave it again. When the Elector of Hanover died a few months later, she wrote to the Duke of Celle to condole with him over the death of his brother, and petitioned him for the restitution of her property. Her efforts were in vain. She continued to live in Brunswick until 1706, when nineteen-year-old Sophie Dorothea, daughter of the divorced Electoral Princess, married the Crown Prince of Prussia and Brandenburg, and took her mother's lady-in-waiting with her to

Berlin. There Mlle Knesebeck lived peacefully to the end of her life, never marrying, writing her own version of Sophie Dorothea's life. From her memoirs came the story of how Count Platen, when interrogating the Princess for the first time, suggested that she was pregnant by Königsmarck; how the Princess haughtily answered that he was surely confusing her with his own wife; how she took the sacrament to prove her innocence, and how, to the horror of the whole court, she then challenged Countess Platen to do the same. Mlle Knesebeck's memoirs, written many years after the events of 1694, differed somewhat from the evidence she gave during her interrogation, and even from the declarations she made immediately after her escape. But in substance they were the same, exonerating Sophie Dorothea of all possible guilt. The Confidante died as she had lived, protesting her mistress's innocence to the last.

While Hanover was enjoying the carnival season of 1695, Sophie Dorothea was lying ill and helpless at Lauenau. As long as her future was in the balance she held on, conferring with her lawyer, signing papers, burying herself in legal business. Once the case was over, reaction set in. The horror of her lover's murder, the tension and fears of the past few months, the physical stress of her confinement, everything she must have tried to repress, suddenly erupted. She broke down, a physical and mental wreck. She was too ill and too downtrodden to remind the authorities that they had no right to hold her in Hanover territory. Cresset noted in his despatches how the weeks went by, with the Princess still confined at Lauenau. It seemed as if the Elector was deliberately holding her under his direct jurisdiction, to avoid any possible unpleasantness at Celle. Again he reckoned without Duchess Eleonore. She constantly evoked the agreement he had signed with her husband, according to which Sophie Dorothea was to be returned to her father's territory after the divorce. At last the Elector gave way. On 28 February 1695 Sophie Dorothea was escorted under heavy guard from Lauenau to Ahlden, where she was given the rank and style of Duchess. She was twenty-eight when she was taken to the castle. With one brief interlude of a few months, she lived there under guard for the next thirty-two years, until the day of her death.

Duchess of Ahlden

The consistorial court which found the Electoral Princess of Hanover guilty of wilful desertion passed no sentence on her other than a prohibition on re-marriage. Restrictions on her freedom of movement were never mentioned in any of the court proceedings, nor were they demanded by the prosecution. Indeed, there were no legal grounds to condemn the Princess to confinement of any sort. By law, she should have been free to go and live wherever she wished.

Unfortunately a free Sophie Dorothea constituted a political risk. She might have gone to Saxony and persuaded Augustus the Strong to reopen the Königsmarck case. She might have gone to the Emperor in Vienna and challenged the legality of the divorce in order to win some concessions for herself; or she might have contended that the dissolution of her marriage also meant the annulment of the contract which had transferred her inheritance to a person who was no longer her husband. She might even have gone to France, and as a naturalised French subject, sought Louis XIV's protection against the Elector of Hanover. Once out of reach, the Princess could have caused incalculable damage and furnished Hanover's enemies with further excuses for acts of hostility. She had to be rendered harmless before she recovered from her stupor and began to understand her rights.

In his far-sighted way, Ernest Augustus had weighed this up even before divorce proceedings were started. Taking advantage of his brother's momentary grievance against his daughter, he persuaded him to sign an agreement confining her for the rest of her life to the castle of Ahlden, as a means of safeguarding the future integrity of the ninth Electorate. No power in the land could challenge the sovereign's right to dispose of the life of a subject. Ernest Augustus did not need any legal pronouncement to enable him to keep a potential trouble-maker out of mischief. Nobody in Hanover would have questioned an order to put a disgraced Princess under house-arrest, just as nobody had batted an eyelid when an uncooperative lady-in-waiting was sent to prison without trial. The Elector's power was absolute.

But even an absolute sovereign like Ernest Augustus had to have a face-saver. His agents spread a rumour that a plot was being hatched to abduct the Princess, and that she was therefore kept under guard. In one of his despatches the English envoy Cresset reported that the Duke of Celle was beginning to soften towards his daughter, when Ernest Augustus immediately sent to inform him that Sophie Dorothea was in league with certain foreign powers, which were plotting to attack Ahlden and release her by force. To keep up the myth, instructions were given to fortify the castle against an imminent invasion. Cresset gave his own version of the proceedings:

> They sent a small engineer from Hanover, to throw up a little dirt and stick in a few pales, which they call fortifying Ahlden, where they keep the Princess a prisoner. Wackerback, her jailer, often alarms the garrison with a body of men coming in disguise to carry her off. It must be the Emperor in the moon that sends 'em, for they cannot now pretend but that Saxony has something else to doe.[1]

Although there is no authentic record of Sophie Dorothea's intimate thoughts during her first months at Ahlden, it is not difficult to imagine what she must have gone through. Her letters to Königsmarck show her to have been passionate, emotional and highly-strung. Her terrible suffering at the murder of her lover must have been equalled by her hatred for the people she suspected of having caused it, and her desire for revenge. She was ill for a long time. She wrote pathetic letters to her mother, who was not allowed to come and see her. She lived in a daze, functioning like an automaton. The routine that was established around her must have eventually helped her to regain her equilibrium and adjust herself to her new surroundings.

Once the Princess was out of the way, the Elector saw no reason to deny her the luxuries that her rank entitled her to; on the contrary, allowing her to maintain her own household kept up the official version that she had retired to Ahlden of her own free will. Accordingly the castle was provided with elegant furniture and every effort was made to give it the semblance of a real court. The Duchess of Ahlden, as she was styled by those who meant to eradicate all traces of her past existence, was entitled to her own establishment. She had a marshal, a garrison of forty soldiers, infantry and cavalry, two or three ladies-in-waiting, two pages and one or two gentlemen-in-waiting. Her household consisted of two valets, a butler, three cooks, a confectioner, a head groom with several boys under him, a coachman, fourteen footmen and twelve maids.

Although she maintained the staff out of her own allowance, she had no say in their appointment. Before entering service, every one of them had to take an oath not to permit anything to happen which might be prejudicial to what was discreetly termed 'the unity of the Family'. They were encouraged to spy on their mistress and report anything suspicious to the governor of the castle. The governor himself was under direct orders from the Elector to watch the Princess's every move and see that she had no contact with the outside world. Although she had no friends left beside her mother, strict precautions were taken to prevent any attempt at escape. The castle, flanked on one side by the river Ahler and protected on the other by a moat, was surrounded by sentries who kept guard day and night. The Princess was not allowed out-of-doors, and only when her health deteriorated for lack of fresh air was she permitted a short stroll in the back garden of the castle. Once, when fire broke out in her quarters, she was left to pace frantically up and down a long gallery, clutching her jewel-box to her heart, until a signed order from the governor authorised her evacuation to a place of safety.

Her daily routine kept her tolerably busy. Every day she wrote her instructions for the cook and butler with her own hand. On certain days she held her official *levées*, to which the local clergy and village dignitaries were invited. On Sundays the chaplain conducted a service in her apartments. Sophie Dorothea and her ladies prayed in one room, while the rest of the household, including the soldiers off duty, prayed in the next, with the adjoining doors wide open.

The Princess had always been religious, if not profoundly so, and now, in her loneliness, she turned to religion for consolation. During her first days at the castle, even before the divorce, she was visited by the chaplain Casaucau and talked to him about repentance. As she settled down, she often sought his company, and through him turned to good works. She gradually became the acknowledged benefactress of Ahlden. The woman who had once been so self-centred that a flooded village meant no more to her than an irritating delay in receiving her lover's letters, now learnt to show compassion for the plight of others. She distributed charity, contributed towards the education of poor children, and gave money to re-build the village after a fire. She enriched the local church with costly gifts, a silver candlestick, a pulpit cushion, an altar-cloth.

But religion alone was not enough to comfort a young woman who had no particular vocation. Feminine even in times of stress, she kept up her morale by taking great care over her appearance. Her allowance enabled her to dress as lavishly as ever, and ordering materials and selecting fashions must have taken her mind off sad thoughts. She spent much time in front of her mirror, choosing the jewels to go with her dresses as if she were about to entertain distinguished guests, or meet a lover. Perhaps deep down she never ceased to hope Königsmarck was still alive and would one day turn up to fulfil his promise to take her away and marry her. In later years, when by special dispensation she was allowed to go out for a drive in her coach, she used to put on her most splendid clothes, with diamonds gleaming in her hair. She would drive at top speed towards the bridge on the west approach of the village, which was just within the six-mile limit allowed to her. As soon as she reached it she would turn back and drive towards the castle, then reverse and drive again to the bridge, while the entire castle cavalry galloped behind her with their swords drawn, ready to stop any attempt at escape.

All her activities and all the comings and going in the small court were regulated by orders from above. Nobody from outside Ahlden was allowed to visit her. Her incoming and outgoing mail was censored. Her plea to be allowed to see her children was ignored. Her request to permit her mother to visit her was refused. She was completely cut off from the world. It was only after several months of constant pleading that Duchess Eleonore eventually succeeded in wrenching from Duke Ernest Augustus permission to visit her daughter. A mother's love was all she could bring her, for no other concessions were ever granted. From then on until her death Duchess Eleonore was Sophie Dorothea's only link with the outside world. From her the Princess heard about political developments in Europe, which the Duchess followed with great interest, always wondering how they might affect her daughter's chances of liberation. The next few years offered her several opportunities to act on her behalf.

In October 1697 the Treaty of Ryswick was signed between Louis XIV and the Emperor Leopold, bringing to an end the nine-year-long war between France and the Grand Alliance. England, Spain and Holland had signed the treaty a month earlier.

To the Elector of Hanover peace meant the discontinuation of the costly campaigns in Flanders. To French-born Duchess Eleonore it meant that Louis XIV was no longer an enemy, and resuming cordial relations with him was the order of the day. Years earlier, when still a plain Mme de Harburg, she had sought and obtained his promise of protection for herself and her daughter. Now, although a Duchess, she felt just as insecure. Her husband was seventy. If he were to die, his widow and his daughter would be for ever at the mercy of the Hanover relatives, who now had more reason to hate them.

Weighing all this in her mind, Eleonore decided to appeal again to the kindness of the King of France. This time she could no longer count on the cooperation of her husband. Instead, she discussed her idea with her old friend and ally, Duke Anthony Ulric, who throughout Sophie Dorothea's trial kept assuring her mother that he believed in her innocence. The Duke promised to help.

When diplomatic relations were resumed between France and the three Brunswick courts, Anthony Ulric cautiously broached the subject with the new French envoy du Héron. He hinted that if, after the demise of the Duke of Celle, his widow and his daughter were allowed to settle in France, they would probably embrace the Catholic religion. There was no indication on Eleonore's part that she ever thought of doing so; on the contrary, she continued to give Huguenot refugees a warm welcome in her court, and even persuaded her husband to allow them to build a place of worship in Celle. But Anthony Ulric was too much of a politician to let a thing like that stand in the way of a diplomatic mission. Perhaps he half-believed that Eleonore would see the light one day, as he himself did towards the end of his life. In any case, he convinced the French envoy of Eleonore's goodwill and merit. The Sun King was pleased at what he heard, and in April 1699 instructed du Héron to give the Duchess the required assurance:

> If the Duchess of Celle and her daughter the Duchess of Hanover decide to come to my country, after the demise of the Duke of Celle, and to embrace the Catholic faith, I would gladly give them my protection. You can also assure Duke Anthony Ulric of my pleasure in the kind sentiments he has shown them.

In the midst of her negotiations with France, another event occurred which momentarily raised Duchess Eleonore's hopes for her daughter's release. It was the death of the Elector of Hanover.

In January 1698, after many years of ill-health, Duke Ernest Augustus died at the age of sixty-nine. His last few months were particularly painful. He suffered loss of sight in one eye and loss of speech. Writing to one of her nieces, the Electress Sophia said that he was in a state of nervous debility and that, as a last resort, it was decided to consult a Dutch quack. For many months she never left her husband's side, except when he was asleep. He died much regretted by her and by Duke George William, who had come from Celle to be with his brother in his last hour.

Ernest Augustus had been a skilful and astute ruler, an apt imitator of the great French prototype that so many German princes of his time kept before their eyes. He lived extravagantly to suit his tastes, but he knew how to turn his extravagance to advantage. If he was despotic, he was also enlightened; and if he was ruthless, he was far-sighted. He formed a dynasty and firmly guided it towards grandeur and fame. In his seventeen years as ruler of Hanover he had turned it from a provincial capital into a centre of power. He never lost sight of his ultimate goal, which was the greater glory of Hanover, and on his death-bed he made his elder brother promise to carry on his lifework after him.

As soon as the news of the Elector's death reached Ahlden, Sophie Dorothea, no doubt advised by her mother, wrote two letters of condolence and supplication, one to her former husband, the new Elector, the other to his widowed mother. Her letter to the Electress Sophia must have been the easier to write:

Ahlden, 29 January 1698

Madam,

It is my duty as well as my natural desire to assure Your Highness how deeply I share your grief over the loss of the Elector your husband. I pray God with all my heart to console you and keep you for many years to come in prosperity and good health. I beg of you once again to forgive all I have done which may have offended you and to intercede on my behalf with your son the Elector. I implore him to grant me the pardon I so painfully long for and to allow me to embrace my children. My fervent desire is also to kiss Your Highness's hands once more before I die, and if you grant me this favour I shall be overwhelmed with gratitude. I beg you, Madam, to do me the honour of believing that nothing could ever equal the respect with which I remain,

Your Highness's most humble and most obedient servant,
Sophie Dorothea[3]

Writing to George Louis required an even greater show of submission and repentance, but three years of captivity had taught Sophie Dorothea to swallow her pride. She grovelled like a beggar:

Ahlden, 29 January 1698

Sir,

I take the liberty of writing to Your Highness to assure you how deeply I share your grief over the death of the Elector your father.

I pray God to console you, to bless your reign with his most gracious favours and to comfort Your Highness with all forms of prosperity. These prayers I shall say every day of my life. I shall never stop regretting having displeased Your Highness. I beg you to forgive me for my past mistakes, which I am asking you on my knees, from the bottom of my heart. My sorrow at having offended you is so deep and so bitter that I can hardly express it. The sincerity of my repentance should move Your Highness to pardon me, and if, to crown your kindness, you would allow me to see you and embrace our dear children, my gratitude for such highly-desired favours would know no bounds, for there is nothing I desire as fervently as the fulfilment of my request, after which I should die contented. In the meantime I pray God a thousand times to give you long life and good health, and I am,

> Submissively and respectfully,
> Your Highness's most humble and most obedient servant,
> Sophie Dorothea[4]

The two letters indicated a deep change in Sophie Dorothea's attitude to her children. It was natural that she should long to see them, but her desperate clinging to them was something new. It was the result of her long confinement and the vacuum created in her heart by the loss of the man she loved. They became the most important thing in her life.

She had never been a particularly devoted mother. By the time her second child was born she was so full of bitterness against the hostile court that her main concern was to leave Hanover in order to stay peacefully with her parents for as long as she could. She seemed perfectly content to leave the upbringing of her son and daughter to governesses and governors, as indeed she was expected to do. In the whole of her correspondence with Königsmarck she never mentioned their illnesses or their progress. She never wrote of rows with governesses or in-laws about the children's diet or education. She never indicated whether they accompanied her on her prolonged visits to her parents at Celle, Epsdorff, Luisburg or any of their other residences. She never mentioned sitting with them for a court portrait, that must have been commissioned by Ernest Augustus after very careful consideration of the cost. The only reference she ever made to the children was in reply to a letter Königsmarck had written in the summer of 1693. She was at Celle at the time, while he was in Hanover. Teasing her for her jealousy, he wrote to tell her how he had spent a whole evening at court being attentive to a young lady who reminded him of her. Sophie Dorothea immediately made enquiries from eye-witnesses, and was greatly relieved to learn that the young lady in question was none other than her own little daughter, who had been allowed to stay up, together with her brother. Königsmarck had spent the whole evening making card-houses for the two children. In gratitude, Sophie Dorothea wrote to thank her lover for not giving her any cause for complaint.

Yet she must have been tender with her children on the not-too-frequent occasions when court routine and her own turbulent state of mind allowed her to be with them. They would not have remained as loyal to her as they did, had she not been warm and loving. Her son somehow managed to get hold of a full-length portrait of her, which he kept in his rooms and later smuggled away with him to England; while her daughter, when she grew up, secretly corresponded with her. They never condemned their mother and, whatever they heard to the contrary, their impressions of her must have been based on confidences extracted from loyal servants to whom the Electoral Princess had shown kindness.

The letters of supplication proved to be a waste of time. The Electress Sophia had little influence over her son. He had never taken much notice of her advice, and although he was scrupulous in his show of respect towards his widowed mother, he made it clear that he was not going to be ruled by her. Not that the old Electress would have recommended granting Sophie Dorothea's request to see her children. As the grandmother in charge of their upbringing, she felt it was essential to prepare them for their future life without any interference from the past. Young George Augustus, heir to the Electorate and possibly to the throne of England, had to be particularly protected from the influence of a disgraced mother. All the Electress's old prejudices against the d'Olbreuse family revived. Her correspondence with her niece in Versailles showed quite clearly that she had no compassion for her former daughter-in-law.

As for George Louis, he hated Sophie Dorothea with all the coldness of his sullen nature. He saw no reason to forgive a woman who had made a cuckold of him. Nor was he going to allow her to see his children and prejudice them against their father. Too much was at stake. Immediately on his accession to the Electorate, George Louis asked his uncle to reaffirm his pre-divorce undertaking to keep the Princess permanently confined to the castle of Ahlden. Duke George William, deeply moved by his brother's death and true to his promise to maintain the unity of Hanover and Celle, solemnly agreed to respect a decision whose sole object he believed to be the safeguarding of the political future of the ninth Electorate. As on the previous occasion, the undertaking was softened by an increase in Duchess Eleonore's dowry, which the new Elector raised from eight thousand thalers a year to twelve thousand. But Eleonore would not be bought. While continuing her visits to her daughter, she watched out for the next opportunity to ask for her release. It came towards the end of that year, when King William paid a visit to Hanover and Celle.

The Duke of Celle had long been on cordial terms with William of Orange, and when the latter became King of England, kept up a correspondence with him and supported his efforts to form the Grand Alliance. William, for his part, rewarded his old friend and ally by conferring on him in 1691 the Order of the Garter, long before he considered it for Ernest Augustus. The Duchess of Celle too had much sympathy for William, in spite of her French orientation. She had never forgotten that it was he who had discreetly advised Ernest Augustus and Sophia, on their accession to the Duchy of Hanover, to recognise her newly-won title of Duchess. Unlike Sophia, Eleonore was allowed to have a say in her husband's political deliberations, and she won William's respect by her tactful championing of his cause. It was tacitly accepted in Hanover that her credit with him was higher than Duchess Sophia's.

As the English succession became more of a reality with every royal death at the court of St James, Hanover was determined to win William for the just claims of the Electress Sophia. After Ernest Augustus died it was thought politic to entrust the further courting of William's favour to the Duchess of Celle. She applied herself to the task with her usual tact and charm, hoping to win the throne of England for her grandson.

William arrived during the winter of 1698–9, and according to plan, went to Celle first. Eleonore impressed on him the advisability of recognising the Electress Sophia, grand-daughter of James I, as in line of succession to the English throne. At the same time Eleonore discussed with him the chance of arranging a match between her grand-daughter Sophie Dorothea and the ten-year-old William of Gloucester, Princess Anne's sickly son, who was to have succeeded his mother after William's death and hers. The King viewed Eleonore's approaches favourably. When he left Celle for Hanover, his mind was made up. Before returning to London he gave the Electress Sophia a definite promise to recognise her claim.

Duchess Eleonore was in great favour for her successful negotiations. Early in the new year Leibnitz, in his capacity of court historiographer and diplomat, wrote to congratulate her on the success of her mission. He must have done so with the full consent of his master, the Elector George Louis, who would not deign to write in person to the mother of his hated former wife, although he had reason to thank her for her achievement.

Throughout William's stay at Celle, there were speculations as to whether Duchess Eleonore would ask him to say something in Hanover in favour of her daughter. The French envoy du Héron discussed her chances of success in his despatch to Louis XIV:

Her Highness the Duchess of Celle will try to persuade the King to speak on behalf of the Princess of Hanover; but the ministers, who are no friends of either the mother or the daughter, have brought so much pressure to bear on the Duke [of Celle], that it is to be feared he will indicate to the King of England it would not give him pleasure if he interfered in the Princess's affairs.[5]

With her husband set against involving William in her daughter's fate, Duchess Eleonore may not have dared to confront him with a request that was bound to have unpleasant repercussions, and even prejudice the success of her other negotiations. If she did, there was nothing to show for it. All Sophie Dorothea gained from William's visit was a detailed account by her mother of the future grandeur that might one day come to her children.

There was one last opportunity for Duchess Eleonore to intercede on her daughter's behalf, and this time she nearly succeeded in getting Sophie Dorothea out of Ahlden once and for all.

For several years Louis XIV had been considering the advisability of allowing a French Bourbon to succeed to the throne of Spain, after the foreseeable death of Carlos II without an heir. Louis realised that such a step would be firmly opposed by the Emperor Leopold of Austria and William III, but Spain was too great a prize to let slide for such considerations. While the issue was still in the balance, William approached some of the members of the former Grand Alliance, and formed a coalition against France. When Carlos II died in November 1700, naming Philip of Anjou, Louis XIV's grandson, as his successor, William was ready to strike. The War of the Spanish Succession began.

But hostilities started even before the opening of Carlos II's will. In the spring of 1700 some Saxonian and French troops marched together through Brunswick territories—the three Brunswick Dukes siding as usual with William—and made a few successful attacks. It was feared they might march on Ahlden, which lay in their path.

The danger was negligible, but Duchess Eleonore made the most of it. She represented to her husband how disgraceful it would be if French troops occupied the undefended castle of Ahlden and took as a hostage a Princess whose son could one day become King of England. The only way to avert the danger, the Duchess contended, was to transfer Sophie Dorothea to a fortified castle, where any attack could be easily rebuffed. No place was better suited to meet such a contingency than Celle.

Eleonore's argument was so well presented, that even the wily Bernstorff, who saw through it, could say nothing to refute it. The Elector George Louis was notified, and although he was very much against moving Sophie Dorothea out of Ahlden, he could suggest no other way of meeting the French danger. He gave his grudging consent, while reminding George William of his solemn promise never to see his daughter. Bernstorff was instructed to keep an eye on the old Duke and at the slightest sign of softening on his part, to use his influence to dissuade him from a reconciliation.

And so, one April evening of 1700, Sophie Dorothea left the castle of Ahlden and was escorted to Celle, where she and her small retinue arrived very late at night and were immediately sent to their special quarters. She was installed in her childhood apartment, which, ironically, was so full of memories of clandestine meetings with Königsmarck only a few years earlier. Her arrival was kept as quiet as possible, and the court was not supposed to take any notice of it. But it was impossible to ignore it altogether. Her mother visited her constantly, and she must have talked quite openly of her hopes of keeping her at home indefinitely. On 29 July, the Duchess of Orléans wrote from Versailles to her aunt in Hanover:

The Duchess of Celle has lost no time in having her daughter brought to Celle. I should think that her father must be very much embarrassed about this, for it will grieve him to send his daughter away again without seeing her, and yet the honour of the house does not permit him to let her remain at Celle, and there is the fear that the Elector would take it ill.[6]

On 8 August the Duchess of Orléans wrote again, with her usual touch of malice:

I should like to know if the Elector will allow the Duchess of Ahlden to remain at Celle or if he will send her back to Ahlden. I hear that the Princess leads a very solitary life, but all the same she is splendidly dressed, and when she takes a walk on the ramparts at Celle she always covers her face with a veil. I imagine she hopes to touch the heart of her husband by her decorous life, so that he may take her as his wife again.[7]

The French danger was short-lived. As soon as the troops retreated from their foray into Brunswick territory, George Louis instructed the Duke of Celle, through Bernstorff, to arrange for the return of his daughter to Ahlden. Duchess Eleonore was not satisfied that the danger was over and insisted on detaining her daughter. The instructions were repeated. The Duchess, whose word could not be openly doubted, for she was the only person officially allowed to visit the Princess, claimed that her daughter was too ill to be moved. It became a tug-of-war between Eleonore and George Louis, with Sophie Dorothea kept again in a state of tension and suspense. On 26 August the Duchess of Orléans gave her own opinion of the situation:

I hear the Duchess of Celle has received orders to send her daughter back to Ahlden, but they have not been carried out. The people of Celle are not to be blamed for lamenting on account of their Princess, but her father deserves praise for exhibiting such firmness.[8]

In the end Eleonore ran out of pretexts, and her husband felt honour-bound to stand by his agreement with George Louis. As the gates of Ahlden castle closed behind her, Sophie Dorothea knew that her last chance of freedom had vanished. She was never to be allowed out further than the village bridge.

Elector into King

From the moment of his accession in 1698, George Louis took the reins of government firmly into his own hands. He had already had some experience of administration during his father's last illness, and he had no difficulty in asserting his authority over his ministers, including Count Platen. He successfully rebuffed a fresh attempt by his brother Prince Max and Duke Anthony Ulric to undermine the law of primogeniture, and had himself confirmed by the Emperor Leopold as the Elector of Hanover. He set out to consolidate the gains made by his father, and within a very short time put his administration on a solid, if rather uninspired, basis. His court was less dazzling than his father's, but more sober. John Toland, a member of the English delegation that came to Hanover about three years after George Louis's accession, left the following description of the forty-year-old Elector:

> He's a perfect Man of Business, exactly regular in the Economy of his Revenues, reads all Dispatches himself at first hand, writes most of his own Letters, and spends a very considerable part of his Time about such Occupations in his Closet, and with his Ministers. I hope therefore that none of our Countrymen will be so injudicious

as to think his Reserv'dness the Effect of Sullenness or Pride, nor mistake that for State which really proceeds from Modesty, Caution and Deliberation; for he's very affable to such as accost him, and expects that others shou'd speak to him first, which is the best Information I cou'd have from all about him, and I partly know to be true by Experience. And as to what I said of his Frugality in laying out the public Mony, I need not give a more particular Proof, than that all the Expenses of his Court (as to Eating, Drinking, Fire, Candles, and the like) are duly paid every Saturday Night; the Officers of his Army receive their Pay every Month, as likewise his Envoys in every part of Europe; and all the Officers of his Household, with the rest that are on the Civil List, are clear'd off every half Year. His Administration is most equitable, mild, and prudent. He's the most belov'd by his Subjects of any Prince in the World.[1]

To suggest that George Louis was beloved by all his subjects was a courtier's natural exaggeration; but the Elector was certainly loved, or at least accommodated, by a growing number of willing mistresses. He was at the prime of life, powerful and lascivious. At last he was in a position to indulge his amorous inclinations with the same ease that his father had before him. Although he retained Mlle Schulenburg as his first lady to the end of his life, later creating her Duchess of Kendal, he had other mistresses. Most prominent in his new entourage was Sophie Charlotte Kielmansegg.

The suggestion that she was his mistress was put forward and denied with equal vehemence. It was based on the fact that she was a favourite, that she followed George Louis to England, and was later created Countess of Darlington. It was disputed on the grounds that she was the daughter of Countess Platen and Ernest Augustus, and therefore George Louis's half-sister; and it was contended that whatever favours he bestowed on her must have been due to brotherly affection.

She was born in Osnabrück when George Louis was fifteen and about to take part in his first battle. Because of her paternity and her mother's unchallenged position at court, she was accepted as a natural member of the ducal household. The Electress Sophia embroidered a cushion cover for the young lady's regular seat at the Leine Palace audience chamber. Sophie Charlotte had inherited her mother's looks and wit, and when Count Königsmarck first arrived in Hanover, there was talk of arranging a match between them. She married Baron John Adolph Kielmansegg at the comparatively late age of twenty-six.

By that time her mother, the once powerful Countess Platen, was dead. After George Louis's accession, she had to relinquish her proud position at court and retire to Monplaisir. There she eked out her existence, nursing her disease, until she died, two years after Ernest Augustus. Tradition had it that on her deathbed she confessed to her part in Königsmarck's murder. Towards the end of her life she went blind, but she could still see 'Königsmarck's ghost by her wicked old bed', as Thackeray later wrote.

When Sophie Charlotte married Kielmansegg, shortly after her mother's death, George Louis had been the Elector of Hanover for over three years. Whether his half-sister was his mistress or not, he spent much of his time with her. He advanced her husband and made him Master of the Horse. The couple lived in a beautiful house called Fantaisie, where the young Baroness entertained so extravagantly that she was soon at the mercy of creditors. She had four children; her defenders say they were all by her husband, others suggest that at least two were by George Louis. When the Elector of Hanover went to England to become King, Baron Kielmansegg was chosen to be in his retinue, while the Baroness was left behind, as a hostage to creditors. She escaped their watchful eyes by disguising herself and succeeded in joining her husband and her half-brother in time to cross the Channel with them. She lived at court, and as Countess of Darlington survived Kielmansegg by many years.

After his accession to the Electorate George Louis became involved with yet another member of the Platen family. She was the young Countess Platen, wife of Countess Platen's son Ernest Augustus. Toland described her as a great beauty, who would be noticed in any court. George Louis however had failed to notice her, until she thrust herself on his attention and forced him to make amends for his oversight. Like her mother-in-law, she was notoriously flirtatious, but complained bitterly when anybody suggested that she was. Her association with George Louis was not of the lasting kind, but there was no shortage of candidates aspiring to step into her shoes. With the growing importance of Hanover at the court of St James, there began a steady influx of beautiful visitors from London, who were most anxious to win the favour of a potential king.

In July 1700 Prince William, Duke of Gloucester, the only surviving son of the future Queen Anne, died of measles at the age of eleven. His mother, who was to succeed William III, was not expected to bear any more children, so the question of the further succession had to be resolved well in advance. The choice lay between the direct line of the exiled Catholic Stuarts, enjoying the hospitality of Louis XIV at St Germain, and the remote line of the Protestant Stuarts, as represented by the house of Hanover. There was little doubt that the choice would fall on the Protestant descendants of James I, foreign as they were, rather than on the Catholic ones.

An Act settling the succession on the Electress Sophia and her heirs was passed by both Houses of Parliament, and in the summer of 1701 became law. The following year Lord Macclesfield headed a delegation despatched to Hanover to present the Electress with a copy of the Act. His party included several peers, a chaplain, a physician, and a budding diplomat and author, John Toland, who later wrote a detailed account of the visit.

In honour of the occasion, George Louis overcame for once his 'Frugality in laying out the public Mony' and offered the entire party of thirty or forty gentlemen free travel within his domains as well as free board and lodgings. The delegation was met at the frontier by ministers and court officials, then escorted to Hanover. Its members were cossetted and feasted, and any Englishman who happened to be in Hanover and visited them in their hotels was equally well entertained. Every morning the Elector sent his own servants to wait on them, giving them the use of the Palace plate for their tea and coffee. Even the servants of the English were treated like honoured guests, with a liberal daily allowance, so that they would not have to feed on the leavings of their masters' table.

The climax came with a grand banquet and ball, during which Lord Macclesfield ceremoniously presented the Electress Sophia with a copy of the Act of Settlement, and invested George Louis with the Order of the Garter. For Sophia, at seventy-two, the reading of the Act must have been the proudest moment of her life. She must have particularly thrilled to the clauses which named her in person:

. . . Therefore for a further provision of the Succession of the Crown in the Protestant line, we your Majesty's most dutiful and most loyal Subjects, the Lords Spiritual and Temporal, and Commons, in this present Parliament assembled, do beseech your Majesty, that it may be enacted and declared, and be it enacted and declared by the King's most Excellent Majesty, by and with the Advice and Consent of the Lords Spiritual and Temporal, and Commons, in this present Parliament assembled, and by the Authority of the same, That the most Excellent Princess Sophia' Electress and Duchess Dowager of Hanover, Daughter of the most Excellent Princess Elizabeth, late Queen of Bohemia, Daughter of the late Sovereign Lord King James the first, of happy Memory, be and is hereby declared to be next in Succession in the Protestant Line, to the Imperial Crown and Dignity of the said Realms of England, France and Ireland, with the Dominions and the Territories thereunto belonging, after his Majesty and the Princess Anne of Denmark, and for Default of issue in the said Princess Anne, and of his Majesty respectively: And that from and after the decease of his said Majesty, our now Sovereign Lord, and of her Royal Highness the Princess Anne of Denmark, and for Default of issue of the said Princess Anne, and of his Majesty respectively, the Crown and regal government of the said Kingdoms of England, France and Ireland, and of the Dominions thereunto belonging with the Royal State and Dignity of the said Realms, and all Honours, Stiles, Titles, Regalities, Prerogatives, Powers, Jurisdictions and Authorities, to the same belonging and appertaining, shall be, remain and continue to the said most Excellent Princess Sophia, and the Heirs of her body, being Protestants: And thereunto the said Lords Spiritual and Temporal, and the Commons, shall and will, in the Name of all the People of this Realm, most humbly and faithfully submit themselves their Heirs and Posterities; and do faithfully promise that after the Deceases of his Majesty, and her Royal Highness, and the failure of Heirs of their respective Bodies, to stand to, maintain, and defend the said Princess Sophia, and the Heirs of her Body, being Protestants, according to the limitation and Succession of the Crown in this Act specified and contained, to the utmost of their Powers, with their Lives and Estates, against all persons whatsoever that shall attempt any Thing to the contrary . . .[2]

After the ceremony, Lord Macclesfield paid a courtesy visit to Celle, then returned to Hanover to take his leave. There was a general exchange of presents. The Electress Sophia, soon to call herself Heiress of Great Britain, presented his Lordship with her portrait set in diamonds; George Louis gave him a huge basin and ewer in massive gold; and the Duke of Celle gave him a precious collection of gold medals. There were also presents for the other members of the delegation, and not one was forgotten. They returned to London with wonderful tales about the liberality of the house of Hanover.

In all these proceedings Sophie Dorothea's name was never mentioned. Even Toland, who traced delightful pen-portraits of each of the Electoral family, never hinted at her existence. That same year the Duchess of Orléans summed up the general attitude, behind which the Electoral family salved their consciences:

As the Duchess of Ahlden often sees her mother and other ladies, and can also go out for drives, she is not so much to be pitied.[3]

In his eighty-first year, not having seen his daughter for ten years, Duke George William decided that the time had come for him to try and ensure her future after his death. There was no question of her immediate release, but with her eventual liberty in mind, he added a codicil to his will, making her the residual legatee of his fortune. Duchess Eleonore was also allowed to make a will in her daughter's favour, leaving her a vast sum deposited in the banks of The Hague and Amsterdam, as well as the Olbreuse property in Poitou.

As for his widow's future, the Duke had taken his precautions long ago. Fully aware that on his death Celle would become the property of the Dukes of Hanover, and that Eleonore would have to vacate the castle, he had started building her a home of her own. As early as 1692 he commissioned an Italian architect to go to Paris to study the latest designs and ideas, and over the years he had him build a residence at

Luneburg, where the Duchess of Celle would be able to retire. George William also left her his favourite hunting lodge of Wienhausen, which she, in her will, and with his approval, left to Sophie Dorothea.

With all the legal provisions properly dispensed with, there remained only the question of a father's conscience. After ten years of captivity, Sophie Dorothea could no longer be considered a political danger. There was no reason why the Duke of Celle should not accompany his wife on one of her regular visits to Ahlden. But even after so many years Bernstorff was still apprehensive. A reconciliation between father and daughter was not to be allowed. He dared not oppose an old man's wish to see his daughter before he died; instead he invented excuses to put the visit off. George William was in no hurry. He was wonderfully well preserved, and at eighty-one still an active hunter. He agreed to wait. In the summer of 1705 he went on a shooting expedition, and caught a severe chill. He died in Wienhausen in Eleonore's arms, without having made his peace with his daughter.

George William's death brought about the official unification of Celle and Hanover under the Elector George Louis. The process was achieved quite smoothly. For many years the foreign policy of the two duchies had been identical, and no major administrative adjustments were necessary. The castle of Celle was taken over by the Elector, and the Dowager Duchess Eleonore left for Luneburg. George Louis however went on residing in the Leine Palace in Hanover, and Celle remained unoccupied.

Her husband's death spurred Duchess Eleonore to make her last attempt to have her daughter released. She asked the Elector to allow Sophie Dorothea, now aged thirty-nine, to come and live with her widowed mother at Luneburg. Her request was refused. The old Duchess, whose health was seriously affected by George William's death, continued her sad journeys to Ahlden, which were now made more difficult by the extra distance. She braved poor health and the cruel buffeting on the bad roads to bring her daughter the comfort of her devotion. During those visits she told her of two forthcoming marriages. One was between Sophie Dorothea's son and Caroline of Ansbach; the other between Sophie Dorothea's daughter and Prince Frederick William of Brandenburg, heir to the throne of Prussia.

When the young English diplomat Toland visited Hanover for the presentation of the copy of the Act of Settlement to the Electress Sophia, he wrote a detailed description of her two grandchildren, the Electoral Prince George Augustus, and his sister the Electoral Princess Sophie Dorothea.

According to Toland, the Prince combined good looks with a pleasant personality. He was of medium height, fair with light brown hair; and he had a winning social manner. He also had an inquisitive mind, and at nineteen was considered to have acquired a solid groundwork of learning. He was judged a great master of history and Latin, which, Toland wrote, he spoke as fluently as his father. From his grandmother, the Electress, he learnt English, and from his grandfather the Duke of Celle the art of hunting. The young man got on well with Duke George William.

His inquisitive mind led him to an escapade that brought on him his father's wrath. When out hunting one day near Luisburg, he broke away from the party and rode at full speed to Ahlden. His escort caught up with him within a few miles of the castle, and stopped him just in time from forcing his way in.

According to another version, the Prince actually got as far as Ahlden, but was refused entry by the governor of the castle. Undeterred, the young man stood on the right bank of the Ahler, until his mother appeared at her window and waved to him. As soon as he recognised her he plunged into the river, determined to swim it and climb up to her apartment through a window. His companions caught up with him just in time to drag him out of the water and forced him to ride back to Hanover. That was, so the story goes, the beginning of the lifelong hostility between George I and the future Prince of Wales.

In 1705, only a few months after his grandfather's death, George Augustus married Caroline of Ansbach, who became Queen Caroline when he succeeded to the throne as George II.

His sister Sophie Dorothea, at fifteen, was described by Toland as one of the most lovely and charming ladies he had ever seen. She was tall and well-built for her age, with a clear complexion, fine brown hair and very lively blue eyes. She had been educated by her grandmother, the Electress, and, although no great scholar, was considered a young lady of sense and sensibility. She was particularly noted for her even temperament. Of the many attractive matches that were proposed for her, the choice eventually fell on her cousin Frederick William of Brandenburg, Crown Prince of Prussia. From a political point of view it was a splendid match. In 1701 the Elector of Brandenburg became the first King of Prussia, and his only son, born to him by Sophie Charlotte of Hanover, was due to succeed him. Whatever bitterness the Duchess of Ahlden may have felt against her former sister-in-law, she must have suppressed it in the pleasant expectation of seeing her own daughter become Queen of Prussia. The reigning Queen of Prussia did not live to see the marriage. She died prematurely, about the same time as the Duke of Celle.

After the wedding, which took place in Hanover in 1706, young Sophie Dorothea moved to her husband's court in Berlin, where she immediately showed her independence of her father by openly inviting Mlle Knesebeck to come and be her lady-in-waiting. She also started a secret correspondence with her mother at Ahlden. Further than that she dared not go. She never went as far as visiting her, although she had an opportunity of doing so when, as Queen of Prussia, she came back to Hanover for visits.

The marriage of her children was not officially communicated to the Duchess of Ahlden, and her only source of information was again her mother, who had attended both weddings. From her Sophie Dorothea also learnt that her old enemy, Count Platen, died in 1706, blind and unlamented. His post as chief minister to the elector of Hanover was filled by Bernstorff, who was raised to the rank of Count. If George Louis needed any support in his savage condemnation of his former wife to a life-sentence of house arrest, Bernstorff gave it to him. Nothing could bring any change in Sophie Dorothea's existence. She sought what comfort she could from her mother's visits and letters, her good works, the administration of her property, her drives and her toilette. The Duchess of Orléans commented in a latter she wrote to her aunt in 1710:

That the Princess always sits before her looking-glass may be forgiven to her, but it proves that she is a coquette by nature.[4]

The death of William in 1702 and the accession of Anne to the throne of Great Britain brought the Electress Sophia within practical reach of her cherished goal. Although she was thirty-five years older than Queen Anne, the Electress was determined to outlive her and see herself crowned. Her supporters in England, wishing to pre-empt any treacherous move by Queen Anne in favour of the St Germain Stuarts, advised the elderly Electress and her son to pay a visit to their future kingdom and make themselves known to the people. Sophia felt too old to travel, but was persuaded it would be wise for her son and grandson to do so. George Augustus had already been created Duke of Cambridge by Queen Anne, and was therefore entitled to take up his seat in the House of Lords. In 1714 the Hanoverian minister to the court of St James was instructed to apply for a writ summoning the Duke of Cambridge to attend Her Majesty's pleasure in the House.

When the request was transmitted to the Queen, she was so incensed at the possible Hanoverian infiltration during her lifetime that she acted in what was later described as 'an extraordinary manner'. She accused the Hanoverian minister of having acted without authorisation from Hanover, and banned him from St James. She then wrote three strongly-worded letters, to the Electress, to George Louis and to George Augustus, warning them that any attempt on their part to set foot on English soil during her lifetime might lead to most undesirable results.

The letters reached Hanover at the beginning of June. At eighty-four, the Electress Sophia could be easily agitated by unpleasant news, in spite of her seemingly robust constitution. The blunt refusal to allow her heirs to see their promised land was too much for her. She cried that she would not survive such a blow, and she did not. Mollineux, the Duke of Marlborough's agent in Hanover, gave the following account of her death:

The letters were delivered on Wednesday at noon. When I came to Court she was at cards, but she was so full of these letters that she got up and ordered me to follow her into the garden, where she gave them to me to read, and walked and spoke a good deal in relation to them. I believe she walked three hours that night. The next morning, which was Thursday, I heard that she was out of order, and on going immediately to Court, she ordered me to be called into her bedchamber. She gave me the letters I sent you the copy; she bid me send them the next post, and bring them afterwards to her to Court. This was on Friday. In the morning, on Friday, they told me she was very well, but seemed very chagrined. She was dressed, and dined with the Elector as usual. About four she did me the honour to send to town for some other copies of the same letters, and then she was still perfectly well. She walked and talked very heartily in the Orangery. After that, about six, she went out to walk in the garden and was still very well. A shower of rain came, and as she was walking pretty fast to get to shelter, they told her she was walking a little too fast. She answered, 'I believe I do', and dropped down on saying these words, which were her last. They raised her up, chafed her with spirits, tried to bleed her; but it was all in vain, and when I came up she was as dead as if she had been four days so.[5]

Sophia missed being Queen of Great Britain by fifty-three days. She died on 8 June 1714, Queen Anne on 1 August. In London the Elector of Hanover was immediately proclaimed George I, and a delegation was sent to bring him to his kingdom across the water.

He took with him a large retinue which included his marshal of the court, several physicians, the indispensable Mustapha and Muhammed, four pages, two trumpeters, a carver, twelve footmen, eighteen cooks, two housemaids and a washerwoman. His political staff included Count Bernstorff, and his household was made up of such familiar figures as Baron Kielmansegg and Count Ernest Augustus Platen. Mlle Schulenburg took along her two daughters, politely referred to as her nieces; Mme Kielmansegg sent hers with her husband. Altogether, with women and children, George's German retinue numbered some hundred and fifty people.

They arrived at Greenwich on a fine September day, and were met by the English nobility, who had turned out to welcome their new sovereign in a splendid procession of two hundred coaches, each drawn by six horses. At London Bridge the King was ceremoniously invited by the Lord Mayor to enter the City. Bells pealed, bands played and guns were fired in salute. When he reached St James, George I expressed his surprise and gratification at the sight of the vast crowds that had lined the streets to see him.

Soon however the same London crowds began to make fun of his two German companions, whose appearance was most unprepossessing. Walpole later wrote that one was as corpulent and ample as the other was long and emaciated. As their position at court became known, the crowds did not hesitate to mock 'so uncommon a seraglio' and booed them during their drives in the park. One of the ladies—Walpole did not record which prided herself most on her command of the language —leaned out of her coach window one day and asked in her heavily-accented English: 'Good people, why you abuse us so? We come for all your goods.' 'Yes, damn you', a fellow in the crowd shouted back at her, 'and for all our chattels too.'[6]

The passing of years

One of Sophie Dorothea's chief occupations during her thirty-two years of captivity was writing. She had always been an easy and fluent writer, and during her long solitude she must have written hundreds of letters. Many of them were business communications addressed to various court officials who helped her with the administration of her property. They showed her in a new light; practical, calm, and matter-of-fact. Thus in November 1707, having just learnt that she had become a grandmother, she wrote pleasantly to Councillor R. [Ramdohr?] of Hanover, first discussing with him the unfinished business of her late father's will:

> I could not answer your letter by the previous post, because I spent such a long time over my letter to my mother. I agree with you that during President Goertz's absence my business in Hanover, in connection with my late father's will, cannot easily be resolved and finished. We shall therefore wait for his return to clear the matter up and finish with it, if possible.
>
> I shall also be pleased, before you take any further steps, to hear what your opinion is on the subject, as you tell me you would like

me to know it. At the same time you might enlighten me on the subject which I have very much at heart, and about which you give me such high hopes that I am absolutely delighted. I am very grateful to you for having acted in accordance with my wishes and I am very much obliged to you. I am sending you the receipt for eleven hundred *écus* which you let me have last Sunday. Your son also sent me five hundred and fifty *écus*, the receipt for which I had signed and sent him in advance.

I thank you for sharing my joy over my daughter's safe delivery. What crowns my happiness is that God has favoured her with a son. From what it seems, she certainly does not need anything else to make her perfectly happy, except a long life. Divine Providence, which takes such good care of my children, will also grant their mother what is deemed best. I put my entire trust in Providence in everything that concerns me, knowing that I will never find myself in better hands. You no doubt know that General Finck has left Hanover to pay a visit to my mother. I end here, Sir, assuring you that I would be more than pleased to have an opportunity to be of some service to you.[1]

There were no special difficulties about the Duke of Celle's will, for he had not left his daughter anything that might have been disputed. All the same there was something of a scuffle before Sophie Dorothea was allowed to have transferred to Ahlden the silver plate her father had left her. She set much store by it. She must have been less impressed with the Duke's library, which he also left her. It was an odd collection of fishing and hunting manuals, history books, travel accounts, military text-books and old-fashioned novels.

Her letters to her mother may have been less controlled than her business ones. The first were 'pathetic', the English envoy Cresset recorded in one of his dispatches. Later they may have become more restrained. They could not have contained anything disloyal, or they would not have been passed by the governor of the day—there were three of them during her long years at Ahlden. In essence however the whole correspondence between mother and daughter was considered undesirable evidence, and after the deaths of the two women, it was destroyed by the order of George I. Not one letter survived.

Sophie Dorothea must have inherited her ease of writing from her mother, who had an extensive correspondence with kings and princes. Even in her widowhood she continued to exchange cordial letters with Louis XIV, King Frederick I of Prussia, Duke Anthony Ulric and his son, Leibnitz, and many exiled French Huguenots. She had become a venerable old lady, whose kindness and tact had won her many grateful admirers. Her elegantly-furnished court at Luneburg attracted some distinguished visitors, among them the Crown Prince of Prussia and his wife. The Young Sophie Dorothea took the opportunity of asking her grandmother a great many questions about the mother she had not seen since the age of seven. It was probably during that visit that she started her secret correspondence with Ahlden, with Duchess Eleonore serving as a willing messenger.

Although the Young Sophie Dorothea had made a splendid marriage, it was not a happy one. Frederick William, who at eighteen was very much in love with his beautiful cousin, gradually cooled off. A year younger than his wife, he found other company while she was busy presenting him with children. When, at the age of twenty-five, the Crown Prince succeeded his father to the throne of Prussia as Frederick William I, his first act was to dismiss every unnecessary official and introduce the most stringent economy into the palace. One of his daughters later described how he used to threaten to send the family to the country, where further domestic saving could be induced by forcing the Queen to do her own cooking.

As King of Prussia Frederick William proved an excellent administrator and ruler, and on his death he left the country economically far sounder than he had found it. His preoccupation with money had started long before his accession. While his young wife pressed her grandmother at Luneburg for information about her mother's life, the Crown Prince asked for information about her assets. On his return to Berlin he sought legal advice as to whether the Duchess of Ahlden was entitled to bequeath her property to her children, or whether, if she pre-deceased her former husband, it would revert to him. Satisfied that it would not, he set out to win her goodwill by hinting that he might use his influence with his father-in-law to obtain her release. He went as far as to turn a blind eye on his wife's correspondence with her mother. But while dangling the promise of freedom before the captive, in order to encourage her to leave more of her wealth to her daughter than to her son in England, the Crown Prince was careful not to antagonise the King of Great Britain by asking him to release his hated former wife.

Not aware of her son-in-law's calculations, Sophie Dorothea began to hope again. In a letter attributed to 1709, she reminded him of her longing to be freed. To gain her freedom, the middle-aged woman did not hesitate to shower hackneyed flatteries on the twenty-one-year-old prince.

Sir,

I could not possibly express all the joy I felt when I received the kind letter Your Royal Highness had done me the honour of writing to me. I thank you for it with all my heart, and I beg you to believe that my answer would not have reached you before me had I dared follow my inclination. My unhappy situation must excuse me. The kindness that Your Royal Highness shows me is my consolation. I truly deserve it, Sir, for it is not possible to love and respect Your Royal Highness more than I do. I should die contented if I had the happiness of telling you so myself, for I desire more than words can express to see such an accomplished Prince, who is so dear to me for all the reasons in the world. I ask Your Royal Highness to continue to favour me with your friendship which is so precious to me. My own actions will prove mine to you, as well as my boundless gratitude for the interest you take in everything that concerns me. I am, Your Royal Highness, with much zeal,

Your very humble and very obedient servant
and your devoted mother,
Sophie Dorothea[2]

In 1716 King George I made the first of his many return visits to his Electorate. He stayed at the Leine Palace or Herrenhausen, happy to be back among his Hanoverian subjects, away from the turmoil of English politics. His court in Hanover was as pleasant as it had been in its heyday, with elegant ladies adorning his dinner table. Lady Mary Wortley Montagu arrived with her husband from Vienna, and besides leaving some very entertaining descriptions of the court and its ladies, also succeeded in impressing the King. He became very attentive. Once in a benevolent mood, he granted Duchess Eleonore's request to return to Celle, which had been left untenanted since the death of Duke George William.

The following year, after nearly twelve years of exile, Eleonore returned to the castle that had been her home throughout her married life. She was old and virtually blind, but she still maintained a small court, consisting chiefly of French Huguenots. Of her old friends only Anthony Ulric was still alive. She added a codicil to her will, leaving him and the Duchess of Wolfenbüttel a small legacy. She spent her few remaining years putting her affairs in order, giving away her possessions. She continued her tiring journeys to Ahlden to the very last year of her life. She died at the beginning of 1722, at the age of eighty-five, and was officially mourned in the courts of Hanover, Prussia and Great Britain. Even her old enemy, the Duchess of Orléans, herself an old lady now, was moved to write to a relative that the Duchess of Celle had had her good points after all.

In accordance with her wishes, Eleonore was buried without pomp. The funeral took place a week after her death, at midnight. Twelve pages with lighted torches preceded the coffin to the church of Celle, where she was buried next to her husband; but the niche above, which should have held her statue, remained vacant. For generations to come visitors to the church were told that the reason for the omission was the Duchess's inferior rank at birth.

Sophie Dorothea was fifty-six when her mother died. She took her death sensibly and immersed herself in the long business correspondence concerning the winding-up of the estate. A few months after the funeral the will was opened in the presence of representatives sent by the three main beneficiaries—Sophie Dorothea, the Queen of Prussia and the Prince of Wales. There were many small legacies to distant relatives and friends, and Sophie Dorothea tried as much as she could to see that they were properly executed. She wrote many letters about them to her two Ahlden bailiffs, Ludemann and Chappuzeau, sadly complaining of 'the ill use and abuse people have made of my mother's kindness and generosity'.[3]

After her mother's death, Sophie Dorothea had to re-adjust herself to a life without the loving visits that had supported her for nearly twenty-seven years. It must have taken a great deal of self-discipline to keep up the daily routine and not let herself sink into indolence and despair. She devoted more time than ever to good works, sending money to the village poor, liberal gifts and pensions to her father's old servants, help to exiled French Huguenots in Holland. For many years past, she had been allowed to attend the local church on Sundays instead of having the service held in her own apartments. She attended regularly, taking a great interest in the church's funds and having it rebuilt at her own expense when it was burnt down. She also presented it with an organ inscribed with her name.

The Sunday visits to church, although under guard, gave her a much-needed opportunity to see and be seen by people outside her immediate narrow entourage, still chosen for her by the Hanoverian government. In her mid-fifties, she had gone stout and grey, but she was still a very elegant woman. She never lost her love of beautiful clothes and jewels. She went on ordering rich materials from Holland, buying new jewels—with those she had inherited from her mother she had a brilliant collection—and having elaborate dresses made. Without realising it, she emulated Duchess Sophia of Hanover in insisting on etiquette and full court dress for her ladies.

She busied herself as much as she could with household accounts, the revenues from her estates, the wages of her staff. She did not pretend to understand all the intricacies of her finances, and put her trust in her agents. She once wrote to one of them, Count de Bar, that she did not like signing documents without understanding what they were about; but she realised that if she put off signing, she would only have more documents thrust upon her later on. Yet she was not unworldly. She had a pretty shrewd idea of how to make her money increase. Keeping her eye on the stock exchanges abroad, she instructed Count de Bar when to sell her bonds. Her instructions were clear and practical, as the following letter shows:

Ahlden, 27 October, 1724

After having carefully considered the current high price of Dutch bonds, according to the information sent by Count de Bar to Ludemann the bailiff in his letter of the 14th instant, stating that those on The Hague exchange are at par, that is one hundred for one hundred, and those at the Amsterdam exchange are at one hundred and nine to one hundred, depending on the buyers' terms, I have decided to sell all my bonds on the two exchanges of The Hague and Amsterdam. The current price seems to be so high and so favourable that it is not likely to rise any higher; on the contrary, it may drop considerably.

I therefore order the bailiff to send Count de Bar in Holland the six letters I signed, granting the Count power of attorney to sell the bonds in my name.

I also desire that the money realised from the sale, over and above the thirty thousand crowns I have already disposed of, should be put in safe keeping, until I find a suitable chance to invest it profitably at interest, provided this could be done in such a manner that at any time, in peace or war, I may always have the money at my disposal without hindrance.

While waiting for a suitable opportunity to invest it, I am satisfied that it could be deposited in the bank of Amsterdam for the necessary precautions and security.[4]

From her distant castle, Sophie Dorothea tried to follow the fortunes of her children and their families. She had no direct communication with her son, the Prince of Wales, who was too engrossed in his quarrels with his father to find time to indulge in a secret correspondence with his mother. Whatever information she had about him was imparted by the Queen of Prussia, who kept up her unofficial correspondence with her mother, in spite of the risk.

Four people were involved in the exchange of letters, messages and even presents between mother and daughter. On the Ahlden side there were Count de Bar, and Ludemann the bailiff. They both travelled frequently on the Princess's business, and could take letters in and out of the castle without the governor's knowledge.

In Berlin, the Queen of Prussia entrusted her letters to Privy Councillor Ludwig, and to an attendant called Frederick. Secrecy had to be observed at all times, for the King, although tolerant of the correspondence for the sake of the expected inheritance, was not to be trusted too much. Sometimes the Queen would not dare write at all; instead she would give a verbal message to Frederick or Ludwig, to be passed on to de Bar or Ludemann, who would then make a note of it and take it to Ahlden. Sophie Dorothea, an old hand at clandestine correspondence, was also on her guard. When a letter once reached her not through Ludemann, but through a chain of unknown messengers, she checked the handwriting against a previous letter. Although it looked genuine enough, she suspected it was a forgery and warned her daughter that something had gone wrong.

A subject that exercised both mother and daughter was the marriage of the grandchildren. The Queen of Prussia had set her heart on marrying two of her children to two of her brother's in England. Wilhelmina and Fritz—later Frederick the Great—were to marry their English cousins Frederick and Amelia. For some reason Sophie Dorothea was not in favour of the project, and wrote to her daughter to tell her so. Why her opinion mattered is a matter for conjecture. She had no say in anything, and her views could not have interested anybody. But she was a wealthy woman, in control of her bank accounts. The Queen of Prussia, always kept on a tight budget by her economy-conscious husband, no doubt needed ready money to buy the favour of influential people towards her double-marriage scheme. Her mother's disapproval therefore meant no financial aid from that quarter. The Queen then tried threats. Having promised her mother to intercede for her with the King to obtain her release from George I, she sent word to Ahlden that she would not continue her efforts unless the double-marriage deal came off. Sophie Dorothea did not budge. The Queen realised that she had gone too far and sent a message through Ludemann, assuring her mother of her filial devotion and affection. To show her good intentions, she sent along some presents, including miniatures of two of her children. Sophie Dorothea returned the presents, but hung on to the miniatures.

Another project that occupied Sophie Dorothea's mind was the possible visit of her daughter to Ahlden. Twice during her married life did the Queen of Prussia come within visiting distance of the castle, and twice she had to abandon any hope of going there. The first opportunity arose in 1720, when George I was visiting Hanover and invited his daughter and her husband to come and stay at Herrenhausen. The second occurred in 1725, when the King of Prussia joined George I in Hanover to discuss a political treaty with France. On both occasions it was inconceivable that the Queen should abuse her father's hospitality and drive to Ahlden to see a person he hated. Sophie Dorothea must have been bitterly disappointed to have her daughter so near, and yet as remote as ever.

She desperately needed somebody to talk to; not a hireling of the Hanoverian administration, but a friend whom she could trust and rely on. In Count de Bar she felt she found the man she needed.

He had come to her from Celle, where he had served her father. He was debonair and aristocratic and knew how to flatter her. He manifested great devotion to her person and wooed her with small presents which he brought back from his business trips. She once graciously rebuked him for sending her some snuff; not because she did not take it, but because the quantity was extravagant. She was completely won over. She let him handle all her affairs.

Neither de Bar nor his colleagues Ludemann offered their services to the aging Princess out of sheer loyalty. They were both men of the world, and they went into the risky business of her correspondence with Berlin only after they had made sure they could benefit from it. They took advantage of their position of trust to keep back some of the Princess's revenues that passed through their hands. In due course the Queen of Prussia became suspicious and warned her mother against them. After repeated accusations, Sophie Dorothea was persuaded that Ludemann had betrayed her trust in one way or another. But she would not hear anything against Count de Bar. He had become indispensable to her. He was the only person from the outside world who could still come to see her. She clung to him with all the tenacity of her passionate nature. She gave him a chance to refute her daughter's accusations and accepted his explanations without a doubt. Her reply to his plea was hardly less emotional than some of the love letters she wrote more than thirty years earlier:

27 September, 1725

I will begin by saying that your kind assurances and protestations restored my peace of mind. I shall make use of the same words, if you can still recollect them, to express my own feelings towards you, and were it possible to go beyond them, I would certainly do so. Words cannot express all I feel, all I have always felt and all I shall continue to feel until my last breath. For God's sake, be always the same to me, as I shall continue to be to you until my dying day.[5]

Having retained her confidence, de Bar continued to represent the Princess in Holland. Communication between them was infrequent. Sophie Dorothea dared not write to him too often, for fear of arousing the suspicion of her household, her dragons and harpies, as she called them. She longed for him to come and see her at Ahlden, as she openly wrote in one of her last letters to him:

> Ahlden, 3 August, 1726
>
> If it were in my power, Sir, to answer your letter of 20 December last the moment it was delivered to me, I would have done so. Words can hardly express all I feel. I have a thousand things to tell you, but I will keep them until I see you again. Heaven grant that it may be soon. I pray constantly for that happy day and await it with impatience. Come soon, Sir, I beg of you. You know how much I need you, on all imaginable accounts. But come in a way that will leave us nothing to fear from the incredible injustice and fury of my enemies.
>
> May I assure you again of my esteem and my gratitude, which increase every day of my life. Both are boundless and to put it briefly, they are proportionate to what you deserve. They are above all that ever was in this world and ever will be.[6]

The Count preferred to stay away, carrying on with his profitable financial transactions on the stock exchange. He eventually succeeded in appropriating most of the money he had realised from the sale of Sophie Dorothea's bonds. When incontrovertible proof was brought to her of his fraudulence, she agreed to allow court proceedings to be started against him. Fortunately for her aching old heart, she did not live long enough to see the end of the case, which failed to make de Bar give up his loot.

Unforgiven

When George I arrived in London in 1714 accompanied by a son and heir but not by a wife, it became necessary to explain her absence. Yet no official explanation was ever given. Some of the King's German entourage gave out that His Majesty was a widower; others that his wife was mad and had to be left behind; and some whispered she was a Papist. Neither George nor Count Bernstorff, who continued to be his trusted adviser, made any attempt to inform the court or the public that a divorce had taken place. Instead, they allowed wild conjectures and rumours, which they neither confirmed nor denied.

In a country like England, accustomed as it was to royal divorce, this was a strange attitude to take, unless there was some very compelling reason to do so. From the King's subsequent efforts to destroy all the secret papers connected with the trial, it would appear he had serious misgivings as to the validity of the proceedings that led to his divorce in 1694. The English had long been pictured in the Hanoverian mind as a people who had little respect for their kings. They were quite likely to query a verdict that in Hanover had gone unquestioned. If no official reference to the royal divorce was ever made in London, it was no doubt in order to prevent any possible probing into what might have been exposed as a miscarriage of justice.

Rumours were therefore not discouraged. Even when they were critical of the King's behaviour, they were preferable to facts. The popular belief was that Sophie Dorothea had allowed one of her gallant courtiers to kiss her hand while she was still in bed, and that the enraged husband condemned her for that small indiscretion to a life of imprisonment. The theme of the cruel husband and the innocent wife became a frequent indictment against the King, and was often brought up against him at public demonstrations held annually on the anniversary of Queen Anne's death. Even then there was no comment from the court of St James. Walpole wrote in his reminiscences that nobody knew for certain whether the King was divorced or not. He personally tended to think he was not, for there was no other way to explain the absolute power he had over the life of the Duchess of Ahlden.

The theory that Sophie Dorothea was still the King's wife became so widely accepted in England, that a hundred and twenty years later Thackeray gave it expression in a few satirical lines he published in *Punch*, under the title of *George the First—Star of Brunswick*:

> He preferred Hanover to England
> He preferred two hideous mistresses
> To a beautiful and innocent wife.
> He hated all art and despised literature
> But he liked train-oil in his salads;
> And gave an enlightened patronage to bad oysters.
> And he had Walpole for a minister:
> Consistent in his preference for every kind of corruption.[1]

There was another reason for George's constant efforts to suppress the evidence connected with the trial. Königsmarck's disappearance had by no means been forgotten; indeed it had become a constant source of highly dramatised accounts, all compromising the name of Hanover. It was essential to eliminate any document that might point to a possible connection between the events of 1 July 1694 and the King of Great Britain. Getting rid of the trial papers was not enough. On George's instructions his mother's letters to Leibnitz during that period were also destroyed. So were the letters written by her to the Duchess of Orléans, who agreed to have them burnt at the King's explicit request. The despatches of the English envoys to Hanover and Dresden must have also been tampered with, for there are some telling gaps in their otherwise regular reporting. After Sophie Dorothea's death, her correspondence with her mother was destroyed. Only a few documents escaped the *auto da fé*; some letters between Platen and Bernstorff; copies of some of the original court documents, made by Councillor Thies and preserved by his descendants; and Sophie Dorothea's letters seized in Königsmarck's house, which were kept sealed by the Hanover administration, and must have been considered too inaccessible to constitute any danger. A few letters by Leibnitz also survived, in which he alluded to the confiscated letters and summarised part of their contents.

But the destruction of documented evidence did not seem enough to George, who feared that Sophie Dorothea might still escape from Ahlden and rouse the world to the injustice of her position. He did not trust the friendship between Duchess Eleonore and the old intriguer Anthony Ulric, and was equally wary of the King of Prussia's lack of hostility towards his mother-in-law. Although there was not the slightest indication that any of these parties would ever contemplate anything rash, George was not running any risks. Before leaving for England, he left instructions to intensify the security precautions at Ahlden. The guards were ordered to watch the Princess's movements more closely than ever, and communication with the outside world became a hazard. While her mother lived, Sophie Dorothea could fill in the gaps in her information through her visits; after her death she was completely cut off. In 1726, when writing to Count de Bar at three o'clock in the morning in order to avoid spying eyes, she complained:

> I am entirely ignorant of what is going on in the world, except for what I gather from the general political news. I am closely guarded, and more pains than ever are taken to stop me learning anything.[2]

After the King's departure for England, Sophie Dorothea began to have new fears. From the court of St James came rumours of Mlle

Schulenburg's growing importance in English society. While in Hanover she was no more than a resident mistress, in London she seemed to become a power to reckon with. It was whispered that the King might want to marry her. There was no reason to suppose that an ancestry-conscious Hanoverian, who had once spurned Anne of York and the Princess of Celle on account of their faulty genealogy, would marry a Schulenburg. But Sophie Dorothea was disturbed. It was no use telling herself that if George wanted to re-marry he was free to do so without first getting rid of her. In her agitated state of mind everything seemed feasible. The word poison crept into her secret correspondence. Again it was her mother who found a solution, which although far-fetched, turned out to be effective.

Like so many Germans of his time, George was highly superstitious. When a well-known French 'prophetess' was particularly recommended to him for her power to read the future, he commanded her to read his. Self-professed prophets and visionaries were in vogue at the time both in Germany and in England, and there was nothing unusual in the King's command.

Duchess Eleonore, who had been known to spurn such prophets when they came to Celle, was not above using their skill when it concerned the life of her daughter. With a handsome gift judiciously presented from afar, she induced the London prophetess to tell the King something which would help Sophie Dorothea. Accordingly the French Debora, as Walpole called her, warned George to take good care of 'his wife' if he wanted to live long, for he would only survive her by a year and a day.

Crude as the scheme was, it must have had some effect. During the last years of her life, Sophie Dorothea had the best medical care available. Apart from her own resident doctor, she was visited by court physicians from Hanover, who examined her at regular intervals and reported on her state of health. In spite of years of confinement, with hardly any exercise except the escorted drives in her coach, she kept reasonably fit. Her illnesses, in her middle age as in her youth, were more a result of nervous strain than physical disorder. In her fifty-ninth year she wrote to Count de Bar:

My health is good, and better than might be expected in my

constantly agitated state of mind. The God of mercy looks after me in a way that can only be described as miraculous. I take good care of myself, since I have friends who are kind enough to take an interest in my welfare.[3]

Her life expectancy should have been high, for both her parents lived to be well over eighty. But her nerves gave way under the perpetual strain that, like a pendulum, swung her from one extreme to another, from high hopes to utter despair. In 1726 she suffered two added blows, one after the other. One was the failure of her daughter to visit her during her recent stay at Hanover; the other was Count de Bar's proved fraudulence. That was the last straw. The future held nothing in store. The best medical care in Hanover could not re-kindle the will to live in an aging woman who felt betrayed, deserted and forgotten. With remarkable self-discipline she tried to carry on as usual, writing her daily instructions to the butler, her letters of charity, her courteous messages of sympathy to her parishioners. But the old resilience had gone. On 18 October her hand, usually so firm, began to tremble; and the lines of her letters, usually so even, became disordered. Four days later she took to her bed, never to leave it again. She died on 13 November 1726, at eleven o'clock at night, in her sixty-first year.

When the news of her death became known, the courts of Hanover and Prussia went into deep mourning; Hanover in deference to the memory of the Duke and Duchess of Celle, Prussia in deference to a Queen whose mother was known to have left her a large inheritance. Only London treated her death as a matter of no importance. The day George received the news, he went to see an Italian comedy at the Haymarket, accompanied by the Duchess of Kendal and Lady Darlington. The following day he commanded a special performance at the King's Theatre. The *London Gazette* made only the briefest allusion to the demise of the Duchess of Ahlden. A sharp rebuke was sent to the court of Hanover for its misguided show of grief, with an order to remove any signs of mourning. A message written in the same spirit was also sent to Prussia, but failed to achieve any results. Even the Prince of Wales was not allowed to show any grief for his dead mother. Lady Cowper, lady-in-waiting to the Princess of Wales, noted down in her diary a few lines of verse that were supposed to portray the son's anger against his father's heartlessness:

> A mother dead, and am I from the throne
> Commanded not to show myself her son?
> Well, since the decent sable I'm denied
> For her, my parent on the surer side,
> Remember, George, 'twill be my turn some day,
> This, and all former favours to repay;
> And when that long-expected time I see,
> Let Kendal, at her peril, mourn for thee.[4]

While Prussia was in mourning and the court of St James was manifesting an unusual zeal for the theatre, Sophie Dorothea's body was put in a leaden coffin and temporarily deposited in the Ahlden vaults, awaiting the King's instructions about the funeral arrangements. None came for several weeks. Instead, her will was seized and destroyed, thus making her property go to her former husband, instead of her son and daughter. Her papers were partly burnt and partly packed in strong cases and sent to Hanover. The household was disbanded, the furniture dispersed.

Early in the new year an envoy arrived from London with the Royal Command, instructing the governor to bury the Duchess of Ahlden in the castle garden. Unfortunately it was a rainy winter, and the river Ahler had overflowed, turning the garden into a swamp. It was impossible to dig a grave. After several attempts to sink the coffin into the waterlogged hole, it was returned to the castle vaults, and a despatch was sent to London to inform His Majesty of the unsuitability of the terrain.

It was only in May that instructions from London were received to transfer the coffin to Celle and bury it in the ducal vaults of the church. It was put on a carriage and driven to Celle by night, where a small group of local residents awaited it with lighted torches. Four workmen lifted it off the carriage and took it down to the vaults, where it was deposited without as much as a prayer. A small tablet of identity was later affixed to the right-hand corner of the coffin, bearing the dead woman's name, with the dates of her birth and death. None of her titles was mentioned. In death, as in life, Sophie Dorothea was condemned to obscurity.

In June 1727, only a few weeks after the burial, George set out for Hanover and Osnabrück, where he was to be the guest of his brother Ernest, who had become its secular bishop. He sailed from Greenwich with the Duchess of Kendal, then drove to Delden in Holland for an overnight stop. He had a heavy meal, and spent a restless night, which he attributed to indigestion.

At seven o'clock on the following morning, leaving the Duchess of Kendal to follow him later, he set out for Osnabrück. On the way he had an attack of what seemed to be apoplexy. His right arm was paralysed, his tongue hung out of his mouth, and he fell backwards. The coach was stopped, his surgeon bled him and suggested returning to Delden. With his left hand the King motioned that he wished to go on to Osnabrück. The procession of coaches arrived at ten o'clock at night. According to one version George was carried in and bled again, but died within a few minutes in his brother's arms, without regaining consciousness. According to another version he was dead on arrival. He was buried in state in Hanover.

The Duchess of Kendal, who was following him at a more leisurely pace, heard of his death on the road. She went to Brunswick and mourned for him for three months, after which she returned to England and retired to Kendal House. Walpole wrote that soon after her retirement a black fowl of some sort, possibly a raven, took to visiting her garden. Superstitious as she was, she took it to be the reincarnation of the late King. She fed the bird every day until death parted them— Walpole was not sure which of them died first.

About eight or ten weeks after George's death, copies of a strange letter began to circulate through the courts of Europe. Nobody knew who the author of it was, but it was passed from hand to hand in great secrecy, until it reached George Lockhart of Carnwath, a Jacobite who was visiting the Pretender at Aix-la-Chapelle. Lockhart translated it from French into English, for the benefit of readers in England. The contents of that letter have since become an integral part of the Sophie Dorothea apocrypha.

It claimed that before she died, the Princess became delirious and spent her last night raving and ranting against the King. She called him cruel and unjust, and cursed him before God. A few hours before she died she rallied sufficiently to sit up in bed and write to him in her own hand. It was a short letter, in which she cursed him again, and summoned him to appear before God's throne of justice within a year and a day of her own death. She then entrusted the letter to one of her attendants, asking him to deliver it to the King, and died.

The attendant did not dare to go to England, nor could he hope to be able to hand it to the King with impunity during his projected visit to Hanover. He therefore hit on the idea of delivering the letter *en route*, where he would be out of the King's jurisdiction.

It was customary for petitioners to await the King along the royal route and thrust their petitions into his coach. The messenger waited not far from Delden, and when he saw the royal coach approach, beckoned with the white paper in his hand. The coach slowed down, a hand stretched out to receive the petition, and the messenger was left behind, never to be recognised.

The letter gave the King a terrible shock. The summons to appear before the throne of justice within a year and a day of Sophie Dorothea's death echoed the warning pronounced years earlier by the French prophetess. He fell backwards, half-paralysed, barely managing to whisper that he wished to be driven on to Osnabrück, his childhood home. Throughout the rest of the frantic drive the words of the curse kept ringing in his head. He died in great agony of mind and body, within a year of his wife's death. Sophie Dorothea's curse had come true.

George Lockhart, who brought this version to the attention of the English court, felt the story could have been fabricated by the King of Prussia or even by George II, both of whom had a grudge against George I. But how such a letter, circulated in secrecy in the courts of Europe, could have harmed the late King, remains unclear.

On the other hand, it may well be that Sophie Dorothea did write a deathbed letter to her former husband, protesting her innocence and his injustice to the last. Amongst her attendants there was one who might have been trusted to deliver it posthumously. It was Chapuzzeau, who like his father before him, had been a loyal servant of the Duke of

Celle. He might have respected a dying woman's last wish, and taken the first reasonable opportunity to deliver the letter. George had already had one attack of apoplexy a few years earlier, and the shock of reading such a letter, coming on top of his illness of the night before, might have hastened his end, although it need not have caused it. The incident must have been hushed up, and it was two or three months before it leaked out. In the circumstances it was natural that it should reach the courts of Europe before it crossed the Channel.

Whichever was the cause of his death, George I died unlamented. When the Prince of Wales heard of his father's demise, one of his first acts was to produce two portraits of his late mother, which he had been storing in secret, and have them hung in his wife's apartment. One was a full-length portrait of Sophie Dorothea in what Walpole described as 'royal robes', the other a half-length. They both faced the courtiers from Caroline's dressing-room and bedroom walls, when they came in to pay their respects to the new King and Queen of Great Britain. Later they passed on to one of the King's daughters.

George II said on one or two occasions that had his mother survived his father, he would have brought her over to England and made her Queen-Dowager. As it happened, he was never called upon to live up to his promise. But during her lifetime he did try to plead for her with his father, as did his sister. If they failed, it was not their fault, as the Queen of Prussia sadly wrote to him about a year after his accession:

Neither you nor I could ever persuade our late father to allow our mother to leave Ahlden.[5]

George II must have heard a great deal about his mother's disgrace, but like his sister, who taught her children that 'the Duchess of Ahlden had been less guilty than imprudent', he gave her the benefit of the doubt. When he paid his first royal visit to Hanover, he sent for her papers, including the letters seized in Königsmarck's desk, and went through them. If his intention had been to vindicate her honour, the letters must have undermined his romantic notion. He had them burnt, and did not speak of his mother ever again.

Both father and son thus followed the same course. George I

destroyed documentary evidence in order to protect himself against suspicion of tampering with the course of justice; George II did so in order to protect his mother's honour. Vindictiveness on the one side, over-sensitiveness on the other, robbed her of her due place in history. Ancestress of the dynasty that reigns over Great Britain to this day, Sophie Dorothea alone was made to pay for the early sins of the house of Hanover.

APPENDIX: THE LETTERS

The original French manuscripts of the correspondence between Sophie Dorothea and Königsmarck are preserved partly in the University Library of Lund, in Sweden, and partly in the Royal Secret State Archives of Berlin. Their authenticity, once questioned, has been established beyond doubt by archivists and historians, one of the earliest among them being W. H. Wilkins, who in his *The Love of an Uncrowned Queen* (1900 and 1903) gave a polished translation of the Lund letters, the only ones he was able to examine.

The two collections, totalling nearly three hundred letters, form only part of the correspondence that extended over four years, beginning in July 1690 and ending sometime in June 1694. Many—we shall never know how many—must have been lost; the wide gaps in an otherwise very regular correspondence bear witness to that. Sophie Dorothea's last extant letter dates from August 1693; Königsmarck's from November of that year. Their later letters were seized and presumably destroyed, as were some of their earlier ones.

Realising that they were not safe in their possession, and yet loth to destroy them, the lovers formed the habit of entrusting the letters to Aurora Königsmarck, the Count's sister. After Königsmarck's disappearance Aurora must have passed them on to her sister Amelia, Countess Lewenhaupt, whose husband served in the Celle and Hanover army, and who later returned with his wife to his native Sweden. One of the descendants of the Lewenhaupt family bequeathed the correspondence in 1848 to the University Library of Lund.

The provenance of the Berlin letters has yet to be traced; presumably they are those which the lovers, for one reason or another, did not put in Aurora's hands. Their last owner was Frederick the Great, grandson of

Sophie Dorothea, who sometime during his reign (1740–86) sent them to the Royal Archives, in one packet, on top of which he had written with his own hand: 'Correspondence between Princess Sophie Dorothea and Count Königsmarck in the Royal Secret State Archives of Berlin.' This batch is much smaller than the Lund collection, and its span shorter, but its contents dovetail the Lund letters. Frederick the Great must have got it from his mother, Sophie Dorothea's daughter; but how she came to have the letters is not known.

The Berlin letters were published for the first time by A. W. Ward, in the appendix to his 1909 edition of *The Electress Sophia and the Hanoverian Succession*, where he reproduced them in French exactly as they were written, with every idiosyncrasy of spelling. The Lund ones were published earlier, but only in fragments; the most comprehensive selection was published in 1914, by G. du Boscq de Beaumont and M. Bernos in their *Correspondance de Sophie Dorothée*, where they corrected the faulty spelling for the benefit of the readers. In my translation of the letters I have tried to resist the urge to improve stylistic faults and strived to be faithful to the spirit of the writers, retaining their spontaneity, their uninhibitedness, their lack of polish and their occasional grossness.

Most of the letters, both in the Lund and the Berlin collections, are insufficiently dated; sometimes they are only marked with the day of the week, sometimes with the date of the month, without stating which month; the year is never recorded. To make the letters coherent, it was obviously necessary to establish their chronology. In that I leaned heavily on Professor Georg Schnath's *Der Königsmarck Briefwechsel*, 1952, where, without quoting any, he catalogued every single one available, both published and unpublished, with notes as to probable dates, place of writing and events referred to.

While Sophie Dorothea's letters were literate by any standard, if repetitive, Königsmarck's must have been a written replica of the way he spoke. A. Greenwood, in her *Hanoverian Queens of England*, suggested that his French, to judge by his spelling, must have been so badly mispronounced that it was a miracle the Princess ever understood his conversation. In fact he had an excellent command of French, which he had studied from childhood, and which became his natural language. He certainly used both its elegancies and its colloquialisms with perfect ease. His spelling was erratic, but so was George Louis's, later King George I. When one considers that Königsmarck was a Swede, to whom the French sound of *eu* sounded like the Swedish *ö*, it is easy to understand why he spelt *heureux* as *horos*. Similarly, when one considers that the sound value of the Swedish *J* is something like *i*, it is easy to understand why he wrote *jl* for *il*. His spelling was most unorthodox, but at least it was consistent in its phonic application. His pronunciation, far from being unintelligible, must have been accurate; and his fluency in the language must have been such that even to his mother he sometimes wrote in French, while she always answered in German. I cannot resist giving some examples of his spelling, chosen at random:

Rien nay plus innosang	Rien n'est plus innocent
jattang de vous leur du rendevous	J'attends de vous l'heure du rendezvous
que ne soufertong cant jl faux se separrer de vous	Que ne souffre-t-on quand il faut se séparer de vous
les laistres d'yair	Les lettres d'hier
vostre fidail amang	vo(s)tre fidèle amant
astor	à cette heure

Altogether there are over two hundred letters written by Königsmarck to Sophie Dorothea, while only seventy or so of hers have survived. Whether he was more conscientious than the Princess in the destruction of incriminating evidence we shall never know. What we do know is that such letters as have come to us bear witness to a love, which although not great in the classical sense, is moving in its uninhibited manifestation of human frailty.

BIBLIOGRAPHY

BAILY, F. E., *Sophia of Hanover and her Times*, 1936.

BEAUCAIRE, H., *Une Mésalliance dans la Maison de Brunswick*, 1884.

BECKMAN, K. A., *Aurora Königsmarck och Hennes Bröder*, 1948.

BODEMAN, E., *Aus den Briefen der Herzogin Elisabeth Charlotte von Orleans und die Kurfürstin Sophia von Hannover*, 1891.

BOSCQ DE BEAUMONT, G. and BERNOS, M., *Correspondance de Sophia Dorothée*, 1914.

BROWN, JOHN, *Anecdotes and Characters of the House of Brunswick*, 1821.

BRUNET, M. G., *Correspondance Complète de Madame Duchesse d'Orléans*, 1904.

COLBURN, H., *Memoirs of Sophia Dorothea*, 1845.

CRAMER, F. M., *Biographische Nachrichten von der Gräfin Maria Aurora Königsmark*, 1833.

CRAMER, F. M., *Denkwürdigkeiten der Gräfin Maria Aurora Königsmark*, 1836.

CREVELIER, J., *La Vie Romanesque d'Aurore de Königsmarck*, 1929.

DAMNERT, R., *Aurora von Königsmarck*, 1936.

DRAPER, S., *The Princess of Zell*, 1796.

FORESTER, H., *Memoirs of Sophia Electress of Hanover*, 1888.

George I, The Character of, 1719.

GILDE, L., *Die Reichweite der Prinzessin von Celle*, 1966.

GILDE, L., *Graf Königsmarck*, 1967.

GREENWOOD, A. D., *Lives of the Hanoverian Queens of England*, 1909.

HONE, W., *Sophia Dorothea Princess of Zell*, 1820.

KLOPP, O., *Der Fall des Hauses Stuart und die Succession des Hauses Hannover*, 1875–88.

KLOPP, O., *Die Werke von Leibniz*, 1864–73.

KOECHER, A., *Die Prinzessin von Ahlden, Historische Zeitschrift*, edit. H. Sybel, 1882.

KOECHER, A., *Memoiren der Herzogin Sophia*, 1888.

KÖNIGSMARCK, AURORA, *Memoirs of the Love and State Intrigues of the Court of Hanover*, 1743.

LEE, J., *Sophia Dorothea Princess of Zell*, 1820.

LEISTER, D.-J., *Bildnisse der Prinzessin von Ahlden*, Niedersächsischen Jahrbuch, 1954.

LOCKHART, G., of Carnwath, *The Lockhart Papers*, 1743.

MALORTIE, C. E., *Der Hannoversche Hof*, 1847.

MALORTIE, C. E., *Beiträge zur Geschichte des Braunschweig-Lüneburgischen Hauses und Hofes*, 1860–72.

MELVILLE, L., *The First George*, 1908.

MONTAGU, LADY MARY WORTLEY, *The Letters and Works of*, 1861.

MORAND, P., *Ci-gît Sophie Dorothée de Celle*, 1968.

PALMBLAD, W. F., *Aurora Königsmark*, 1846–9.

PLUMB, J. H., *The First Four Georges*, 1956.

POELNITZ, Baron, *Histoire Secrette*, 1732.

POELNITZ, Baron, *Histoire Secrette*, 1764.

POELNITZ, Baron, *La Saxe Galante*, 1735.

REDDAWAY, W. F., *A History of Europe 1610–1715*, 1959.

REDMAN, A., *The House of Hanover*, 1960.

SCHAUMANN, A. F. H., *Sophie Dorothea Prinzessin von Ahlden und Kurfürstin Sophie von Hanover*, 1879.

SCHNATH, G., *Sophie Dorothea—der Königsmarck Briefwechsel*, 1952.

SCHNATH, G., *Der Fall Königsmarck*, 1963.

SCHNATH, G., *Eleonore v.d. Knesebeck*, Niedersächsichen Jahrbuch, 1955.

SCHULENBURG-KLOSTERRODA, *Die Herzogin von Ahlden*, 1852.

SICILIANOS, D., *Old and New Athens*, 1960.

TOLAND, J., *An Account of the Courts of Prussia and Hanover*, 1705.

WARD, A. W., *The Electress Sophia and the Hanoverian Succession*, 1909.

WILKINS, W. H., *The Love of an Uncrowned Queen*, 1900.

WILKINS, W. H., *The Love of an Uncrowned Queen*, 1903.

Zeitschrift des Historischen Vereins für Niedersachsen, 1882.

REFERENCE NOTES

CHAPTER 1

1. KOECHER, A., *Memoiren der Herzogin Sophie*, p. 39.
2. Ibid., p. 50.
3. Ibid., p. 55.
4. Ibid., p. 59.
5. Ibid., p. 60.
6. Ibid., p. 61.
7. Ibid., p. 63.

CHAPTER 2

1. KOECHER, A., *Memoiren der Herzogin Sophie*, p. 65.
2. Ibid., p. 70.
3. Ibid., p. 71.
4. WARD, A. W., *The Electress Sophia and the Hanoverian Succession*, p. 160.
5. KOECHER, A., *Memoiren der Herzogin Sophie*, p. 90.
6. Ibid., p. 90.
7. Ibid., p. 90.
8. Ibid., p. 25.
9. Ibid., p. 91.
10. Ibid., p. 25.
11. Ibid., p. 92.
12. Ibid., p. 25.

CHAPTER 3

1. KOECHER, A., *Memoiren der Herzogin Sophie*, p. 21.
2. BEAUCAIRE, H., *Une Mésalliance dans la Maison de Brunswick*, p. 271.

3. KOECHER, A., *Memoiren der Herzogin Sophie*, p. 98.
4. Ibid., p. 102.
5. Ibid., p. 69.
6. Ibid., p. 105.
7. Ibid., p. 107.
8. Ibid., p. 28.

CHAPTER 4

1. KOECHER, A., *Memoiren der Herzogin Sophie*, p. 29.
2. Ibid., p. 110.
3. Ibid., p. 121.
4. Ibid., p. 29.
5. After WILKINS, W. H., *The Love of an Uncrowned Queen*, Vol. I, 1900, p. 58.
6. BEAUCAIRE, H., *Une Mésalliance dans la Maison de Brunswick*, p. 118.
7. Ibid., p. 119.
8. Ibid., p. 121.
9. KÖNIGSMARCK, AURORA, *Memoirs of the Love and State Intrigues of the Court of Hanover*, p. 14.
10. COLBURN, H., *Memoirs of Sophia Dorothea*, p. 99.
11. BEAUCAIRE, H., *Une Mésalliance dans la Maison de Brunswick*, p. 122.
12. KLOPP, O., *Die Werke von Leibniz*, Vol. V, p. 97.

CHAPTER 5

1. MONTAGU, LADY MARY WORTLEY, *The letters and works of*, Vol. I, p. 260.
2. WARD, W. H., *The Electress Sophia and the Hanoverian Succession*, p. 194, footnote.

CHAPTER 6

1. BEAUCAIRE, H., *Une Mésalliance dans la Maison de Brunswick*, p. 106.
2. GREENWOOD, A. D., *Lives of the Hanoverian Queens of England*, Vol. I, p. 27.
3. DRAPER, S., *The Princess of Zell*, Vol. I, p. 77.
4. Ibid., p. 80.

CHAPTER 7

1. CREVELIER, J., *La Vie Romanesque d'Aurore de Königsmarck*, p. 310.
2. GILDE, L., *Die Reichweite der Prinzessin von Celle*, p. 81.

3. KÖNIGSMARCK, AURORA, *Memoirs of the Love and State Intrigues of the Court of Hanover*, p. 17.
4. GILDE, L., *Die Reichweite der Prinzessin von Celle*, p. 131.
5. WILKINS, W. H., *The Love of an Uncrowned Queen*, p. 101.
6. Ibid., p. 101.
7. Ibid., p. 103.

CHAPTER 8

1. BOSCQ DE BEAUMONT, G., and BERNOS, M., *Correspondance de Sophie Dorothée*, p. 30.
2. Ibid., p. 31.
3. Ibid., p. 34.
4. Ibid., p. 33.
5. Ibid., p. 36.
6. WARD, A. W., *The Electress Sophia and the Hanoverian Succession*, p. 471.
7. BOSCQ DE BEAUMONT, G. and BERNOS, M., *Correspondance de Sophie Dorothée*, p. 38.
8. WARD, A. W., *The Electress Sophia and the Hanoverian Succession*, p. 472.
9. BOSCQ DE BEAUMONT, G. and BERNOS, M., *Correspondance de Sophie Dorothée*, p. 39.
10. WARD, A. W., *The Electress Sophia and the Hanoverian Succession*, p. 473.
11. BOSCQ DE BEAUMONT, G. and BERNOS, M., *Correspondance de Sophie Dorothée*, p. 40.

CHAPTER 9

1. BOSCQ DE BEAUMONT, G. and BERNOS, M., *Correspondance de Sophie Dorothée*, p. 42, with WILKINS, W. H., *The Love of an Uncrowned Queen*, 1903, p. 147.
2. WARD, A. W., *The Electress Sophia and the Hanoverian Succession*, p. 482, with SCHNATH, G., *Der Königsmarck Briefwechsel*, p. 35, No. 18 and footnote.
3. WARD, A. W., *The Electress Sophia and the Hanoverian Succession*, p. 483.
4. BOSCQ DE BEAUMONT, G. and BERNOS, M., *Correspondance de Sophie Dorothée*, p. 43.
5. Ibid., p. 45.
6. Ibid., p. 47.
7. GILDE, L., *Die Reichweite der Prinzessin von Celle*, p. 168.
8. BOSCQ DE BEAUMONT, G. and BERNOS, M., *Correspondance de Sophie Dorothée*, p. 48.

9. Ibid., p. 50.
10. WARD, A. W., *The Electress Sophia and the Hanoverian Succession*, p. 489.
11. BOSCQ DE BEAUMONT, G. and BERNOS, M., *Correspondance de Sophie Dorothée*, p. 50.
12. Ibid., p. 52.
13. PALMBLAD, W. F., *Aurora Königsmark*, Vol. II, p. 263, No. 18.

CHAPTER 10

1. WARD, A. W., *The Electress Sophia and the Hanoverian Succession*, p. 456.
2. BOSCQ DE BEAUMONT, G. and BERNOS, M., *Correspondance de Sophie Dorothée*, p. 56.
3. PALMBLAD, W. F., *Aurora Königsmark*, Vol. II, p. 269, No. 35.
4. BOSCQ DE BEAUMONT, G. and BERNOS, M., *Correspondance de Sophie Dorothée*, p. 55.
5. Ibid., p. 57.
6. PALMBLAD, W. F., *Aurora Königsmark*, Vol. II, p. 157.
7. Ibid., Vol. II, p. 269, No. 38.
8. BOSCQ DE BEAUMONT, G. and BERNOS, M., *Correspondance de Sophie Dorothée*, p. 54.
9. PALMBLAD, W. F., *Aurora Königsmark*, Vol. II, p. 268, No. 35.
10. BOSCQ DE BEAUMONT, G. and BERNOS, M., *Correspondance de Sophie Dorothée*, p. 61.
11. After WILKINS, W. H., *The Love of an Uncrowned Queen*, p. 167.

CHAPTER 11

1. After WILKINS, W. H., *The Love of an Uncrowned Queen*, p. 170.
2. WARD, A. W., *The Electress Sophia and the Hanoverian Succession*, p. 460.
3. BOSCQ DE BEAUMONT, G. and BERNOS, M., *Correspondance de Sophie Dorothée*, p. 63.
4. Ibid., p. 66.
5. Ibid., p. 73.
6. Ibid., p. 79.
7. Ibid., p. 68.
8. Ibid., p. 82.
9. Ibid., p. 82.
10. Ibid., p. 70.
11. Ibid., p. 76.
12. Ibid., p. 89.
13. Ibid., p. 90.

14. Ibid., p. 95.
15. Ibid., p. 98.
16. Ibid., p. 101.
17. Ibid., p. 105.

CHAPTER 12

1. BOSCQ DE BEAUMONT, G. and BERNOS, M., *Correspondance de Sophie Dorothée*, p. 107.
2. WARD, A. W., *The Electress Sophia and the Hanoverian Succession*, p. 469.
3. BOSCQ DE BEAUMONT, G. and BERNOS, M., *Correspondance de Sophie Dorothée*, p. 111.
4. Ibid., p. 114.
5. Ibid., p. 119.
6. Ibid., p. 121.
7. Ibid., p. 162.
8. Ibid., p. 130.
9. WARD, A. W., *The Electress Sophia and the Hanoverian Succession*, p. 483.
10. Ibid., p. 466.
11. BOSCQ DE BEAUMONT, G. and BERNOS, M., *Correspondance de Sophie Dorothée*, p. 153.
12. WARD, A. W., *The Electress Sophia and the Hanoverian Succession*, p. 486.

CHAPTER 13

1. BOSCQ DE BEAUMONT, G. and BERNOS, M., *Correspondance de Sophie Dorothée*, p. 156.
2. After WILKINS, W. H., *The Love of an Uncrowned Queen*, p. 240.
3. Ibid., p. 243.
4. BOSCQ DE BEAUMONT, G. and BERNOS, M., *Correspondance de Sophie Dorothée*, p. 170.
5. After WILKINS, W. H., *The Love of an Uncrowned Queen*, p. 247.
6. Ibid., p. 248.
7. Ibid., p. 248.
8. Ibid., p. 249.
9. Ibid., p. 250.

CHAPTER 14

1. MELVILLE, L., *The First George*, Vol. I, p. 30.
2. WILKINS, W. H., *The Love of an Uncrowned Queen*, p. 156.

3. BOSCQ DE BEAUMONT, G. and BERNOS, M., *Correspondance de Sophie Dorothée*, p. 177.

CHAPTER 15

1. BOSCQ DE BEAUMONT, G. and BERNOS, M., *Correspondance de Sophie Dorothée*, p. 59.
2. PALMBLAD, W. F., *Aurora Königsmark*, Vol. II, p. 266, No. 30.
3. WARD, A. W., *The Electress Sophia and the Hanoverian Succession*, p. 458.
4. BOSCQ DE BEAUMONT, G. and BERNOS, M., *Correspondance de Sophie Dorothée*, p. 60.
5. Ibid., p. 219.
6. Ibid., p. 201.
7. Ibid., p. 194.
8. Ibid., p. 211.
9. SCHNATH, G., *Der Königsmarck Briefwechsel*, p. viii.
10. WARD, A. W., *The Electress Sophia and the Hanoverian Succession*, p. 454.
11. BOSCQ DE BEAUMONT, G. and BERNOS, M., *Correspondance de Sophie Dorothée*, p. 219.
12. Ibid., p. 267.
13. PALMBLAD, W. F., *Aurora Königsmark*, Vol. II, p. 260, No. 10.
14. Ibid., p. 269, No. 37.
15. BOSCQ DE BEAUMONT, G. and BERNOS, M., *Correspondance de Sophie Dorothée*, p. 235.

CHAPTER 16

1. BOSCQ DE BEAUMONT, G. and BERNOS, M., *Correspondance de Sophie Dorothée*, p. 301.
2. Ibid., p. 307.
3. WARD, A. W., *The Electress Sophia and the Hanoverian Succession*, p. 480.
4. BOSCQ DE BEAUMONT, G. and BERNOS, M., *Correspondance de Sophie Dorothée*, p. 310.
5. Ibid., p. 271.

CHAPTER 17

1. KÖNIGSMARCK, AURORA, *Memoirs of the Love and State Intrigues of the Court of Hanover*, p. 109.
2. WILKINS, W. H., *The Love of an Uncrowned Queen*, p. 365.
3. Ibid., p. 369.

CHAPTER 18

1. *Zeitschrift des Historischen vereins für Niedersachsen 1882*, p. 169.
2. KOECHER, A., *Die Prinzessin von Ahlden*, Historische Zeitschrift 1882, edited H. Sybel, p. 195.
3. Ibid., p. 215.
4. Ibid., p. 228.
5. GREENWOOD, A. D., *Lives of the Hanoverian Queens of England*, Vol. I, p. 115.
6. KOECHER, A., *Die Prinzessin von Ahlden*, Historische Zeitschrift 1882, edited H. Sybel, p. 225.
7. Ibid., p. 250.

CHAPTER 19

1. GREENWOOD, A. D., *Lives of the Hanoverian Queens of England*, Vol. I, p. 116.
2. BEAUCAIRE, H., *Une Mésalliance dans la Maison de Brunswick*, p. 181.
3. *Zeitschrift des Historischen Vereins für Niedersachsen*, p. 255.
4. Ibid., p. 254.
5. BEAUCAIRE, H., *Une Mésalliance dans la Maison de Brunswick*, p. 167.
6. WILKINS, W. H., *The Love of an Uncrowned Queen*, p. 407.
7. Ibid., p. 407.
8. Ibid., p. 408.

CHAPTER 20

1. TOLAND, J., *An Account of the Courts of Prussia and Hanover*, p. 70.
2. MELVILLE, L., *The First George*, Vol. II, p. 206.
3. WILKINS, W. H., *The Love of an Uncrowned Queen*, p. 411.
4. Ibid., p. 419.
5. COLBURN, H., *Memoirs of Sophia Dorothea*, p. 300.
6. BROWN, J., *Anecdotes and Characters of the House of Brunswick*, p. 172.

CHAPTER 21

1. BEAUCAIRE, H., *Une Mésalliance dans la Maison de Brunswick*, p. 254.
2. Ibid., p. 262.
3. Ibid., p. 195.
4. After COLBURN, H., *Memoirs of Sophia Dorothea*, p. 343.

5. Ibid., p. 357.
6. Ibid., p. 367.

CHAPTER 22

1. MELVILLE, L., *The First George*, Vol. I, p. 217.
2. COLBURN, H., *Memoirs of Sophia Dorothea*, p. 369.
3. Ibid., p. 363.
4. MELVILLE, L., *The First George*, Vol. II, p. 67.
5. BEAUCAIRE, H., *Une Mésalliance dans la Maison de Brunswick*, p. 189, footnote.

INDEX